Chekhov and the Vaudeville

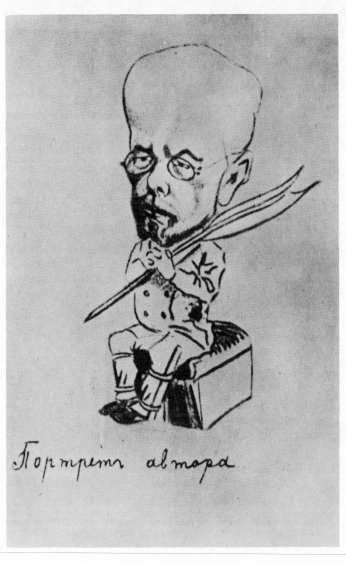

Портретъ автора

1. Chekhov's self portrait.

(Бобриковъ)

Chekhov and the Vaudeville

A Study of Chekhov's One-Act Plays

VERA GOTTLIEB

Senior lecturer in drama
University of London, Goldsmiths' College

CAMBRIDGE UNIVERSITY PRESS

Cambridge

London   New York   New Rochelle

Melbourne   Sydney

Published by the Press Syndicate of the University of Cambridge
The Pitt Building, Trumpington Street, Cambridge CB2 1RP
32 East 57th Street, New York, NY 10022, USA
296 Beaconsfield Parade, Middle Park, Melbourne 3206, Australia

First published 1982

Printed in Great Britain at the University Press, Cambridge

Library of Congress catalogue card number: 81–18142

British Library Cataloguing in Publication Data
Gottlieb, Vera
Chekhov and the vaudeville.
1. Chekhov, A. P. – Criticism and interpretation
I. Title
891.72'3   PG3458
ISBN 0 521 24170 7

*To my mother
and in memory of my father*

The Artist [Chekhov]

He crunched along gray pebbles, passing
A sloping garden, glanced at reservoirs,
And sat on a bench . . . Behind a new white house
The ridge of Yaila rises close and heavy.

All weary from the heat, a slate gray crane
Is standing in the bushes. Lowered crest,
And legs like canes. . . . He says, 'Well, bird?
Not bad to go to Yaroslavl, to the Volga!'

And, smiling then, he thinks of death,
How they will take him out – how gray like doves
The mourning *rizae* in the sun
The yellow fire is, the white on blue a house.

'The bulky priest, with censer, leaves the porch
And leads the choir out. . . . The frightened crane
Begins to jug, appealing from the fence –
And, well, to dance, to rap his beak against the bier!'

A tickle in the chest. The dust from off the road
Is hot, particularly dry.
Removing his pince-nez, he coughs and thinks,
'Ye-es, vaudeville. . . . All the rest is tripe.'

Ivan Bunin

Translated by Joyce Vining from *Shakespeare: Time and Conscience* by Grigori Kozintsev, London, 1967.

Contents

Contents

Illustrations

Introductory note

In recent years an increasing number of Western and Soviet productions of Chekhov's full-length plays have begun to challenge the effect of several decades of productions and criticism in which the emphasis was primarily on Chekhov's 'melancholy' and 'nostalgia'. It is, of course, only in the theatre that the delicate balance between tears and laughter may be truly tested, but this book is an attempt to explore Chekhov's 'sad comicality', and the validity of Chekhov's often-expressed view of himself as a writer of comedies. The medium chosen for this exploration is Chekhov's one-act plays: these farce-vaudevilles, dramatic studies, plays and monologues reveal many of the comedy and 'distancing' techniques to be found in *Ivanov*, *The Seagull*, *Uncle Vanya*, *The Three Sisters* and *The Cherry Orchard*; and it is these apparently conventional one-act plays which illustrate Chekhov's indebtedness to his contemporary popular theatre and inherited comedy techniques. It is, perhaps, exactly because of their seemingly conventional nature, their brevity, and the natural theatrical and literary emphasis on the great full-length plays, that these short plays have received scant critical attention. But Chekhov's one-act plays were written within the period from 1885 to 1903 which produced most of his literary masterpieces and all but the last of his full-length dramatic works; and, as this book attempts to illustrate, the short plays reveal as much about Chekhov's philosophy as they do of his use of theatre.

It is, in fact, the scarcity of critical material on these aspects of Chekhov's work which gives added value to the sources which have influenced this book. I am indebted to a chapter in G. Berdnikov's book, *Chekhov-dramaturg*, entitled 'Chekhov's Vaudevilles'; to the articles written by A. S. Dolinina and E. S. Smirnova-Chikina on *Tatyana Repina*; to V. V. Uspensky and N. Shantarenkov for their collections of Russian vaudevilles; to R. Simonov's account of Vakhtangov's production of *The Wedding*; to Yu. Yuzovsky for his account of Meyerhold's production of *The Bear*, *The Proposal* and *The*

Anniversary, and to Peter Brook's brief but illuminating comment on Chekhov's technique in the chapter called 'The Rough Theatre' in his book *The Empty Space*.

I am glad to record my considerable debt and gratitude for the advice, suggestions and help given to me in different yet equally invaluable ways by George Brandt, Sari Feldman, Henry Gifford, Margot Heinemann, Nesta Jones, John Northam and Peter Thomson. In particular, I am indebted to Edward Braun under whose expert guidance this book emerged in its present form, and who generously supplied the photographs from Meyerhold's *33 Swoons*. I am deeply grateful for his generous help and patience with me over a period of some years. I wish also to thank Irene Slatter and, above all, my mother, Nora Gottlieb, for her endless patience, encouragement, and expert criticism. None of those I have mentioned, however, is responsible for the remaining errors and inadequacies – those are entirely my own.

I am grateful also to University of London Goldsmiths' College for granting me a term's sabbatical leave which enabled me to complete this book.

A note on the text

All quotations from Chekhov's plays are taken from the first three volumes of *The Oxford Chekhov*, translated and edited by Ronald Hingley (Vol. 1, 1968; Vol. 2, 1967; Vol. 3, 1964). By permission of Oxford University Press.

References to quotations are abbreviated accordingly:

H. (Hingley), 1, 2 or 3 (volume number), followed by the page number. Thus, Hingley, Volume 1, page 9 is abbreviated as: H.1.9.

The translation of Chekhov's little-known plays or sketches given in Appendices 1 and 2 is, however, my responsibility.

1

Objectivity and commitment: the evolution of a philosophy

In life, there are no clear-cut consequences or reasons; in it, everything is mixed up together; the important and the paltry, the great and the base, the tragic and the ridiculous. One is hypnotised and enslaved by routine and cannot manage to break away from it. What are needed are new forms, new ones.[1]

Chekhov's words, as reported by Alexander Kuprin,[2] provide a crucial explanation of Chekhov's philosophy and of his motivation and technique as a writer. Thus, Chekhov's refusal to view life in terms of 'absolutes' and to ignore the often contradictory complexities of life, produced literary and dramatic techniques which could not simply or explicitly be concerned with expressing 'a moral' or 'a lesson' presented by means of 'heroes' and 'villains'. Equally, the co-existence, as Chekhov saw it, of 'the tragic and the ridiculous' made it impossible for him to write in accordance with one or other of the artificially created and artificially divided categories of 'tragedy' or 'comedy'. It was exactly this awareness of what he called 'the sad comicality of everyday life' which motivated Chekhov's search for 'new forms'.

It was in this, however, that Chekhov was perhaps most misunderstood both by his contemporaries and by later critics and producers: concentrating on the content, many critics have reached mutually contradictory conclusions as to the tone and intention of Chekhov's work; underestimating the significance and motivation of his technique, many critics have failed to relate Chekhov's characteristics as a writer to the content of his work.

It is perhaps a commonplace that content and form are inseparable, but Chekhov's philosophy and motivation cannot be separated from the evolution of his dramatic technique.

On 28 July 1904, a few weeks after Chekhov's death, Lev Tolstoy gave an interview to the journal *Slovo* in which he stated:

To evoke a mood you want a lyrical poem. Dramatic forms serve, and ought to serve, quite different aims. In a dramatic work the author ought to deal with some problem that has yet to be solved and every character in the play ought to solve it according to the idiosyncrasies of his own character. It is like a laboratory experiment. But you won't find anything of the kind in Chekhov.[3]

Tolstoy, looking for an explicit 'message', underestimates a dramatic form which works through ironic implication; in contradiction, however, Gorky found 'a message' and wrote that Chekhov 'pounds on the public's empty heads'.[4] The critic Nikolai Mikhailovsky, looking for a social problem play, accused Chekhov of indifference, while Chekhov has also been called 'the poet and apologist of ineffectualness'[5] and 'the poet of hopelessness'.[6]

Few of Chekhov's contemporaries recognised in his plays the creation of an innovatory dramatic form. Gorky, writing to Chekhov about *Uncle Vanya*, recognised that '*Uncle Vanya* is a completely new species of dramatic art' but continued 'You know, I feel that in this play you are colder than the devil to human beings. You are as indifferent toward them as snow, as a blizzard.'[7] Stanislavsky, seizing almost exclusively on what he saw as the 'naturalistic' elements of the plays, produced Chekhov's comedies and dramas as tragedies – thus providing his own emotional tone and philosophical attitude. As Meyerhold points out:

The naturalistic director subjects all the separate parts of the work to analysis and fails to gain a picture of the *whole*. He is carried away by the filigree work of applying finishing touches to various scenes, the gratifying products of his creative imagination, absolute pearls of verisimilitude; in consequence, he destroys the balance and harmony of the whole.[8]

And it is Meyerhold who quotes a revealing discussion between Chekhov and some of the actors of the Moscow Art Theatre on the question of verisimilitude in the theatre:

On the second occasion (11 September 1898) that Chekhov attended rehearsals of *The Seagull* at the Moscow Art Theatre, one of the actors told him that off-stage there would be frogs croaking, dragon-flies humming and dogs barking.
'Why?' – asked Anton Pavlovich in a dissatisfied tone.
'Because it's realistic' – replied the actor.
'Realistic!' – repeated Chekhov with a laugh. Then after a short pause he said: 'The stage is art. There's a genre painting by Kramskoy in which the faces are portrayed superbly. What would happen if you cut the nose out of one of the paintings and substituted a real one? The nose would be "realistic" but the picture would be ruined.'[9]

Using this and other examples, Meyerhold writes: 'One need hardly amplify Chekhov's indictment of the naturalistic theatre implicit in this dialogue.'

In this, however, Chekhov defines the difference between 'art' and 'life' in terms not dissimilar from Pushkin's *Notes on Popular Drama*, written in 1830:

Verisimilitude is still considered to be the principal condition of dramatic art and to form its basis. What if it were proved to us that it is precisely verisimilitude which is excluded by the very essence of dramatic art? Reading a poem or a novel, we can often lose ourselves in the thought that the events described are fact and not fiction. Reading an ode, or an elegy, we can think that the poet portrayed his real feelings in actual circumstances. But wherein lies the verisimilitude in a building divided into two parts, of which one is filled with spectators?...

The truth concerning the passions, a verisimilitude in the feelings experienced in given situations – that is what our intelligence demands of a dramatist.[10]

Common to both Pushkin and Chekhov is the view that the pursuit of 'truth', and the objective depiction of that 'truth', need not imply or assume verisimilitude in presentation.

Writing retrospectively about Chekhov, Nemirovich-Danchenko concluded: 'There is no denying that our theatre was at fault in failing to grasp the full meaning of Chekhov...*Chekhov refined his realism to the point where it became symbolic*...maybe the theatre simply handled him too roughly.'[11] It is significant, however, that the few of Chekhov's contemporaries or later theatre practitioners who did welcome the innovatory nature of Chekhov's dramatic art were themselves innovators, and themselves rejected the verisimilitude required by naturalism. Thus, in an article called 'The Two Chekhovs' (1914), Vladimir Mayakovsky wrote of Chekhov's 'new forms of expressing an idea', while Vsevolod Meyerhold recognised that the 'malaise of that decadent intelligentsia'[12] was, in fact, ridiculed by Chekhov and was not, as others thought, dramatised as tragedy. In more recent years, Peter Brook has significantly placed his discussion of Chekhov's plays in the chapter called 'The Rough Theatre' in his book, *The Empty Space*, and he wrote:

It is an easy mistake to consider Chekhov as a naturalistic writer, and in fact many of the sloppiest and thinnest plays of recent years called 'slice of life' fondly think themselves Chekhovian. Chekhov never just made a slice of life – he was a doctor who with infinite gentleness and care took thousands and thousands of fine layers off life. These he cultured, and then arranged them in an exquisitely cunning, completely artificial and meaningful order in which part of the cunning lay in so disguising the artifice that the result looked like the keyhole view it had never been.[13]

As Chekhov said himself: 'the stage demands a degree of artifice'.[14]

In *My Life in Art*, Stanislavsky acknowledged that 'Anton Pavlovich was a man of the theatre'.[15] By 1896, the year of *The Seagull*, Chekhov was fully conversant with the arts of the theatre, whether visual or aural. He was aware of the dangers of the 'incredible' whether in melodrama or – as Meyerhold makes clear – in naturalism carried to its logical conclusion. Chekhov was also well aware of the new dramatic forms of Maeterlinck, of Ibsen, Strindberg, and Hauptmann,[16] and the dramatic theories of both Zola and Tolstoy; but as a contributor to, for example, Nikolai Leykin's magazine, *Fragments*,[17] he spent some time in Moscow theatres where adaptations from French melodramas, 'well-made' plays and farces were the staple diet.

His knowledge of contemporary theatre is clearly evidenced in numerous short stories, in reviews, letters and – of course – in his own plays; but inseparable from Chekhov's comments on theatre and dramatic literature in general, is his own evolution as a playwright. And the evolution of Chekhov's dramatic technique is also the evolution of a philosophy – a philosophy concerned with the very questions which Tolstoy raises: what is art? What is the writer's obligation to society? What is the writer's obligation to his art? These questions, in turn, relate to the controversy over Chekhov's content: is he, as some of his contemporary critics thought,[18] so lacking in commitment and so objective, that his plays 'say' nothing; or as some Western critics have thought, so subjective that his is truly 'the voice of twilight Russia'?[19]

In one of his early stories, *The Drama*, written between 1882 and 1886, two smug old gentlemen – Poluekhtov, a Justice of the Peace, and his friend Fintifleyev, a colonel on the General Staff – are 'sitting over a cosy snack together and discussing the Arts'. Poluekhtov says:

The contemporary playwright and the actor are trying – now, how shall I put it? – are trying to be true to life, realistic. You see on the stage what you'd see in real life. But is that what we're looking for? We want, don't we, some sort of histrionic element? Anyway, people are fed up with real life, sick and tired of it, it's got stale. People need something to make their nerves quiver, to make their insides turn over. The old-time actor used to speak in a forced, sepulchral voice, he would thump his breast with his fist and shout with all his might, he would disappear through the floor, but, all the same, he did get something across. And in what he said, too, something was communicated! He spoke about Duty, and Humaneness and Freedom. In every scene there would be examples of selflessness, heroic exploits, suffering, frenzied passion. But nowadays? Now, you see, what we want is realism! Think of the stage and you'll see...faugh!

This speech is shortly interrupted by a ring at the door. Poluekhtov's sister has sent her small boy to his uncle, with a note requesting him to give the boy a thrashing for a bad mark in Greek. Poluekhtov carries out his sister's request, beats the boy with a belt, and sending him off in tears, returns to his friend to drink a toast to 'Art and Humaneness'. The discrepancy between ordinary conduct and idealistic standards is presented vividly in the story, but characteristically the 'moral' of the story is by implication only: the point of the story emerges through the juxtaposition of what is said with what is done, or the discussion about ideals, and the action which interrupts it. This method, with variations, is characteristic of all Chekhov's work, whether literary or dramatic: a point is not made explicit, but it is made structurally, through juxtaposition. Thus our understanding of Poluekhtov and Fintifleyev (whose name is associated with 'Bagatelle') is deepened and altered by their non-reactions to a real but apparently negligible drama.

This story was written in the period of *Platonov* (1881?), *On the High Road* (1885), the first version of *Smoking is Bad for You* (1886), and literally hundreds of other short stories, such as *Stage Manager under the Sofa*, *The Malefactor*, *Sergeant Prishibeyev*, *The Witch*, and *The Mire*. Chekhov's aims in his literary work of this period are made explicit by him in numerous and often-quoted letters, but these relate more specifically to literature than to the theatre. Thus whereas most critics normally date Chekhov's literary maturity from 1886, his dramatic maturity is usually dated as ten years later, with *The Seagull*. Philosophically, however, the primary aim was common to both his early stories and his early plays: objectivity.

On 17 April 1883, Chekhov wrote a letter to his brother Alexander, in which he listed the necessary 'ingredients' for a short story:

1. The shorter the better.
2. A bit of ideology and being a bit up to date is most à propos.
3. Caricature is fine, but ignorance of civil service ranks and of the seasons is strictly prohibited...

Three years later, however, in another letter to Alexander Chekhov, on 10 May 1886, the 'list' has become more significant, and Chekhov is less facetious about his own work:

1. Absence of lengthy verbiage of political-social-economic nature.
2. Total objectivity.
3. Truthful descriptions of persons and objects.
4. Extreme brevity.
5. Audacity and originality: free the stereotype.
6. Compassion.

Significantly, Chekhov's last point, compassion, does not, as far as he was concerned, rule out 'total objectivity'. That the one does not contradict the other is at the heart of his philosophy as a writer, and is borne out by the stories and plays of this period. This combination, however, was not understood by Chekhov's critics. Commenting on *The Steppe* and *The Name-Day Party*, one critic complained of 'Chekhov's inability or unwillingness to write as required by literary theories.'[20] Chekhov was also accused of lacking an ideology in *The Name-Day Party*, as his letter of 9 October 1888 to Pleshcheyev makes clear: 'But doesn't the story protest against lying from start to finish? Isn't that an ideology? It isn't? Well, I guess that means either I don't know how to bite or I'm a flea.'[21]

The early plays of the period (with the exception of *Ivanov* (1887) and *The Bear* (1888)[22]) did not come under the same attack, which indicates two crucial points: first, the *apparently* much more conventional or acceptable nature of the early plays; second, the fact that neither Chekhov nor the critics took such plays as *The Proposal* or *The Wedding* seriously enough to warrant critical analysis. To Chekhov, the theatre was still very much 'a noisy, impudent and tiresome mistress', while literature was his 'legal wife'.[23]

In 1888, Chekhov's views on the role and responsibility of the writer were explicitly stated in several well-known and often-quoted letters. Writing to Suvorin on 30 May, Chekhov answered a criticism of his story *Lights:*

You write that neither the conversation about pessimism nor Kisochka's story help to solve the problems of pessimism. In my opinion it is not the writer's job to solve such problems as God, pessimism, etc.; his job is merely to record who, under what conditions, said or thought what about God or pessimism. The artist is not meant to be a judge of his characters and what they say; his only job is to be an impartial witness. I heard two Russians in a muddled conversation about pessimism, a conversation that solved nothing; all I am bound to do is reproduce that conversation exactly as I heard it. Drawing conclusions is up to the jury, that is, the readers.[24]

A few months later, on 4 October 1888, Chekhov wrote to Pleshcheyev:

The people I'm afraid of are the ones who look for tendentiousness between the lines and are determined to see me as either liberal or conservative. I am neither liberal, nor conservative, nor gradualist, nor monk, nor indifferentist. I would like to be a free artist and nothing else, and I regret God has not given me the strength to be one. I hate lies and violence in all of their forms...Pharisaism, dullwittedness and tyranny reign not only in merchants' homes and police stations. I see them in science, in literature, among the younger generation...

I look upon tags and labels as prejudices. My holy of holies is the human body, health, intelligence, talent, inspiration, love and the most absolute freedom imaginable, freedom from violence and lies, no matter what form the latter two take. Such is the program I would adhere to if I were a major artist.[25]

In this 'statement' Chekhov, was in fact, expressing similar views to those written nearly sixty years earlier by Pushkin in the work cited earlier, *Notes on Popular Drama*:

What is necessary to a dramatist? A philosophy, impartiality, the political acumen of an historian, insight, a lively imagination. No prejudices or pre-conceived ideas. *Freedom*.[26]

But the idea of the writer as 'an impartial witness', of 'tags and labels as prejudices', and of the reader as judge and not the writer, was a considerable part of what Chekhov's contemporaries condemned in his work. It was partly this which provoked accusations of 'indifference'. What many Western critics have not always understood, however, was that in the eyes of his contemporaries, Chekhov was in a sense placing himself outside the mainstream of the Russian literary tradition in which there were two constant characteristics: realism and a committed statement about what was realistically depicted. This realism may have taken the form of satire, of parody, or of the grotesque, but never before had irony and understatement been used as Chekhov did in his stories and plays. Irony is more detached than satire or parody, and it is certainly more subtle, more implicit. But the use of irony does not mean indifference to the subject; as Chekhov wrote in 1892: 'The more objective you are, the greater the impression you will make.'[27] To students of Brecht's plays and theories, this is not a new concept, but at the end of the last century the idea of 'objective commitment' was neither immediate nor acceptable.

Chekhov never refused 'to soil his imagination with the dirt of life',[28] and, like Zola, he draws an important and recurrent analogy between the scientist and the writer:

To a chemist the notion of dirt does not exist. A writer must be as objective as a chemist. He must renounce every subjective attitude to life and realise that dunghills play a very honourable part in a landscape and that vicious passions are as much a part of life as virtuous ones.[29]

In his famous 'Preface to the Second Edition' (1868) of *Thérèse Raquin*, Zola had expressed an almost identical view:

The writer is simply an analyst who may have become engrossed in human corruption, but who has done so as a surgeon might in an operating theatre.... In the world of science an accusation of immorality proves nothing whatsoever.

Chekhov's understanding of 'analysis' and the 'objective' did not, however, result in cold dissection or, more specifically, vivisection, nor the often artificially 'set-up' case history. In another letter, of 27 October 1888, Chekhov wrote to Suvorin:

I sometimes preach heresies, but I haven't once gone so far as to deny that problematic questions have a place in art. In conversations with my fellow writers I always insist that it is not the artist's job to try to answer narrowly specialised questions...We have specialists for dealing with special questions; it is their job to make judgments about the peasant communes, the fate of capitalism, the evils of intemperance...The artist must pass judgment only on what he understands; his range is as limited as that of any other specialist – that's what I keep repeating and insisting upon. Anyone who says the artist's field is all answers and no questions has never done any writing or had any dealings with imagery. The artist observes, selects, guesses and synthesizes. The very fact of these actions presupposes a question; if he hadn't asked himself a question at the start, he would have nothing to guess and nothing to select...if you deny that creativity involves questions and intent, you have to admit that the artist creates without premeditation or purpose, in a state of unthinking emotionality. And so if any author were to boast to me that he'd written a story from pure inspiration without first having thought over his intentions, I'd call him a madman.

You are right to demand that an author take conscious stock of what he is doing, but you are confusing two concepts: *answering the questions* and *formulating them correctly*. Only the latter is required of an author.[30] There's not a single question answered in *Anna Karenina* or *Eugene Onegin*, but they are still fully satisfying works because the questions they raise are all formulated correctly. It is the duty of the court to formulate the questions correctly, but it is up to each member of the jury to answer them according to his own preference.[31]

In Chekhov's view, 'formulating the questions correctly' presupposes a balanced, non-partisan approach. This was not, however, Tolstoy's view as he expressed it in the preface to his *Improving Tales for Children* (1887):

He does not write the truth who describes only what has happened and what this or that man has done, but he who shows what people do that is right – that is, in accord with God's will; and what people do wrong – that is, contrary to God's will.

It is not, perhaps, too glib to say that whereas Chekhov's stance was a scientific one, Tolstoy's philosophy was based on morality. It was not until 1894 that Chekhov crystallised the influence that Tolstoy had on him – and his disagreement with Tolstoy:

Tolstoy's philosophy moved me deeply and possessed me for six or seven years. It was not so much his basic postulates that had an effect on me – I had been familiar with them before – it was his way of expressing himself, his common sense, and probably a sort of hypnotism as well. But now something in me protests. Prudence and justice tell me there is more love for mankind in electricity and steam than in chastity and vegetarianism.[32]

In 1890, Chekhov had made his well-known journey across Russia to the penal colony of Sakhalin, an experience which clearly had a significant effect on him. As he wrote to Suvorin on 17 December 1890:

Before my trip, *The Kreutzer Sonata* seemed a major event, but now I find it ridiculous and confused. Either the trip has matured me or I've taken leave of my senses.

On his return from Sakhalin, Chekhov wrote *Gusev* (1890), *In Exile* (1891), and *Ward 6* (1891) – stories, among others, with a new tone, and written while Chekhov was also trying to put down his experiences in his book *The Island of Sakhalin*. Objectivity, however, was still the primary aim:

Forget what I have shown you, for it is all false. I kept writing [*The Island of Sakhalin*] and kept feeling I was on the wrong track, until I finally discovered where the false note was. It was in my trying to teach something to someone with my *Sakhalin* and at the same time trying to conceal something and to hold myself back. But as soon as I started to admit how strange I felt while I was on Sakhalin and what swine live there, things became easier and my work surged ahead, even though it is ending up a bit on the humorous side.[33]

For Chekhov, 'teaching' or 'preaching' was alien; but this is not to say, as Tolstoy did, that his work is without 'a genuinely governing idea'. Chekhov's combination of 'objectivity' and 'compassion' allowed him to suggest and imply, rather than moralise: while he explicitly depicts 'life as it is', Chekhov also implies 'life as it should be'. And it is partly this which clarifies a significant and major difference between Chekhov's philosophy from 1890 onwards and that of Zola. In *Le Naturalisme au Théâtre* (1881), Zola wrote:

Naturalism, in literature... is the return to nature and to man, direct observation, correct anatomy, the acceptance and depiction of that which is.

In a letter to Suvorin on 25 November 1892, Chekhov made it clear that more is required of the writer than 'the depiction of that which is':

the writers whom we consider immortal or even just good, the writers who have the power of keeping us enthralled, all possess one highly important characteristic in common: they get somewhere and they call upon us to go with them, and we feel not only with our reason but with the whole of our being that they have some aim...some of them, according to how great they are, have aims that concern their own times more closely, such as the abolition of serfdom, the liberation of their country, politics, beauty, or simply vodka; others have more remote aims, such as God, life beyond the grave, human happiness, and so on. The best of them are realists and depict life as it is, but because every line they write is permeated, as with a juice, by a consciousness of an aim, you feel in addition to life as it is, also life as it should be, and it is that which delights you. But what about us? We depict life as it is, but we refuse to go a step further. We have neither near nor remote aims and our souls are as flat and bare as a billiard table. We have no politics, we do not believe in revolution, we deny the existence of God, we are not afraid of ghosts, and so far as I am concerned, I am not afraid of death or blindness either. But he who wants nothing, hopes for nothing and fears nothing cannot be an artist.

The Seagull, written four years later, dramatises these very questions, and one is reminded of Dorn's warning to Konstantin in Act 1:

And then a work of art must express a clear, precise idea. You must know why you write, or else – if you take this picturesque path without knowing where you're going you'll lose your way and your gifts will destroy you. (H.2.246.)

Kostya, Yartsev and Yulia Sergeyevna in *Three Years*, written in 1895, debate similar questions on the role and function of art. And in the same story, Yartsev, a chemist, voices a recurrent point in Chekhov's work: 'I simply want to live, and dream, and hope, and miss nothing... Life, my dear fellow, is very short, and we must make the most of it.' The extent to which people do or do not make the most of life is a leitmotif in Chekhov's plays.

On 11 October 1899, Chekhov complied with a request from Dr Gregory Rossolimo, who had been a medical student with him, for some autobiographical notes. Chekhov wrote:

There is no doubt in my mind that my study of medicine has had a serious impact on my literary activities. It significantly broadened the scope of my observations and enriched me with knowledge whose value for me as a writer only a doctor can appreciate. It also served as a guiding influence; my intimacy with medicine probably helped me to avoid many mistakes. My familiarity with the natural sciences and the scientific method has always kept me on my guard; I have tried wherever possible to take scientific data into account, and where it has not been possible I have preferred not writing at all. Let me note in this connection that the principles of creative art do not always admit of full accord with scientific data; death by poison cannot be represented on stage as it actually happens. But some accord with scientific data should be felt even within the boundaries of artistic convention, that is, the reader or spectator should be made to realise that convention is involved but that the author is also well versed in the reality of the situation. I am not one of those writers who negate the value of science and would not wish to be one of those who believe that they can work out everything for themselves.[34]

Chekhov's presentation of his characters is that of a doctor who, in diagnosing a complaint, either regards his patient as curable, or recommends a change of life-style. As he describes it himself, it is 'the sad comicality of everyday life' which provides the content of his plays; but in that phrase, the form of the plays is also indicated: 'sad comicality' summarises the juxtaposition of one with the other to avoid sentiment, to provoke thought, and to ensure an objective awareness on the part of the spectator. The perspective is always shifting: when a Chekhov character lacks a sense of proportion, the spectator does not. Utilising elements of the nineteenth century popular theatre, Chekhov makes something quite new out of the conventions and stock situations; incorporating certain essentials of naturalism – namely, 'direct observation, correct anatomy' – he extends the strict definition of naturalism by making symbols organic to his dramatic structure. Melodrama is used to reveal the melodramatic; farce deflates and heightens the tragic; vaudeville tricks can reveal unhappiness – and irony allows the combination of objectivity and compassion.

A comment made by Chekhov just before his final medical examination is, perhaps, analogous to his dramatic method and purpose:

First of all, I'd get my patients into a laughing mood, and only then would I begin to treat them.[35]

2

Conventions and innovations in Russian comedy

1. Chekhov and his theatre of the 1880s

In 1886 Chekhov wrote a short story called *Dramatist*, in which the playwright, 'a dim personality with lustreless eyes and a catarrhal physiognomy', is shown paying a visit to his doctor:

His complaints include breathlessness, belching, heartburn, depression and a bad taste in the mouth.

'What do you do for a living?' asked the doctor.

'I am a playwright,' the individual replied not without pride.

The doctor, filled with respect for his patient, smiled deferentially. Since such an occupation implied great nervous strain, he asked his patient to describe his mode of life. The playwright told him that he usually got up at twelve, and at once smoked a cigarette and drank two or three glasses of vodka. After breakfast he again had some beer or wine, the choice depending 'on his finances'. Then he usually went to a pub and after the pub he had a game of billiards. At six o'clock he went to a restaurant to have his dinner, but his appetite was so bad that to stimulate it he was forced to have six or seven glasses of vodka. Then at the theatre he felt so nervous that he again had to consume large quantities of drink. From the theatre he went to some night-club where he usually stayed till the morning.

'And when do you write your plays?' asked the doctor.

'My plays?' the playwright shrugged.

'Well, that depends... First of all, I get hold of some French or German piece either by accident or through some friends (I haven't got the time to keep an eye on all the new foreign plays that are published myself). If the play is any good, I take it to my sister or hire a student for five roubles. They translate it for me and I, you see, adapt it for the Russian stage: I substitute Russian names for the names of the characters and so on. That's all. But don't run away with the idea that this is easy. It isn't at all easy!' the 'dim individual' declared, rolling up his eyes and heaving a sigh.[1]

This story is one of several by Chekhov which have as their subject or background the prevalent conditions of the Russian stage,[2] and it clearly illustrates Chekhov's knowledge of contemporary plays and play-writing methods. Moreover, it expresses a satirical attitude to the custom of the 'popular' theatre, the imitation and adaptation of foreign plays, particularly French, for the Russian stage. This imitation of foreign models, although customary since the eighteenth century, had by the 1880s and 1890s produced a situation in the theatre in which 'convention' and 'formulas' were more in demand than innovation and originality. The 'degeneration' of the theatre applied to the privately-owned and the provincial theatres, and equally to the Imperial and the privately-owned theatres of Moscow and Petersburg; even the theatre considered by Nemirovich-Danchenko as 'the best',[3] the Maly Theatre, had become atrophied and stereotyped:

Why did Chekhov not find a place on the official stage – on, for example, the famous stage of the Moscow Maly Theatre which was then at the peak of its reputation? There were two kinds of repertoire: comedy and drama which primarily meant Ostrovsky's plays, and then plays by, for example, Schiller or Hugo...By this time, with the death of Ostrovsky, the contemporary repertoire was under the control of five or six 'masters' of the drama to whom the art of the Maly Theatre and the requirements of the lead actors was second nature. At the head of the company were Fedotova and Yermolova – every play was invariably written for one or the other and when they both played together, the Maly Theatre was sold out...These writers – called 'juror' dramatists by the critics – had absolute job security and control: they simply informed the stage director, Tchernevsky, when a new play would be ready and how to cast it, and he would schedule the repertory accordingly.

The theatre's administration was not controlled by theatre people but by government officials, and thus the manager, when appointed, did not need to know anything about the theatre: he was an officer of the Guards, a position he obtained through his wife. The modest role of the stage director, on the other hand, involved neither a creative function nor an educative contribution, and the actors listened to him only out of courtesy...Thus the understanding of stagecraft, of casting, or of what constituted a good part was inhibited and stereotyped...In a word, it was the old story of academic conservatism.

This resulted in a rigid distinction in the theatre between 'dramatist' and 'writer': the dramatist might be in popular demand at the Maly Theatre, but counted for little amongst real writers, while his box-office successes never interested the editors of journals and periodicals. Equally, however, a writer of popular and successful short stories was a mere guest in the theatre. Thus, for example, the unknown Krylov[4] was at home in the theatre because he 'knew the stage', while Turgenev – who did not – was only a respected visitor. The question of 'knowing the stage' was effectively a door closed in the face of the serious writer.

This archaic situation still remained essentially unchallenged, but gradually there was an increasing demand for a *literary* theatre...

The Russian theatre, made justly famous by Gogol and Shchepkin, had become stultified by conservatism and sentimentality; it was like an armoured ship encrusted with barnacles from long rest at anchor.[5]

It was this situation, symptomatic of the general decadence of Russian culture at the end of the nineteenth century, produced by political and economic causes, which prompted Stanislavsky to say: 'in those days [theatre] was controlled by restaurateurs on the one hand, and by bureaucrats on the other'.[6]

It was, in fact, those prevalent conditions of the Russian stage which motivated the significant changes of the late 1880s and the 1890s: in 1888 there was an open challenge to the conventional theatricalism of the Imperial theatres when The Society of Art and Literature was formed by A. F. Fedotov, F. A. Komissarzhevsky, F. L. Sologub, and Stanislavsky. In March 1897 the first All-Russian Conference of Theatre Workers was held in Moscow: the conference discussed the low standard of theatre, but only in the provincial theatres, since the conference had been permitted by the authorities only on the condition that no mention was made of the Imperial theatres.[7] One year later, in 1898, Nemirovich-Danchenko and Stanislavsky founded the Moscow Art Theatre.

Until then the best actors and dramatists had had few outlets for their dissatisfaction and disillusionment, and neither the majority of private theatres nor the Imperial theatres observed even the most basic artistic requirements. The most popular and profitable productions were of farces which reiterated the most risqué and coarsest situations of operetta plots and differed from operetta only in that neither musical ear nor voice was required of the actor. It is scarcely surprising, therefore, that *The Seagull*, first performed at the Alexandrinsky Theatre on 17 October 1896, was withdrawn from the repertoire after the fifth performance. It is in *The Seagull* that Konstantin Treplev voices a very real contemporary criticism of the theatre, a criticism which is not invalidated by his own inability to replace Arkadina's theatre with something expressing 'a clear, precise idea':

the theatre's in a rut nowadays, if you ask me – it's so one-sided. The curtain goes up and you see a room with three walls. It's evening, so the lights are on. And in the room you have these geniuses, these high priests of art, to show you how people eat, drink, love, walk about and wear their jackets. Out of mediocre scenes and lines they try to drag a moral, some commonplace that doesn't tax the brain and might come in useful about the house. When I'm offered a thousand different variations on the same old theme, I have to escape – run for it.[8]

Konstantin provides a specific clue to Arkadina's theatre when he talks in Act I of her 'acting in *The Lady with the Camellias* or *It's a Mad Life*'. Clearly, Arkadina is an actress of the 'establishment' and popular theatre, the theatre of 'a thousand different variations on the same old theme' in which 'formula' plays, melodramas, farces and vaudeville were the staple diet.[9] This was the theatre against which Nemirovich-Danchenko and Stanislavsky reacted, and which Chekhov, in a letter to Shcheglov of 7 November 1888, described in these terms:

The contemporary theatre is like a rash, a bad disease of cities. It is necessary to sweep away this disease with a broom; to like it is not healthy. You'll start arguing with me and repeating the old phrase: the theatre is a school, it educates and so forth. But I'll tell you what I see: the present theatre is not above the crowd – on the contrary, the life of the crowd is above the theatre, more clever than the theatre! Consequently, that means the theatre is not a school, but something else.

Chekhov became increasingly critical of contemporary plays and productions, but it was exactly this theatre with which he was most familiar. His early experience was of the provincial theatre of Taganrog,[10] and the stereotyped theatres of Moscow on which he reported for Leykin's *Fragments*. Thus, to state the obvious, his knowledge of the theatre did not originate with his association with the Moscow Art Theatre, nor were *Ivanov* (1887–9) or *The Wood Demon* (1889) the only plays which preceded *The Seagull*, *Uncle Vanya*, *The Three Sisters* and *The Cherry Orchard*. Before Chekhov became an innovatory force in the Russian theatre, many of the plays he wrote owed a great deal to the popular theatre. Using the long-established form of the farce and the vaudeville, Chekhov initially wrote apparently conventional plays.

It is, perhaps, because of the apparent conventionality of his vaudevilles that Chekhov's short plays have been largely neglected by the critics. As Eric Bentley says: 'It is never wise for an author to give a modest account of himself: the critics accept it.'[11] Chekhov did, in fact, often describe his vaudevilles in frivolous or dismissive terms, as, for example, in a letter of 22 February 1888 to the poet Yakov Polonsky: 'Having nothing to do, I wrote a silly little French vaudeville under the title of *The Bear*.' But there is considerable danger in taking such comments at face value: Nemirovich-Danchenko wrote that 'Chekhov often advised me to write vaudevilles', and adds 'because they were sure to bring me in a good income'.[12] And in a letter to Suvorin in

1894, after Chekhov had written all his one-act plays with the exception of the final version of *Smoking is Bad for You*, Chekhov wrote:

> It is much easier to write a play about Socrates than about a young girl or a cook, which merely shows that I do not regard the writing of vaudevilles as a frivolous occupation. Nor do you consider it as such, much as you may pretend that it is nothing but a lot of frivolous nonsense. If a vaudeville is nonsense, then a five-act play by such a man as Burenin[13] is nonsense.[14]

Chekhov's inherent seriousness towards writing farce-vaudevilles is also made clear by the fact that he was concerned with vaudevilles throughout his creative life: from 1885 (*On the High Road*), to the middle of the nineties (the unfinished *The Night before the Trial*, 1895), to the beginning of the twentieth century (the last version of *Smoking is Bad for You*, 1903). And as his letters make clear, Chekhov often returned to the idea of writing a new farce-vaudeville in the nineties and early twentieth century.

Chekhov started writing vaudeville sketches while he was still at school and, as Derman describes, before Chekhov left Taganrog he wrote vaudevilles which he sent to his brother Alexander in Moscow, in the hope of getting them produced. Also Chekhov's brother, Michael, testifies that 'some time before writing *Ivanov*, Anton Pavlovich took up plays and vaudevilles, but destroyed them himself'.[15] There are, however, some references to these early vaudevilles: titles such as *Not for Nothing Did the Hen Cluck; He had Met his Match This Time*, and *The Cleanshaven Secretary with a Gun*[16] which give an idea as to the tone, but no facts as to the content.[17] The only information about Chekhov's unknown vaudevilles, other than titles, relates to one which he planned in 1885 (the year of *On the High Road*), which would have been called *The Power of Hypnosis* and which is described by Shcheglov.[18]

But however seriously Chekhov took his vaudeville writing, critics have dismissed them as merely the conventional and second-rate workings of a youthful writer. Thus S. D. Balukhaty wrote:

> Chekhov does not start with his vaudevilles some kind of original line in the theatre which could be an innovation. His vaudevilles, both in theme and in composition, correspond to the theme and type of the traditional structure of the vaudeville genre which was popular in the theatre of the '80s.[19]

The traditional aspects of Chekhov's one-act plays form a crucial link between the theatrical conventions of his contemporary theatre and the Chekhov best-known for his last four plays.

But of Chekhov's knowledge of popular conventions there is no doubt, particularly in the light of his list written in 1880, which he called *Things Most Frequently Encountered in Novels, Stories and Other Such Things:*

A count,
A countess with traces of former beauty,
The baron – neighbour,
The littérateur – liberal,
The impoverished nobleman,
The foreign musician,
Stupid footmen, nannies, governesses,
The German manager,
The Esquire and heir from America,
People who are not beautiful, but pleasant and attractive,
The hero – who is rescuing the heroine from a crazed horse, strong in spirit and capable at any convenient occasion of showing the strength of his fists,
The height of the skies, the impenetrable, boundless...distance...incomprehensible, in a word: nature!
Fair-haired friends and ginger-coloured enemies,
The rich uncle, he may be liberal or conservative, depending on the circumstances. For the hero, the uncle's admonitions are not as useful as his death,
The aunt in Tambov,
The doctor with a worried face, arousing hope that there might be a crisis; he often has a walking stick with a cane handle and he is bald. And where there is a doctor, there is rheumatism, incurred from honest labour, there is migraine, inflammation of the brain, care of the wounded in a duel, and the inevitable advice to go and take the waters,
The servant who has been in service with the old masters, who is prepared to go through thick and thin for the master's family, even go through fire. A very witty fellow.
A dog who does everything except talk, a parrot, a nightingale,
A dacha outside Moscow, and a mortgaged estate in the South,
Electricity – in the majority of cases dragged in for no particular reason,
A briefcase out of Russian leather, Chinese porcelain, an English saddle, the gun that does not fire, a medal on your lapel, pineapples, champagne, truffles and oysters,
Incidental eavesdropping as the cause of great discoveries,
An endless number of interjections, and attempts to use an appropriate technical term,
Subtle hints to rather weighty circumstances,
Very often there is the absence of an ending,
Seven Deadly Sins in the beginning and a wedding at the end!
The end.[20]

This list indicates the initial possible origin of certain of the comic elements in Chekhov's plays. One may readily recognise the derivation of the argument between Yat and Zhigalov about electricity in *The*

Wedding, but equally 'the dog who does everything except talk' brings to mind Charlotte Ivanovna in *The Cherry Orchard* whose dog 'actually eats nuts'; the servant 'who has been in service with the old masters' might well be Firs; a 'ginger-coloured enemy' is described in Act 1 of *Platonov* by Shcherbuk when he talks of his wife's 'blasted red-haired lover-boy' called Ginger, and the 'aunt in Tambov' is reminiscent of 'the aunt in Yaroslavl' several times mentioned as a possible source of financial salvation in *The Cherry Orchard*. And where, as is often the case, Chekhov reverses the convention and, for example, either does *not* provide a wedding at the end (as in the case of Varya and Lopakhin), or offers a very dubious wedding as in the case of Lomov and Natasha in *The Proposal*, his innovatory use of convention becomes clarified: Chekhov consciously plays against the audience expectations which he has initially aroused.

Thus, what is often a comic effect in Chekhov's plays is sometimes a parody of a particular theatrical convention as in *The Proposal*, or the very real and credible result of what has now become an artificial situation as in *The Cherry Orchard*, in which the conventional device has much deeper implications.

It is Chekhov's early awareness of 'the artificial' which implies a particular response to convention, a response which lends itself very readily to parody on the one hand, and to the conscious avoidance of artificiality on the other. In an article called 'Chekhov's *Tatyana Repina*',[21] Smirnova-Chikina mentions Chekhov's many parodies on the works of such French writers as, for example, Victor Hugo, Alphonse Daudet, Jules Verne, Gaboriau, or Ponson du Terrail. And she, amongst other critics, puts forward the view that *Tatyana Repina* is itself a parody.[22] An example of Chekhov's 'tone' may be seen in the climax to his parody of a Victor Hugo novel, *A Thousand and One Passions (Tysyacha odna strast')*:

A powerful man, hurling his enemy down the crater of a volcano because of a beautiful woman's eyes, is a magnificent, grandiose and edifying picture! All it needed was lava![23]

Chekhov's avoidance of artificiality is evident in his short stories and his plays, but is also illustrated very clearly at the beginning of his writing career in his reaction in 1881 (a year after noting down his list of conventions and clichés), to Sarah Bernhardt's visit to Moscow. Chekhov wrote reviews of her performance for some Moscow journals:

We watched Sarah Bernhardt and were thrown into raptures by her great industry. There were times in her acting which nearly moved us to tears. If our tears did not flow it was only because the whole charm of her acting was spoilt by its artificiality. But for that wretched artificiality, those contrived conjuring tricks and exaggeration, we should definitely have burst into tears, and indeed the whole theatre would have rocked with thunderous applause.

and:

Every sigh, all her tears, her convulsions in the death scenes, the whole of her acting is nothing more than a cleverly, faultlessly learned lesson...When she acts, she is not trying to be natural, but to be unusual. Her intention is to strike the audience, to astonish and to dazzle.[24]

Chekhov made the same criticism of Russian actors, and stressed their inability to play individualised characters as opposed to conventional 'types':

Our actors never observe ordinary people. They know nothing of landowners, business men, priests, or civil servants. On the other hand, they are quite capable of representing billiard markers, rich men's mistresses, drunken card-sharpers, and generally those individuals whom they happen to observe incidentally during their pub-crawls and drinking bouts. The real trouble is that they are so frightfully ignorant.[25]

On one level, however, the artificiality and stereotyped nature of the Russian stage at this time was an inheritance of the strict censorship which had existed for centuries, and which was still a very real factor in Chekhov's time. As Nemirovich-Danchenko wrote:

When first translated, *Hannele*[26] was forbidden stage production. Two censorships existed simultaneously: one for printed works and one for the stage, and thus while the play was passed for publication, it was prohibited for performance...Another translation was made which was more acceptable for Russian stage performance and the censorship passed it...Then, on the eve of the final dress rehearsal, I suddenly received an order from Trepov, the Chief of Police, to take the play off...I discovered that the play was now forbidden because of a protest by the Metropolitan of Moscow, Vladimir...Independent of government censorship for publications and performances, there was also Church censorship.[27]

Chekhov's *On the High Road* was rejected by the censor on the grounds that 'this gloomy, sordid play cannot be approved for performance'[28] and in fact was not even published during Chekhov's lifetime. In this context, Chekhov could only implicitly suggest in *The Cherry Orchard* that Trofimov's political opinions or activities had resulted in expulsion from the university – as it was, several speeches by Trofimov which were overtly critical of prevalent social conditions were cut by the censor before the first performance of the play, and some of Astrov's speeches in *Uncle Vanya* had suffered the same fate.

This climate of constant surveillance inevitably left a profound mark: for fear of compromising themselves, most people retreated into the frivolous or the superficial and this, undoubtedly, was a contributing factor in the hopelessness and inertia which characterises many of Chekhov's characters, and many others amongst the educated classes. The effect is seen very clearly in Chekhov's short story *The Man in a Case*:

This Greek master at a gymnasium, who tried to surround himself as it were with a shell into which he could retire like a snail, wearing galoshes and carrying an umbrella in the finest weather, hiding himself behind dark spectacles and a turned-up collar, plugging his ears with cotton-wool, was in his shrinking attitude to life the very type of the servile citizen. He kept his mind too as it were in a case. Whatever was forbidden he was quite clear about, but there was always something annoyingly indefinite about other things, so if anything new was suggested, a dramatic circle for instance, he was always very nervous about what might come of it. Any kind of departure from the regulations, even if it had nothing to do with him, made him acutely miserable, and he infected others with his feeling, so that 'people began to be afraid of everything. They were afraid of talking aloud, of sending letters, of making new acquaintances, of reading books, afraid of helping the poor or teaching others to read and write'.[29]

In terms of public taste in the theatre, this created a situation similar to that which had existed forty years earlier in 1842 when Nicholas I suppressed the drama and subjected it to the arbitrary censorship of the Third Division (the Gendarmerie): the plays were so innocuous as to be completely colourless, and playwrights and public alike, wishing to be left alone by the police, required nothing more of the theatre than romantic tales, vaudevilles, melodramas, and translations of 'safe' plays from abroad. If anything, this trend had increased at the beginning of the 1880s – as Turgenev had written in a letter in 1874: 'The reign of mediocrity has started.'

Turgenev had reason to note both the mediocrity and the censorship which encouraged it; himself an innovatory dramatist, play after play of his fell foul of the censors. His two-act comedy *The Parasite*, written specifically for Mikhail Shchepkin and the Maly Theatre, was banned for its 'utter immorality' which, in fact, meant its criticism of the Russian nobility; the one-act comedy-vaudeville *Lunch with the Marshal of the Nobility* (1849), was banned for the same reasons, while the first version of *A Month in The Country* (1850), initially called *The Student*, was also banned for performance on the grounds of immorality. Turgenev agreed to significant changes in the play at the insistence of the censors when it was published – distorted – under the title of *Two Women* in January 1855, and it was only performed as a play for the first time in 1872 in Moscow, and 1879 in Petersburg. Effectively, the combination of the censorship and the narrowness and mediocrity of much contemporary theatre succeeded in making Turgenev doubt his own merits as a dramatist. *A Month in the Country* was the last play which Turgenev wrote, and in the brief introduction to the first edition of his works (1869) Turgenev began the sixth volume which contained his plays with the words: 'I feel it is my duty to ask my readers for their indulgence. Not possessing any dramatic talent...I...thought that my plays, unsatisfactory as they are on the stage, would be of some interest to some person who might like to read them. I may be mistaken even about that; let the public judge.' Even today, perhaps, his radical break with tradition and with conventional playwriting is still under-estimated, as indeed are his merits as a playwright.

Chekhov as the inheritor of a great *literary* tradition is well docu-mented in numerous critical studies,[30] all of which seek to analyse, not minimise, the innovatory features of his work. Added to this, however, Chekhov was also the inheritor of a massive and often second-rate *popular* theatrical tradition of comedy, and this is nowhere more apparent than in his farce-vaudevilles.

2. The farce-vaudeville and comedy techniques

The vaudeville, like so many other forms of comedy and light entertain-ment originating in the eighteenth century, was imported from France on to the Russian stage. The vaudeville as 'a purely French genre' was described by Théophile Gautier in 1844:

If the flame of genuine comedy is still glimmering anywhere, certainly it is not in the big theatres, but on twenty small stages where it is broken up into short scenes fashioned by different hands. This comedy, called vaudeville, is a diversi-fied form, animated and witty, sowing Attic salt in handfuls, and showing customs with a casual yet pointed veracity. Its only shortcomings are its un-civilized tongue and intolerable music. And even though, more than anything else, we treasure perfection of style, we must admit that in this inexhaustible creative pattern there is a certain vigour and originality. This is a purely French genre. The Greeks had their tragedy; the Romans, their comedy; the English ιd the Germans, their drama; but vaudeville is completely ours. It is really to ᵥe regretted that the rules of classicism have prevented many noted men of letters from mastering this form, so pliable and so suited to flights of the imagination, and adaptable to all styles, even poetry.[31]

A number of significant points emerge from Gautier's comment. First, vaudevilles were not written by 'noted men of letters' but instead were 'fashioned by different hands', a practice that no doubt produced a patchwork of often dubious quality which, in turn, possibly explains in part the 'literary' criticisms of the vaudeville both in France and in Russia.[32] Secondly, Gautier indicates that 'the rules of classicism' and the vaudeville were by no means related: the vaudeville created its own 'rules' and conventions, and was not bound by the classical 'unities' or other requirements. As such, it was inherently non-literary in its origins, developing on the one hand, into comic opera or operetta, and into farcical and often satirical comedy on the other. And, finally, Gautier points to the flexibility of the genre: it can show 'customs', and be adapted 'to all styles', inclusive of music, poetry (couplets), dances, farce, and so on. It is clearly a 'mixed genre', not necessarily observing the distinction between tragedy and comedy, or 'the joke' and social comment; and as it developed on the Russian stage, it was characteristic of the vaudeville 'to intermingle the comic, the dramatic, the gay and the lyric'.[33]

In his *Art Poetique* (1674) Boileau describes the vaudeville as 'a satiric and often political ballad', a definition which may well lend credence to one theory of the word's derivation: song of the city streets, or *voix de villes*. Very much a form of 'low comedy', vaudeville was initially performed in the little theatres of the Paris fairs. These *pièces en vaudevilles*, as they were called, had to be staged as dumb-shows (owing to the monopoly of the Comédie Française) and regularly parodied the plays and productions of the legitimate theatre, with musical choruses inserted on well-known themes. It was not until 1792 that the special Théâtre de Vaudeville opened in Paris.

The Danish dramatist, critic, and director of the Royal Theatre, J. L. Heiberg (1791–1860), himself the author of French-influenced vaudevilles, provides an analysis of the vaudeville in his essay published in Copenhagen in 1826 called *On Vaudeville and Its Significance for the Danish Stage*.[34] In the essay, Heiberg clarifies the difference in emphasis between comic opera and ordinary musical comedy on the one hand and the vaudeville on the other: in comic opera and musical comedy the dialogue serves only to link and introduce the music, it briefly replaces the music; in vaudeville, however, the dialogue is the main feature, and it is the music which temporarily replaces the dialogue. And Heiberg explains that:

Vaudeville is drama of situation, with characters loosely outlined...It cannot be tragic, since tragedy depends on character development...It exists mainly in the realm of comedy...The music and the text...should seem inseparable. A vaudeville should not have too broad a scope, nor demand elaborate theatrical effects. I have therefore written all my vaudevilles in one act, with no changes of scene.[35]

It is also Heiberg, defending his own plays and those of Holberg, who offers one of the earliest critical justifications of farce and who points to the relationship between farce and vaudeville: 'Against the charge that his vaudevilles are farces, Heiberg replies that indeed they are, and so were many of Holberg's best plays, and that he regards farce as a legitimate and respectable form of drama.'[36]

A further aspect of the vaudeville which Heiberg admired was the opportunity it offered for the combination of 'the burlesque and the melancholic'. This, and the vaudeville's 'topicality', popularised comedy and 'not merely pleased the Court and higher circles, but was sung at street corners and in cellars, and drew to the theatre persons from the class that never, or seldom, pays to see a comedy...The public has found a new interest in local comedy, and the way has therefore been opened for a new national comedy.'[37]

The opportunity offered by the vaudeville for the development of a 'new national comedy' was rarely seized upon by the majority of Russian vaudeville writers; in the eighteenth century the vaudeville and other forms of French comedy were regarded as impeding the emergence of a Russian national drama. And it was the actor P. A. Plavilshchikov (1760–1812), in his article 'On The Theatre', who formulated the views of many on a repertoire consisting largely of French 'imports':

We have filled our theatre with either imitations or translations which not only do not elevate it, but keep it enslaved and make it crawl before the originals of these translations; moreover, we borrow not from the root but from the branches. French tragedy flourished on the Greek root. Every translation is far inferior to its original, while the translation from a translation is still more inferior.[38]

This view was extended by the nineteenth century critic, Vissarion Belinsky, who wrote:

Vaudevilles translated from the French, or adapted from the French, as announced in theatre programs, are, as a matter of fact, neither translated nor adapted: they are forcibly dragged from the French stage to the Russian. What wonder, then, that they appear before the Russian audiences disheveled and distorted, with dull witticisms, flat jests, and poor verses. Dress a Frenchman in a dark gray tunic, gird him with a belt, put leggings and bast shoes on his legs, tie somebody's bushy beard on his face, and make him even curse in Russian: still he will not be a Russian muzhik, but to his own and your regret will continue to be a Frenchman in the guise of a Russian peasant. Consequently he will be neither a Russian nor a Frenchman, but a caricature of both, with no face of his own.[39]

None of this affected the popularity of the vaudeville, and the very superficiality of the eighteenth century versions made it less vulnerable to censorship; the plays quickly followed one another without lingering in the repertory, and although most were forgotten after a few performances, the passionate admiration for the vaudeville began to take on what some contemporary critics considered 'threatening dimensions'.

The primary aim of the vaudeville was to amuse and to entertain, not to instruct, a further source of criticism given that, from its inception, the Russian theatre was regarded as a school for enlightenment. Catherine the Great had herself described the Russian theatre as a 'national school' of which she was the 'headmistress', and whose purpose was to teach people how to live virtuously and usefully for the State.[40] This attitude is typified by the inscription on the curtain of the Hermitage Theatre: *Ridendo castigat mores*, and implies a philosophy of comedy and its moral function. As Sumarokov put it: 'The comedy is called to better life through laughter; / It must make people laugh, and let them think thereafter',[41] a view similar to that expressed in Boileau's couplet: 'Comedy teaches us to laugh without spite... / It knows how to instruct and how to cure.' The moral function of comedy is a predominant feature in the classics of Russian comedy as distinct from the majority of vaudevilles. Thus, writing eleven years after the premiere of *The Government Inspector*, Gogol stated in *An Author's Confession* (1847): 'With *The Government Inspector*, I resolved to put together everything I knew about Russia at that time that was evil – all the injustices perpetrated in the places and circumstances in which a man is expected to display the highest degree of justice and to have a good laugh at it all, once and for all.' This, in turn, may be related to Chekhov's comment quoted earlier: 'First of all, I'd get my patients into a laughing mood, and only then would I begin to treat them.'

In the early part of the nineteenth century, however, a number of factors combined not only to further increase the popularity of the vaudeville but, more important, to shift its function: given the oppression of both censorship and taste which prevented the production of such plays as Lermontov's 'masterpiece of sophisticated sarcasm' *Masquerade*, the early nineteenth century repertoire consisted largely of eighteenth century revivals and there was a serious shortage of 'permissible' new material. In addition, the well-established custom of 'benefit' performances increased the demand for vaudevilles: actors needed new plays and accepted into their circle anyone who composed even a short play, while, in turn, it became fashionable to claim authorship and a connection with the theatre. More often than not the resulting plays were crudely constructed and badly written:

> Without the vaudeville trash
> There is no benefit night,
> Yet naught but ben'fit cash
> Saves actors from their plight.[42]

Thus the actors themselves welcomed the vaudeville since they gained both material and popular success through the parts which it offered. The famous actor V. N. Davydov (for whom Chekhov wrote the part of Svetlovidov in *Swan Song*) expressed the opinion, however, that 'the vaudeville furnished particularly suitable material for "short-charge" actors, who found it difficult to sustain creative effort during a long theatrical performance, but were able to express themselves fully and brilliantly in a short one-act play'.

From the beginning of the nineteenth century, therefore, the vaudeville developed from being merely a 'curtain-raiser' into a one-act play in its own right. Equally, the nature of the vaudeville became more varied: some were only dramatised anecdotes, others were primarily concerned with portraits of comic and unusual characters (and borrowed elements of the *comédie de caractère*), while others relied heavily on elaborate production and 'effects'. More important was that from 1810 onwards the potential for 'serious comedy' was gradually realised: while some authors saw the vaudeville as offering only amusement and entertainment, others 'attempted, through the vaudeville, to influence society by means of art'.[43]

After the 'Decembrist' Revolt of 1825 the Government 'kept an even closer watch on the theatre, and in this atmosphere, some vaudevilles served the Tsarist "ideologists".'[44] It was partly this which prompted Belinsky to write:

The subject of a vaudeville: little passions and weaknesses, funny prejudices, amusingly-eccentric characters, anecdotal events of the private and home-life of society. In a word, if the vaudeville does not trespass its frontiers, and does not wander into spheres alien to it; when it is amusing, light, witty, lively, it can give a very great – though momentary – pleasure both when reading it and when seeing it on the stage.[45]

It is, perhaps, not difficult to see why the vaudeville had such a mixed reputation, ranging as it did from the purely imitative French variety, whether simply translated or roughly adapted, to truly 'national' short plays in which the use of satire, for example, brought it closer to the *comédie de moeurs*.

The various kinds of vaudeville are best seen in the works of writers such as Khmelnitsky (1789–1846), whose main achievement was to provide Russian settings, customs and names for the plays he translated from the French; Pisarev (1803–28), whose gift of characterisation, combination of vaudeville and farce, and early social criticism all single him out as probably the best vaudeville writer; Koni (1809–79), who brought biting satire and social criticism to the vaudeville; the poet and radical Nekrasov (1821–77), who wrote vaudevilles under the pseudonym of Perepelsky; and the actor Vorobyov (1805–60), some of whose plays, written under the name Lensky, were based on works by Scribe.[46]

The popularity of the vaudeville in the first half of the nineteenth century is evidenced, for example, in the repertory of the Alexandrinsky Theatre in 1840: out of the twenty-five plays presented that year, ten were vaudevilles. And by the 1840s, the vaudeville was generally used in three ways: as in the 1820s, it offered superficial entertainment; it was still used as a means of supporting the political *status quo*, for which reason it was allowed; but as the only remaining outlet (with the exception of melodrama, comic opera, and romance) for public performance of 'new' plays, it was gradually used for social criticism. It is this new tendency which motivates historians of the vaudeville to write in terms of 'the progressive and the reactionary vaudeville'. The 'tight-rope' of censorship, in fact, made the 'progressive' vaudeville more potential than actual, but sometimes audiences were surprised by a vaudeville which managed to get past the censor. This is made very clear by Gogol's little clerk, Poprishchin, in his *Diary of a Madman*:

I went to the theatre today. The play was about the Russian fool, Filatka. I couldn't stop laughing. They also put on some sort of vaudeville with some amusing little satirical poems about lawyers, and one Collegiate Registrar in particular. So near the knuckle, I wonder they got past the censor. As fo merchants, the author says straight out that they're swindling everyone and that their sons lead a dissolute life and have thoughts of becoming members of the aristocracy. There was a very witty couplet about the critics, saying they do nothing but pull everything to pieces, so the author asks for the audience's protection. A lot of very amusing plays are being written these days. I love going to the theatre. As long as I've a kopeck in my pocket you can't stop me. But these civil servants of ours are such ignorant pigs, you'd never catch *those* peasants going, even if you gave them a ticket for nothing. One of the actresses sang very well.[47]

Gogol repeatedly spoke out against the vaudeville, condemning it for 'its light mockery at the funny sides of society without a glance at the soul of man'.[48] This entry in Poprishchin's diary also indicates another change in the vaudeville of this time: the change in setting, milieu, and characters.[49]

Until the 1840s, vaudevilles were invariably set in a landowner's mansion or drawing-room; the characters were of the nobility-aristocracy, with the obligatory servants, and the plots almost invariably concerned obstacles to a love affair, problems over dowries and over property. It was in the 1840s that the merchant, the government clerk, lawyers, commoners and 'ordinary people' began to take the noble-man's place on the vaudeville stage (and in the auditorium), while the settings changed to that of a commoner's rooms in the Petersburg Suburb, or a merchant's store. But it was with this development that the 'reactionary' vaudevilles gradually introduced a new element which was to continue in the vaudeville of Chekhov's time: comedy was achieved at the expense of the 'little man'; the comic element was, as a rule, determined by a characteristic dialogue which utilised various deviations from the linguistic and generally cultured norms of educated people; thus 'such scenes turned out to be nothing else but scoffing at simple or uneducated people, mocked at from the position of "polite" society',[50] and it was the way of life and the customs of the merchants and lower-middle classes which provided the main source of amuse-ment.

It is perhaps logical that the very situation which made the vaudeville both popular and acceptable to the censor – namely the political and cultural condition of Russia under Nicholas I, in which freedom of speech and of the press was completely suppressed – simultaneously ensured the dislike and disdain of the vaudeville by the great poets and critics of the time. The vaudeville unexpectedly became one of the few outlets for public dissatisfaction, but the government's theatrical policy fostered pure entertainment and only the most innocent and superficial criticism escaped the censorship. As Gogol put it in a letter of 20 February 1833: 'What good is a play that will never be performed? Drama only lives on the stage. Otherwise it is a soul without a body. All that remains for me to do, therefore, is to invent a subject so innocuous that even a police commissioner would not be upset by it. But what sort of comedy is that, when there is neither truth nor malice?'

The plays written under other influences, such as Shakespeare, Byron or Schiller, remained unperformed. Lermontov, reacting against the rules of French classical tragedy, was influenced by Shakespeare and by Schiller (in particular, *Die Räuber* and the plays of the *Sturm und Drang*), and wrote his famous play *Masquerade* in 1835, but even with an artificially inserted 'happy ending' the play was not allowed performance until 1852.[51] Equally, Pushkin's *Boris Godunov* was only published in 1825 (six years after its completion), and was produced for the first time as late as 1870. Pushkin, influenced by Shakespeare and Byron, made explicit a further reason for the rejection of the French influence in the theatre by the literary 'giants' of the time:

Characters created by Shakespeare are not, as Molière's, types exemplifying some passion or vice, but living beings, compacted of many passions and many vices; and circumstances unfold to the spectators their varied, many-sided personalities. Molière's Miser is miserly – and that is all; Shakespeare's Shylock is miserly, resourceful, vindictive, a fond father, witty.[52]

Pushkin asked for depth of character and not merely the personification of 'vices' and 'virtues', but the treatment of character was only one of the many technical features, common to all forms of Russian comedy, including the vaudeville, which emanated from French originals and which may be found in the earliest comedies of the eighteenth century up to and including comedies by Chekhov's contemporaries. Chekhov therefore inherited stock comic techniques which are to be found both in the often second-rate vaudeville and, albeit with some significant differences, in the greatest classical comedies of the Russian theatre.

The 'stock' treatment of character in eighteenth and nineteenth century Russian comedies originated in the *comédie de caractère* and the models provided by Molière, whether *L'Avare*, *Le Misanthrope*, *Le Malade imaginaire*, or *Le Bourgeois Gentilhomme*:

The aim of a writer of a *comédie de caractère* was to incarnate a complete human type, a universal character; this type provided the play with its focus and at the same time personified a human vice, fault or foible. Eighteenth century theoreticians declared that this central character should 'produce an inevitable crisis in the action' of the play, and this action should itself be devised in such a way as to illustrate the vice, fault or foible satirised.[53]

Thus even when the emphasis in a comedy was not primarily satirical, characters were drawn as the personification of a 'vice' or a 'virtue', and were conventionally divided into hero and heroine, unsuccessful suitor, lover, mistress, and so on, or such characters as 'parent' or 'servant' who were either non-participatory witnesses to the action, or a source of intrigue in it. With few exceptions, the characterisation was two-dimensional or stereotyped. Thus, to return to Pushkin's objection, a miser was *only* a miser: the usurer in Nekrasov's vaudeville *The Petersburg Money-Lender* (1845) personifies his function and his profession.

Another feature common to comic writers, whether mediocre or as major as Gogol, was the use of names for characters which in themselves indicate their natures (as in the English 'Comedy of Humours') or names which made them sound ridiculous. Thus in Fonvizin's *The Minor*, Prostakov may be translated as 'Simpleton'; in Griboyedev's *Woe from Wit*, the name Repetilov is associated with the French 'repeter' and with 'reptile', while in Gogol's *The Government Inspector* many of the names carry grotesque associations, such as Zemlyanika or 'Wild Strawberry'. In Gogol, however, this is less a means of summarising the 'totality' of a character, than of suggesting a 'grotesque' feature, whether physical or mental. Chekhov follows this tradition in some instances in the way he names his characters but, again, not to summarise a whole character, and not to make a character 'grotesque', but to add a further dimension. In *A Tragic Role*, Tolkachov's name stems from the verb 'to push', while in *The Cherry Orchard* Simeonov-Pishchik's name might be translated as 'Simeonov-Squeaker', but there is much more to the character than that might suggest if taken in isolation. Thus where Chekhov's predecessors had used the device to personify or to distort or to make immediately recognisable, Chekhov's occasional use is both a comic 'pointer' and a method of objectivising and making an audience 'question' a character.

An important feature of 'stock characterisation' was the convention of 'speech peculiarities': the type-character was endowed with a mode of speech which was immediately recognisable to an audience as typical of a particular class or profession. In this way, many of the characters in Russian comedy can usually be recognised for what or who they

Far more to.7.

are, through the language they speak. Convention dictated that 'heroes', 'heroines' and 'raisonneurs' should use an elevated, sometimes stilted terminology, and make frequent references to 'heart', 'feeling', 'sense', 'virtue' and 'sensibility', while deviations from cultured norms, or the overt pretensions of the lower classes' speech, was a source of satire. Differentiation of character, therefore, was achieved by means of the convention of language each character was ascribed, but generally in terms of one 'type' distinguished from another 'type' instead of *individual* speech patterns and mannerisms. Equally, 'officialese', often a source of parody, would immediately indicate a lawyer, a doctor or a clerk. By the same token, the use of Franco-Russian jargon was a further source of parody, and would indicate to an audience either a character's class – or pretensions to that class.

This use of jargon, often related both to French-influenced satires *and* to satires on the French influence, was first introduced by Sumarokov in a play of 1750, *An Empty Quarrel*, and may be seen in numerous comedies in the eighteenth and nineteenth centuries. In Nekrasov's 'joke-vaudeville', the one-act comedy *Actor* (1841), his character Italy-anets speaks a lengthy verse (in couplets) in a typical mixture of French and Russian, such as 'trois roubles',[54] and an apparently similar convention is used by Chekhov in, for example, *The Three Sisters* when Natasha characteristically says in Act 2:

Need you really use such language, Masha? A nice-looking girl like you, why, you could appear in the very best society – yes, I really mean it – and be thought quite charming if only you didn't use words like that. *Je vous prie, pardonnez-moi, Marie, mais vous avez des manières un peu grossières.* (H.3.103.)

In Chekhov, however, this use of convention is to indicate and clarify *individual* personality (attitude and mannerisms) in addition to class background: Natasha's French throws the remark intended for Masha directly back to the speaker. 'Speech peculiarities' abound in Chekhov's plays, but are always used as a means of a character's self-revelation which is often comic in effect, partly because it is unconscious. It arises, however, naturally and organically, always motivated by three-dimensional characterisation.

Chekhov, in common with other writers, must have learnt from Gogol's innovatory use of speech peculiarities; in Gogol's work this becomes immensely varied, and a major source of the grotesque comedy. Gogol's method of 'comic alogicality' in language is explained by Gogol himself in *Dead Souls* when he describes how Chichikov's servants, Petrushka and Selifan, carry on conversations:

This class of people has a very odd custom. If you ask them a direct question about something, they can never remember; but if you ask them about something else, right away they come up with the answer to the first question and give it to you in far greater detail than you could possible want.

This method is evident in, for example, Act I, Scene iii of *The Government Inspector:* Bobchinsky's attempt to announce the arrival of the government inspector is endlessly delayed by his own parenthetical details (prompted by Dobchinsky), which range from a hot meat pie stall to Dobchinsky's rumbling stomach and whistling tooth. In this way, 'the babblers in Gogol are comical because they lose the thread of logic, wander off the track, and get bogged down in a mass of parenthetical details that clutter up their talk. The result is a situation in which speech flows on by association and is not governed by logic and relevance.'[55] Thus Gogol's own style of 'stream of consciousness' is illustrated partly by means of his characters' illogic or irrelevance. This 'speech-flow by association' was to be highly developed by Chekhov, but as a vital part of 'subtext': its effect is not 'grotesque' but natural, even scientific. Thus where, for example, Nyukhin in the final version of *Smoking is Bad for You* (1903), experiences a breakdown in logical thinking, what is revealed and explored is a psychological breakdown or disintegration of thought, rather than only a means of characterisation or a 'grotesque' portrait. Nyukhin experiences a kind of release, whereas Bobchinsky or other 'babblers' in Gogol's work exhibit feebleness of thought.

It has been aptly said that Gogol's works are 'a virtual treasury of linguistic monstrosities'[56] and these nearly always express feeble thought-processes on the part of his characters: the comic and grotesque effect comes from muddled thinking and from a breakdown of logic. This method is very different from Molière's method of characterising his garrulous pedants in, for example, *Le Malade imaginaire* or *Le Mariage forcé:* it is verbosity which characterises them, not the absence of logic in what they say.

The use of 'comic illogic' is equally apparent in Gogol's method of constructing dialogue in which he makes a particular use of a comic convention as Chekhov subsequently did: the convention of the 'conversation-of-the-deaf', involving the comic dialogue of the 'mutual-misunderstanding' type. This, a traditional device of comedy, goes back as far as the folk theatre. It is evident in the dialogue between Olivia and Malvolio in Act 3, Scene iv of *Twelfth Night;* in the dialogue between Harpagon and Cléante in Act 4, Scene v of Molière's *L'Avare,* or between Sganarelle on the one hand and Valère and Lucas on the other, in Act i, Scene vi of *Le Médecin malgré lui*. Griboyedov, in *Woe from Wit*, uses exactly the same device in the conversation between Prince Tugoukhovsky and the old countess in Act 3, Scene xx, and the name 'Tugoukhovsky' itself derives from the Russian expression for 'hard of hearing'. This comic convention in the dialogue was particularly exploited by the vaudeville in, for example, P. A. Karatygin's *Wives on Loan* (*Zaemnye zheny*). Examples of this technique in Gogol's work are far too numerous to itemise, but perhaps one example suffices to demonstrate both the comedy and the skill. In *Marriage*, Gogol plays with the Russian word for 'omelette' (*yaichnitsa*) by calling one of his characters Yaichnitsa, and the following dialogue takes place between Yaichnitsa and Zhevakin in Act i, Scene ii of the play:

YAICHNITSA: Ivan Pavlovich Yaichnitsa, serving as an executive clerk.
ZHEVAKIN: Yes, I've had a bite to eat too. I knew it would take a while to get here, and the weather is rather cold. I've had a bit of herring and onion.
YAICHNITSA: I think you've misunderstood. That's my name – Yaichnitsa.
ZHEVAKIN: Oh, pardon me! I'm a bit hard of hearing. I really thought you said you had eaten an omelette.

In the vaudeville, this convention relates to comedy of situation or intrigue and is rarely given a wider application or deeper significance, but in Gogol's hands the convention becomes a method of introducing dramatic irony. Chekhov used the same form of dramatic irony, but also developed it further into irony in its more general sense. Thus, in Act 2 of *The Three Sisters*, Ferapont's inability to hear is both comic and sadly revealing. Andrey says:

If you could hear properly I don't suppose I'd talk to you at all. I must talk to someone, but my wife doesn't understand me and I'm somehow afraid of my sisters, afraid they'll laugh at me and make me look a complete fool. I don't drink and I don't like going into bars, but if I could drop in at Testov's in Moscow right now, or the Great Moscovite Hotel – why, it would suit me down to the ground, old boy.

To this, Ferapont – catching the word 'Moscow' – replies:

There was a contractor at the office a few days back telling us about some businessmen in Moscow. They were eating pancakes, and one of them ate forty and died, or so he said. It was either forty or fifty, I don't rightly remember. (H.3.94)

In Chekhov's last plays, the convention of 'inability to hear' becomes the innovation of 'inability to listen', with all the irony that this implies.

Other techniques originating in the French and Russian comedies of the eighteenth and nineteenth century are to be found in the vaudeville and in Chekhov's plays. The monologue, for example, was traditionally used as a means of explanation and justification; heroes and heroines frequently revealed their feelings about each other in one and, in general, it served as the main source of exposition. The artificiality of this method led, however, to an attempt to provide some motivation for the monologue and thus to the use of the 'false monologue' in which other characters are present on-stage but do not interrupt or respond. By the 1880s, this had developed into a form of vaudeville in its own right, the 'scene monologue', and it may be argued that Chekhov employed the traditional monologue form in *Smoking is Bad for You*. Characteristically, however, his use of the form is quite different: given the role of the 'audience', the play is in fact a 'false monologue' and as such, sets up its own convention; in *Swan Song* the opening monologue by Svetlovidov is also turned into a 'false monologue', again by the role of the 'audience'; and in the same play, the 'false monologue' is utilised in yet a further way with the entrance of Nikita, the Prompter: Svetlovidov is scarcely aware of Nikita, but he makes use of him, and in this a great deal is implied about both characters. A crucial feature of the whole 'twist' at the end of *A Tragic Role* relies for its effect on the silent presence of Murashkin throughout Tolkachov's 'tirade'. In the later plays, Chekhov uses the form to different effect – as at the beginning of Act 2 of *The Cherry Orchard* in which Charlotte's opening speech is a 'false monologue', given the (disinterested) presence of Yasha, Dunyasha and Yepikhodov on-stage; however the effect here is to increase the sense of isolation and loneliness of the character, and to justify her own words: 'I'm longing for someone to talk to, but there isn't anyone. I'm alone in the world.' Often characters 'talk to themselves out loud' with little expectation of a response. This inability to 'connect' is particularly evident between the classes, whether in the misunderstanding between Anfisa and Natasha, and Andrey and Ferapont in *The Three Sisters*, or culminating in the misunderstanding and subsequent treatment of Firs at the end of *The Cherry Orchard*.

Without exception, Chekhov's one-act plays employ unity of time and place, but this observance probably owes as much to the brevity and economy of his short stories as to theatre practice. It is surprising, perhaps, that the fidelity of Russian adaptors to French models did not always extend to observing the unities of time, place and action. The application to comedy of the three unities, deriving as it did from Boileau and Chapelain (not from Aristotle), was regarded flexibly by the Russian comic dramatists; Sumarokov, for example, ignored them completely in his comedies. Only unity of time was adhered to, if only for the purpose of exposition. All of the eighteenth century comedies observed the requirement that the action take place within a stated length of time which, however, varied from three to twenty-four hours. Thus in most types of comedy in this period, there are references to the time of day or night, to meal times, and to the duration of the action in general, but in most cases this took the form of rather obvious and artificial exposition. There were, of course, the usual exceptions: in Turgenev's *A Month in the Country* such references are organically motivated rather than purely expository, while thirty years earlier Griboyedov's use of the three unities in *Woe from Wit* illustrates his employment of the convention to suit his own dramatic intentions. While the action of the play takes place in Famusov's Moscow house, the settings change to several locales within the house; the action occurs over a period of just over twelve hours and there are frequent references to the specific time of day, but such references are not there merely to prove the observance of unity of time – Griboyedov makes 'time' an essential component of the action, and organic to the structure of the play. Equally, Griboyedov ignored unity of action: the play is structured on a 'double intrigue' involving Chatsky's love for Sophie *and* his 'social drama'.[57] Inevitably, the plays which treated action with the greatest ingenuity and flexibility were those in which the 'theme' was more important than 'formula', a point made by Pushkin in his *Draft Note on Tragedy* (1825): 'Since the holding of the audience's attention is the first concern of dramatic art, unity of action must be adhered to. But those of place and time are too arbitrary... And it all does not matter. Is it not simpler to follow the Romantic school, which is marked by the absence of all Rules but not by the absence of art? Interest is All.' There was greater flexibility in comedy than in tragedy, and in all types of comedy the unity of place was variously treated: some comedies were set in a room which remained constant throughout the play, as in Fonvizin's plays; others made use of different rooms within one house, while from the nineteenth century onwards either the entire action or part of the action was sometimes given an exterior setting. In *A Month in the Country*, however, the movement of setting parallels the movement of the action and provides a precedent for Chekhov's similar arrangement of locale: Act 1 is set in the drawing-room; Act 2 takes place in the garden; Act 3 returns to the drawing-room; Act 4 is set in the empty hall between the garden and the main house, while the final act returns, appropriately, to the drawing-room.

Equally, it was Turgenev who structured his play simply by means of acts and did not subdivide *A Month in the Country* into scenes each time a character enters. But in Act 2 of the play there is an interesting example of the 'old-style' staging combined with the 'new': the garden setting with its raspberry bushes is combined with artificial and contrived entrances and exits, and the staging is, in fact, conventional despite the abolition of scenic divisions. In this, however, Turgenev was abandoning a tradition which had been strictly observed by almost all previous playwrights: a new scene began whenever a character entered. Thus in Fonvizin's *The Minor*, the direction reads: Scene VII 'The Same and Valet'; this is then followed by the three lines which comprise that scene, after which there is Scene VIII and the entrance of seven characters. Exactly the same principle was followed by Griboye-dov, by Gogol in *The Government Inspector* in which Scene II, for example, is 'the same' but with the addition of the Postmaster, or by Nekrasov or other vaudeville writers. Chekhov adhered to the same principle until 1889–90: thus, the full-length *Platonov* (1880–1), *Ivanov* (1887–9), and *The Wood Demon* (1889–90) are sub-divided into scenes each time a character enters, as are the one-act *On the High Road* (1885), *Swan Song* (1887–88), *The Bear* (1888) and *The Proposal* (1888–9), but not the one-act plays written after 1889–90 such as *A Tragic Role*, *The Wedding*, or *The Anniversary* or, of course, the full-length plays from *The Seagull* onwards.[58] Traditionally, the number of scenes, and their position in an act and in the play as a whole, had influenced and dictated the rhythm and pace of the play; by 1890, however, Chekhov's development of new means of creating rhythm and pace, and their organic relationship to the structure of his plays, enabled him to discard the convention.

The assumption of 'realism' in the setting of Russian comedy (though not the characterisation) originated in part from the influential *comédie de moeurs*, a genre which became the most 'national' comedy on the Russian stage partly by virtue of its educative value and partly because of the quality of writing it produced. Known as *komediya nravov* (comedy of manners), it was primarily satirical: the emphasis was on depicting contemporary manners and customs in order to expose any faults through mockery, and it was consciously aimed at particular classes of contemporary society. Russian classics of the genre were, for example, Fonvizin's plays, *The Brigadier*, 'the first comedy on our manners',[59] and *The Minor*, which Gogol praised for its 'genuinely social content'. And it is in *The Minor* that the beginnings of a form of comedy peculiarly Russian is to be found: the combination of satire, and what Gorky called 'the socially-critical realistic school'. Thus, from its inception, Russian 'comedy of manners' embraced realism in its depiction and criticism of contemporary society, but the realism was heightened by the use not only of satire and parody but of 'the grotesque'. In this sense there is a direct relationship between Fonvizin's comedies, Griboyedov's *Woe from Wit*, for example, and Gogol's *The Government Inspector* or *Marriage*.

It is also in the contemporary Russian setting in the plays of this genre that 'realistic' features of daily life are to be found: games played by polite society, such as whist, dinner parties on-stage, a gypsy troupe to entertain guests, references to contemporary popular reading and, increasingly, the use of colloquial vocabulary. Thus in *Woe from Wit*, which Pushkin called 'a sharp picture of manners',[60] the evening party and the music and dancing which form the background to the action introduced a new realism to the Russian stage. Twenty-five years later, Turgenev took this aspect of realism further in *A Month in the Country*: Act I opens with a game of preference which continues while other action takes place, and at different moments the card-players' conversation or their attention to another conversation taking place on-stage simultaneously, brings the card-game in and out of focus. Turgenev's dramatic method is natural and credible. Such features are, of course, to be found some years later in Chekhov's plays, where they are more fully developed: the game of lotto at the end of *The Seagull* does not merely depict the characters' way of passing the time, the lunch party in Act I of *The Three Sisters* establishes much more than simply the reality of the Prozorov household, while the party in Act 3 of *The Cherry Orchard* takes place up-stage but forms not so much the background to the play's action at this point, as the counterpoint.

But it was from the comedy of situation, or *comédie d'intrigue*, that the majority of comic dramatists drew their plots. Some critics[61] have indicated the relationship between the *comédie d'intrigue* and the vaudeville:

The 'comedy of situation' in the Russian theatre was usually founded on a simple intrigue provided by the efforts of servants to place obstacles in the way of foolish or disagreeable suitors, and to encourage the courtship of their master or mistress.[62]

And:

Plots in vaudeville almost always revolve around the struggles of the enamored couple with obstacles impeding their happiness, which, in the end, they successfully overcome. Interwoven in the plot are current motifs dealing with customs, literature and, occasionally, social topics.[63]

But as one historian of the vaudeville points out:

one should not exaggerate the closeness of the relationship: comedy of situation is merely entertainment, and it would be wrong to think that vaudeville is necessarily a lower genre: thoughtless entertainment is not in the least *inherent* to the nature of the vaudeville. Thus, in Russia, while not breaking its links with the comedy of situation, the vaudeville often comes close to various types of serious comedy.[64]

It is interesting to note that at the time when comedy of situation became less popular, the vaudeville increased in popularity and potential, but not before it had taken over from comedy of situation a number of technical features: the use of accident and coincidence in the development of the plot or intrigue, the depiction of an amusing oddity in human nature, and the device of a 'comic misunderstanding'. In addition, this genre of comedy allowed for, and centred round, a small cast: namely husband, wife, lover and servant, and – of crucial importance for the vaudeville – it lent itself readily to the use of farce.

The 'stock' situations of the *comédie d'intrigue* were, however, so artificial that the French 'originals' were described as using the *chassé croisé* device, and the emphasis on plot and intrigue consistently over-shadowed characterisation. It was rare, however, for an eighteenth or nineteenth century comic dramatist to use action to illuminate character. Action was usually regarded as the means of providing laughter through the kinds of comic effects to be found in farce – misunderstandings, quarrels, disguises, and so on – and the majority of the comedies of this period provided action only in terms of 'stock' characters in 'stock' situations. In Fonvizin's comedies, or Griboyedov's, action is used to depict character, but in the comedies prior to Chekhov's, it was virtually unknown for character to *produce* the action, or for the emphasis in a play to be on the relationships between characters which produces action.[65] Even in *The Government Inspector* the emphasis is on the situation and the relationships are governed and controlled by that situation. Again, however, it was Turgenev who blazed a trail which Chekhov was to follow: in *A Month in the Country*, characterisation is not based on the traditional *faculté maîtresse* but arises from revelation and, in particular, self-revelation; there is development of character rather than the employment of static features, and the relationships are treated both as the source of the action and as motivation for action. Chekhov's development of 'character in action' is infinitely varied, but initially, in some of the one-act plays, he takes a 'stock' situation with *apparently* 'stock' characters, and radically changes the emphasis: in *The Proposal*, for example, the impediment to a successful proposal is not a situation or an intrigue but the characters themselves.

A further convention common to all forms of comedy, whether of character, manners, situation, or the vaudeville, was the *dénouement:* the happy ending in which all misunderstandings are unravelled. The *dénouement* cut the thread of the intrigue by removing all obstacles to the hero's courtship of the heroine and also resolved the fate of all the other characters. This, of course, assumes the happy resolution of a 'stock' situation. The endings were variously achieved: in the sentimental comedy, or *comédie larmoyante*, the ending often took the form of a *tableau* rather than a *coup de théâtre*, but the method always involved a climax followed by resolution. And it was from the *comédie larmoyante* that Fonvizin adapted and altered the *tableau* ending of *The Minor*, in which after his mother's faint and revival, Starodum brings the play to an end with the curtain-line: 'Behold the just reward of wickedness!' Gogol ends *The Government Inspector* with a grotesque *tableau:* a frozen dumb show in which characteristic attitudes are struck and held for the lengthy stage-time of nearly one and a half minutes. In *A Month in the Country*, however, Turgenev created a completely new ending: instead of a *dénouement*, the play simply 'dissolves'. Chekhov ends *The Bear*, for example, with the *tableau* of a 'prolonged kiss', witnessed by a frozen group of servants, but this is then followed by Chekhov's own equivalent of *le mot de la fin:* conventionally, this 'final word' was addressed to the audience and sums up the 'lesson' of the play, but in *The Bear* it is addressed to the servant, Luka, and neatly encapsulates Popova's *volte-face*. Thus Chekhov sometimes uses the convention in order to reverse it or parody it; in other plays he ends the comedy 'unhappily' or doubtfully, or, like Turgenev, simply does not provide an ending as such. This variety of method relates exactly to Chekhov's use of climax and anti-climax, and in the course of his dramatic development his endings become increasingly unconventional. As Chekhov wrote to Suvorin on 4 June 1892:

I have an interesting subject for a comedy, but I haven't yet devised the ending. Whoever discovers new *dénouements* will have opened up a new era! Those cursed *dénouements* always escape one. The hero either has to get married or shoot himself – there seems to be no other alternative. The title of my future comedy is *The Cigarette Case*.[66] I shall not start writing until I invent an ending as intricate as the beginning.

In his last plays, Chekhov did, in fact, open up a new era, and there is a complete contrast to the traditional *dénouement* because, as in Turgenev's play, before there can be a *dénouement* there must be a plot which can be resolved: the lives of the three sisters, for example, cannot in any stage sense be 'resolved' – their lives continue.

This, however, is organically related to an aspect of comic technique which Chekhov took in a new direction – the extent to which he fuses the comic with the serious (not to say potentially tragic) in both his comedies and his dramas, since, as he put it himself, 'with me the serious always alternates with the trivial'.[67] But in itself, Chekhov's combination of the comic and the serious is not unique in Russian comedy; Fonvizin's *The Minor*, for example, has been justly praised for its wealth of laughter ranging from the hilarious to the tragic. In this respect, however, Fonvizin and some other eighteenth century comic writers brought comedy into their own contemporary era. The classicists, such as Sumarokov, based their plays on the models provided by Racine and Molière, and accepted, with Boileau, that 'Comedy is opposed to sighs and sorrows'. But dramatists such as V. I. Lukin (1737–94), or Plavilshchikov, used much more recent and contemporary models, namely French dramatists such as Beaumarchais, and the mixed genre known in France as the *comédie larmoyante*, or sentimental, tearful comedy. This genre grew in popularity since it increasingly reflected the tastes and the aspirations of the merchant class and bourgeoisie. In a quite different context, Pushkin had advocated 'the mixing of the comic and tragic kinds'[68] in 1825, and, again in a different context, it was the potential for combining the serious and the comic which partly characterised the vaudeville.[69] But in practice, the nature of the 'serious' in eighteenth and nineteenth century comedies is quite unlike anything to be found in Chekhov's work: 'serious' meant either 'sentimental' or 'moral'. And in the great comic dramatists prior to Chekhov, whether Fonvizin, Griboyedov or Gogol, the serious elements are completely bound up with the moral view. Thus, the final words in *The Minor* ring out like a moral sentence, and the same moral sentence is to be found at the end of *The Government Inspector;* equally, Gogol's 'laughter through tears' is quite different either from Chekhov's technique or from his use of the phrase in his stage directions. As the critic Slonimsky puts it:

The play [*The Government Inspector*] is built on the mayor's comic efforts to deceive the inspector general. The failure of these efforts at the very moment when they appear to have met with success is what creates the 'staggering effect' of which Gogol speaks in *An Author's Confession*. It is the very magnitude of this sudden change that sets a tragic stamp on the ending. The mayor is no longer the flat and unsophisticated comic character that he was; he becomes more complex because of normal human emotions, which evoke sympathy on the part of the audience. His language, which has been highly comic, is now tinged with pathos. His concluding monologue reveals the subjective side of humor – a contemplation of events in their totality, an awareness of their general significance. He adopts, as it were, the point of view of the author, who manipulates his characters at will and creates comedy from them: 'Some quill-driver, some scribbler will turn up and stick you in a comedy...and everyone will grin and clap their hands. What are you laughing at? You're laughing at yourselves!'[70]

And the same critic describes Gogol's comic technique in this way:

Look at the whirlwind that precedes the onset of a storm: at first it wafts by, light and low, it sweeps up dust and sundry rubbish from the ground; feathers, leaves, and scraps of paper fly up and whirl about; and soon the whole air is filled with its capricious whirling...At first it is light and harmless, but hidden within it are the tears of nature and a terrible storm. Gogol's comic humor is exactly the same.[71]

In *Dead Souls*, Chapter 7, Gogol himself provides a definition of his 'laughter through tears':

And for a long time to come, I am destined...to contemplate the whole of life as it rushes by in all its immensity, contemplate it through laughter which is perceptible to the world and through tears which are invisible to it and unknown.

And Pushkin's response to Gogol's reading of the first chapters of *Dead Souls* takes definition further; his laughter died away and he commented: 'Lord, how sad our Russia is.'

Gogol's 'laughter through tears' is deeply philosophical and moral; it works through the sharp contrasts which produce the 'grotesque' and the distorted. Gogol's comic-serious effect is gained through the juxtaposition of the exaggerated or the heightened; Chekhov's on the other hand, through the juxtaposition of the understated. In Gogol's plays, where there is laughter there is satire, laughter *at* something, with all the moral purpose that that implies. But in a Chekhov play it is unthinkable that a character would turn on the audience as the Mayor does: the audience does not need to be reproached by Chekhov's characters, because it does not laugh at the characters, but with them. And the seriousness in Chekhov is not from satire, not from a high moral purpose, and not from the contemplation of the 'unknown'; it comes from a recognition of the 'known' and often mundane: from 'the sad comicality of everyday life'. There are no 'staggering effects' in Chekhov's plays and therein lies a characteristic which can first be seen in his vaudevilles.

3. The farce-vaudeville of the 1880s

At first glance, it is understandable that most critics saw nothing very original in Chekhov's vaudevilles: when seen in the context of the 1880s, the external form of Chekhov's vaudevilles approximates very closely to the vaudeville as it had developed by that time. Thus there were a number of 'scene-monologues' which are *apparently* identical in form to *Smoking is Bad for You* – monologues written, for example, by Leo Ivanov, Victor Krylov, or I. M. Bulavtsely and others. Equally, in the vaudeville repertory there were many 'comic scenes of daily life' which, in their subjects, are reminiscent of Chekhov's *The Wedding*. And even more numerous were the one-act 'comedy-jokes' which were regarded as the 'true' vaudeville, and which are apparently identical to *The Bear*.

From this classification it is immediately apparent that the vaudeville of Chekhov's time had become even less varied than the vaudevilles of forty years earlier: by the 1880s it was basically divided into only two varieties – the miniature 'comedy-joke', and the 'comic scene', with the 'scene-monologue' forming a type of 'comic scene'.

The miniature 'comedy-joke' was most probably the kind of play which the patient describes to his doctor in Chekhov's story *Dramatist*, quoted earlier: the plays were invariably translated ones, but with the French or German names changed into Russian names. In this sense, and in their total alienation from contemporary life, these vaudevilles of the 80s displayed the worst features of the earliest and most superficial eighteenth century Russian comedies. In the vast majority of cases, therefore, the vaudeville contemporary with Chekhov ignored both moral and social questions, and centred on the kind of 'love interest' familiar to comedy of situation in which both characterisation and *dénouement* were completely conventional.

Thus a typical vaudeville of this kind has at its centre a couple striving towards a happy union, a union finally achieved at the end of the play. Before the finale, however, the couple have to overcome various obstacles to their match, and the action of the play consists solely in overcoming those obstacles. The play's comic nature is determined only by the author's ingenuity in devising the different situations and obstacles which inhibit the match. In these comedies of situation, the characters are merely 'frozen' into stereotyped masks:

the couple must always be young, one of them must be active and resourceful and thus carry the action, while the other must be passive; generally there is a third character, a relative, who places the obstacles in the way of the match and is, as a result, part of the play's comic structure. And a further source of comedy is often provided by a fourth character, a servant, who contributes both farce and exposition.

The nature of the intrigue, whether in vaudevilles with or without 'love interest', differed only marginally according to the dramatist's skill. Invariably, though, this resulted in mere variations on a conventional theme: misunderstandings over dowries or property (rivalry and litigation between landowners), and love triangles which, in turn, created the conventional 'tangle'. The events and names might differ from one play to another, but the social milieu of the play or the characters' social position, and the place of action were completely standardised. An example of this kind of play is to be found in I. L. Shcheglov's[72] play, *The Summerhouse Husband (Dachny muzh)*. After the production of this comedy the famous theatre critic S. Vasilyev wrote:

What is the 'summerhouse husband'? I have to confess that I understand this word as little now, when I know what it is all about, as before when I had no idea of the content of Shcheglov's play. The summerhouse is not important. The elderly husband of a young woman is portrayed; she does not love him and deceives him...this wife would deceive this husband just as much in town as in the country, in winter and in summer. It is not the locality or the surroundings or the time of year which is significant...[73]

And Chekhov expressed his opinion of the same play:

I am of the opinion that if dear Jean will continue to write in the spirit of *The Summerhouse Husband* then his career as a dramatist will go no further than the rank of captain. One cannot keep regurgitating the same types, the very same towns, the same ladies' bustles. After all, other than bustles and summerhouse husbands, there are still plenty of comic and interesting things in Russia.[74]

Chekhov sought to broaden the scope and subject-matter of the vaudeville, and it was to Shcheglov himself that Chekhov wrote:

You want to have an argument with me about the theatre. By all means, but you will never convince me that I am wrong about my dislike of these scaffolds where they execute playwrights. Our contemporary theatre is a world of confusion, stupidity, and idle talk. The other day Karpov boasted to me that he had shown up 'the silly liberals' in his third-rate *Crocodile Tears*[75] and that was why his play was disliked and abused. After that my hatred of the theatre grew more violent and I grew even more fond of those fanatics who are trying to make something decent and wholesome out of it.[76]

The other common type of vaudeville, 'the comic scene', is described by Berdnikov in these terms:

'The comic scene' – as opposed to the 'comedy-joke' – lacked dynamic action, was static and, more often than not, had neither an internal, logical principle, nor a completion. At best, these types of scenes could – quite vividly – produce the outward appearance of everyday life and everyday types.[77]

At worst, however, it was exactly in these 'comic scenes' that many vaudeville writers fashionably created their comedy at the expense of the 'little man', mocking the uneducated, the ordinary, from a position of superiority.

By this time, the inclusion of couplets, songs and dances was less common in either 'type' of vaudeville, but what remained was still superficial characterisation, contemporaneity, the use of asides and, in the 'comedy-joke', the supremacy of plot in terms of intrigue, mis-understanding or 'obstacles', physical action of a farcical kind, and in the best vaudevilles a rapid pace of action and compactness of form.

The 'monologue-scene' was a version of these comic scenes but, in a very distinctive way, it combined the characteristic feature of each of the common forms of vaudeville: the *situation* of the 'monologue-scene' was taken from the 'comedy-joke' and served as the hero's story; and the comic stereotyped *character* was taken from the 'comic scene' and thus dictated the type of man or woman telling the story. This form of vaudeville can be seen in *Smoking is Bad for You*, but whereas in the first version (1886) both the situation and Nyukhin as a 'type' are conventionalised, in the last version (1903) Chekhov makes something radically different out of the very convention he was using. For this reason both early and late versions of the play must be separately considered: such an examination clearly demonstrates Chekhov's innovatory development of the convention.

It is essential, however, to recognise the relationship and indebtedness of Chekhov's one-act plays to his short stories, not only as the source of material, but as a source of technique. Six of the plays originated as short stories: *On the High Road* was based on the story *In Autumn* (1883), *Swan Song* from the story *Calchas* (1886), *A Tragic Role* was based on *One Among Many* (1887), *The Wedding* from three stories: *The Wedding Season* (1881), *Marrying for Money* (1884) and *A Wedding with a General* (1884), while *The Anniversary* clearly emanates from *A*

Defenceless Creature (1887), and *The Night before the Trial* from the story of that title written in 1886. In dramatising some of his own stories, it is evident that Chekhov relied in his vaudevilles not only on his experience as a prose writer but also on his narrative work. And it is natural that Chekhov set himself the same task with the vaudeville as with his narrative work: 'he strove to take the vaudeville from the literary back-yard onto the wide road of realistic Russian art as he had already done with the short story which hitherto had belonged only to the "small-fry" humorous press.'[78] And simultaneous with Chekhov's search for new literary and dramatic forms, his early creative work makes frequent use of strong elements of parody – parody which also illuminates his contemporary theatre and conventional dramaturgy with its trite themes, characters, situations and language.[79] Chekhov's use of cliché serves, therefore, as a critique *and* as a means of developing his techniques.

In this way, Chekhov achieved for the vaudeville what he also achieved with the short story: he 'humanised' the 'stock' characters and made them realistic complex individuals by avoiding 'retired captains with red noses, drunken press reporters, starving writers, consumptive and hard-working wives, honest young men without a blot on their characters, lofty-minded young ladies, and dear old nannies.'[80] He became increasingly concerned with motive and theme rather than formula: 'You must never put a loaded rifle on the stage if no one is going to fire it.'[81] As a letter of 15 November 1887 indicates, Chekhov consciously learnt the craft of the stage:

The requirements are: (1) complete confusion; (2) each character must possess individual features and idiosyncrasies and must speak in a language of his own; (3) no long speeches; (4) uninterrupted movement; (5) the parts must be written for Gradov, Svetlov, Schmidthof, Kisselevsky, Solovtsov, Vyazovsky, Valentinov, Kosheva, Krasovskaya, and Borozdina;[82] (6) it must be full of criticisms on the prevailing conditions of the stage, for without criticism our vaudeville won't be any use.

Chekhov's phrase, 'for without criticism our vaudeville won't be any use', is crucial to both his method and his purpose.

Chekhov took the vaudeville in a new direction: he decisively broke the traditional concept of the vaudeville as merely a thoughtless 'comedy-joke'; he took the vaudeville beyond its previous boundary of a specific genre of light comedy, and in so doing he also extended the meaning and range of 'comedy' as such. Thus, in a letter of 14 October 1888, Chekov wrote: 'between the big play and the one-act

play the difference is only quantitative. You too should write a vaudeville', and he wrote by the word 'vaudeville': 'a one-act drama or
comedy'.

It is in his vaudevilles that Chekhov begins to erase the distinction
between 'comedy' and 'drama'.

3

The farce-vaudevilles

Chekhov's language is as precise as 'Hullo!' and as simple as 'Give me a glass of tea'. In his method of expressing the idea of a compact little story, the urgent cry of the future is felt: 'Economy!'

It is these new forms of expressing an idea, this true approach to art's real tasks, that gives us the right to speak of Chekhov as a master of verbal art.

Behind the familiar Chekhovian image created by the philistines, that of a grumbler displeased with everything, the defender of 'ridiculous people' against society, behind Chekhov the twilight bard we discern the outlines of the other Chekhov: the joyous and powerful master of the art of literature.[1]

Vladimir Mayakovsky, *The Two Chekhovs* (1914)

On 12 December 1900, Tolstoy was present at a rehearsal of a 'Chekhov evening' arranged by the Society for Art and Literature. Not wishing to be stared at in the auditorium, Tolstoy asked the producer, Nikolai Arbatov, to seat him somewhere in the wings. The vaudevilles *The Bear* and *The Wedding* were being performed and, as an eyewitness reports, 'Tolstoy watched, and all the time a pleased, joyful smile never left his face. At times he roared with laughter as he listened to the incredibly funny lines.' During the interval Tolstoy talked to the actors, and expressed his enthusiasm and amazement over Chekhov's humour: 'After Gogol,' he is reported to have said, 'we don't have such a brilliant, powerful humorist as Chekhov. Sound and powerful humour is absolutely necessary for us. And Chekhov's stories are pearls of beauty.'

It is, of course, scarcely surprising that Tolstoy immediately responded to the social value of Chekhov's one-act comedies, but, in addition, Tolstoy was apparently fully aware of the innovatory nature of Chekhov's dramatic form. After the performance, he went to see Arbatov and began to talk enthusiastically about the virtues of the Russian vaudeville: 'I love the vaudeville, and I think a real Russian vaudeville – and the best I know – is Chekhov's *Wedding*.' Valuing Chekhov's 'dramatic jokes' highly (though none of the full-length plays),[2]

Tolstoy noted the way they differed from the traditional vaudeville, and he pointed out the 'causal' comedy which motivated the action and served as the main driving force of the plays. In addition, Tolstoy praised *The Proposal* for the absence in it of what he called 'the French nonsensical surprises'.[3]

Implicit in Tolstoy's reported remark about the lack of 'the French nonsensical surprises' is an awareness of the different nature of action and plot in Chekhov's one-act plays, a difference which, in turn, opens up further innovatory features. Tolstoy recognised and valued a characteristic of Chekhov's vaudevilles which was significantly lacking in the conventional vaudevilles: 'realism'. This 'realism' relates to the depiction of a milieu and to the credibility of Chekhov's characters, to a particular comic characterisation which prompted Vakhtangov to talk not of caricature but of 'broader realism'.[4] It is to this 'broader realism' that Tolstoy's remark about Gogol and Chekhov may be related: the 'realism' of Chekhov's one-act plays has room for the grotesque and the exaggerated, elements which were heightened to varying degrees by both Vakhtangov in his production of *The Wedding* (1920), and Meyerhold in his programme composed of *The Bear*, *The Proposal* and *The Anniversary* which he called *33 Swoons* (1935). 'Realism' was substantially lacking in the traditional vaudevilles given that the content was dictated by the conventions of the genre, whereas in Chekhov's vaudevilles the content demands and dictates a new form.

This new form manifests itself in all of the one-act plays, whether in the farce-vaudevilles *The Bear* (1888), *The Proposal* (1888–9), *A Tragic Role* (1889), *The Anniversary* (1891), or the unfinished *Night before the Trial* (1890s); in the 'dramatic studies' *On the High Road* (1885), *Swan Song* (1887) or *Tatyana Repina* (1889); in the one-act play *The Wedding* (1889–90), or the one-act monologue *Smoking is Bad for You* (1886–1903). All of these short plays are often referred to as 'vaudevilles', but it is important to note that Chekhov gave each of the plays a precise sub-title indicating the form and, up to a point, the mood, a practice he was to follow in his full-length plays. Partly for this reason the short plays will be considered not chronologically, but under generic 'groups'.

The Bear (1888)

In a letter to Yakov Polonsky on 22 February 1888, Chekhov wrote: 'Just to while away the time, I wrote a trivial little vaudeville in the French manner, called *The Bear*...Alas! when they find out on *New*

Times that I write vaudevilles they will excommunicate me. What am I to do? I plan something worthwhile – and – it is all tra-la-la! In spite of all my attempts at being serious the result is nothing; with me the serious always alternates with the trivial'.

According to Magarshack,[5] Chekhov had, in fact, followed the practice of so many of his predecessors and his contemporaries in 'borrowing' a French play as the source for *The Bear: Les Jirons de Cadillac* by Pierre Berton. The version Chekhov may have seen at Korsh's Theatre, however, had already been adapted from a French to a Russian vaudeville and was performed under the title of *Conquerors are Above Criticism* by a friend of Chekhov's, Solovstov, the actor to whom Chekhov dedicated *The Bear* and who subsequently played the part of Smirnov, Chekhov's 'bear'. The part of Popova was taken by Natalya Rybchinskaya, the actress with whom Solovstov had appeared in *Conquerors are Above Criticism*. Both the French original and the Russian adaptation are conventional comedies of situation: a beautiful society woman tames a vulgar but good-natured sea-dog. The situation is funny, but the characters are stereotypes, and the 'transitions' as unlikely and incredible as those of so many vaudevilles. The only similarity, in fact, between the plot of the original and that of Chekhov's *The Bear* is in the idea of the 'bear' himself, since it is debatable whether Popova does 'tame' Smirnov; she is certainly not a beautiful society woman, and Smirnov is nothing as exotic as a seaman, but simply (and this follows a convention) a rival landowner. Chekhov does, however, replace one convention with another: Popova, though not a society lady, and not a beautiful woman, is a young widow – our first image of her is as she sits 'in deep mourning' – but (and this is crucial to an understanding of Chekhov's technique) she has 'dimpled cheeks'. Chekhov thus immediately sets up the apparently conventional image of a young grieving widow, and simultaneously raises a question as to either the depth and sincerity of her grief, or the 'naturalness' of it. In other words, he is, in a sense, 'under-cutting' his own image.

At first glance, however, this one-act 'joke' appears little other than an extremely funny conventional vaudeville of situation or, in terms of the vaudevilles of the 1880s, 'a comedy-joke': a cast list of three characters composed of a widowed landowner called Popova, a landowner called Smirnov who is in early middle age, and an old man-servant who is called Luka. The names of the characters are common Russian names. Thus Chekhov's audience might well have expected a conventional amorous vaudeville: a man, a woman, a servant who might be there as a source of intrigue and obstacle, and the resulting

2. *The Bear*, a film directed by Annensky, 1938, with O. N. Androvskaya as Popova and M. I. Zharov as Smirnov.

tangle. Moreover, there *are* obstacles in the play: the woman is in mourning for her husband, and has shut herself off from life, while the man has come to claim his debts, and has no respect for the grieving widow. The play reaches a climax in which a duel is nearly fought, but suddenly Smirnov and Popova are in love and the play appears to end happily.

But even when considering the play on the level of plot, a discordant note is sounded: the duel. A duel on-stage was a completely conventional climactic device and source of tension, and invariably involved the rival lovers fighting over the hand of a woman; in *The Bear*, however, the convention of a duel is maintained by Chekhov, but only to be turned inside out given that the participants are Smirnov and Popova herself. Popova's acceptance of Smirnov's furious challenge, and subsequent insistence on fighting are both a reversal of the convention and a parody. As a result, the woman over whom men conventionally fought a duel is no longer the conventionally romantic, passive figure in the background of the action but an active participant in the action. In addition, Chekhov 'plays' with a further device which is implicit in the stock situation of a duel: a love triangle. Here, if there is a 'triangle' at all, it is between Smirnov, Popova and her dead husband, Nikolai. However, any rivalry offered by the dead Nikolai decreases in the course of the play, is in itself a source of irony, and in any case only exists in the mind of Popova; there is, therefore, no impediment to the action of the play except the characters themselves, and no source of action except their attitudes and behaviour. Thus Luka, instead of furthering or impeding the action, cannot, in fact, cope with the clash of characters and becomes an impotent, though sometimes sensible, witness. In the conventional 'comedy-joke' the servant was often at the source of the play's comic structure, and also used to supply exposition for the audience; in *The Bear*, however, Chekhov makes Luka not so much a structural part of the comic action as a witness of the comedy, who thus serves more as a 'norm' or 'touchstone' for the audience. Again, Chekhov's technique is to set up a 'tone' which is then commented on by someone or something within the same structure. But what in the last four full-length plays becomes a complex use of juxtaposition and counterpoint, may, in the early plays, be seen working very simply: Luka, in *The Bear*, provides a sense of proportion.

This 'sense of proportion' is evident at the very beginning of the play, in that what Luka says to Popova is juxtaposed with what the audience sees in the opening *tableau*: Popova, 'in deep mourning, with her eyes fixed on a snapshot', forms an exaggerated visual statement of 'grief'. An audience has no sooner accepted this *tableau* than Luka provides both exposition and exposure:

This won't do, madam, you're just making your life a misery. Cook's out with the maid picking fruit, every living creature's happy and even our cat knows how to enjoy herself – she's parading round the yard trying to pick up a bird or two. But here you are cooped up inside all day like you was in a convent cell – you never have a good time. Yes, it's true. Nigh on twelve months it is since you last set foot outdoors. (H.I.51)

With the opening lines of the play, Luka simultaneously sets up the situation, and exposes the ridiculous: he compares Popova, unfavourably, with the cat. Thus, just as Popova's 'dimpled cheeks' work against her mourning dress, so Luka's opening words work against the opening visual statement. Luka does, therefore, serve his traditional purpose in explaining matters to the audience (weather, time of day, off-stage dramatic world, and so on); but on an innovatory level, Chekhov uses him to indicate to the audience exactly how ludicrous the situation is, an indication which works implicitly through contrasts. The effect, though comic, is immediately three-dimensional, since the ludicrous aspect of the situation rests entirely on Popova's attitude and behaviour: the cat lives normally, but Popova gazes soulfully at a snapshot – not, significantly, a large, dominating oil-painting of the dead husband, but a little snapshot which, in turn, makes its own 'proportional' comment. Popova has abdicated from life: 'My life's finished. He lies in his grave, I've buried myself inside these four walls. We're both dead.' She, to paraphrase Masha in *The Seagull*, is 'in mourning for her life':[6] both Popova and Masha are young women, both are 'role-playing' and self-dramatising, but whereas Popova drops her romantic image and thus remains a comic character, Masha increasingly lives out her role until, with the frustration and pointlessness of her own unrealised, even ill-defined, aspirations, she becomes a tragi-comic figure. Masha never recognises her own initially ridiculous stance, whereas Popova, even before meeting Smirnov, is able to appraise her self-imposed role as the grief-stricken widow, and its value:

LUKA:...You're young, and pretty as a picture with that peaches-and-cream look, so make the most of it. Them looks won't last for ever, you know. If you wait another ten years to come out of your shell and lead them officers a dance, you'll find it's too late.

POPOVA: (*decisively*) Never talk to me like that again, please. When Nicholas died my life lost all meaning, as you know. You may think I'm alive, but I'm not really. I swore to wear this mourning and shun society till my dying day, do you hear? Let his departed spirit see how I love him!

But then Popova explodes her own romantic image as she continues:

Yes, I realize you know what went on – that he was often mean to me, cruel and, er, unfaithful even, but I'll be true to the grave and show him how much I can love. And he'll find me in the next world just as I was before he died.

(H.1.51–2)

In this way, Popova, through self-revelation, deflates her own romantic act, but the pattern of meaning is complex and, correspondingly, psychologically accurate: partly because Nikolai was unfaithful, Popova is determined to play the grieving widow to the hilt, but her realisation of her own role-playing and of the true nature of relations between herself and her dead husband makes her ripe for deflation by the outside world. The situation is therefore set up in which Popova must be exposed; with the arrival of Smirnov the clash between romanticism and vulgarity begins. But this need for 'deflation' also places the situation clearly in the world of comedy. If, in the course of the play, Popova had been led to the realisation of Nikolai's infidelity the play would, at the very least, have been a drama, not a comedy. As it is, Chekhov presents Popova as playing out a drama in a play which is resolutely a comedy. Popova is one of many characters in Chekhov's plays who, intent on playing out a drama, find themselves in a comedy of their own making.

This feature of the play was clearly brought out by Meyerhold's interpretation of *The Bear* in his production: *33 Swoons*. The actress Zinaida Raikh played Popova, a performance described by Yuzovsky:

Recently we saw her in *The Lady of the Camellias*. The dramatic character of Marguerite Gautier which had been revealed by her lyrically – all those half-shades, pauses, the sad play of glances, the voice full of feeling, the hidden feelings – the more hidden, the dearer they were to her. And lo and behold! – maybe it is a risky comparison – but there appeared Marguerite's younger sister. The very same lyricism: half-shades, pauses, play of glances, hidden feelings. But only within the plane of a comedy. It is as if the younger sister were teasing the older one. And the similarity is intensified also because they are both Frenchwomen. Popova-Raikh is, of course, a Frenchwoman – or wants to resemble a Frenchwoman. Everything that there is of a French element, of a Maupassant element, of 'winking', of the slyly ironical in the words 'young widow' opens up in the presentation of Popova. 'The young widow!'...this is a whole culture...a real social type...She hides [vice], but she hides it gracefully, which means she is hiding and showing it, and in this is the whole art: to hide so that it can be seen, otherwise there is no play. What kind of young widow is she? She is also a hypocrite, but hypocrisy is here playing with open cards, that is to say – the revealing of the method.[7]

3. *The Bear* from Meyerhold's *33 Swoons*, March 1935. Nikolai Bogolyubov as Smirnov and Zinaida Raikh as Popova.

Meyerhold did not distort the play in casting and interpreting Popova in this way, as a younger sister to Marguerite Gautier. Instead, he heightened the parody in the play, and made a total interpretation which was justified also by Smirnov's realisation of Popova's 'act':

POPOVA:...I've buried myself alive inside these four walls and I shall go round in these widow's weeds till my dying day.

SMIRNOV: (*with a contemptuous laugh*) Widow's weeds! Who do you take me for? As if I didn't know why you wear this fancy dress and bury yourself indoors! Why, it sticks out a mile! Mysterious and romantic, isn't it? Some army cadet or hack poet may pass by your garden, look up at your window and think: 'There dwells Tamara, the mysterious princess, the one who buried herself alive from love of her husband.' Who do you think you're fooling?

POPOVA: (*flaring up*) *What*! You dare to take that line with me!

SMIRNOV: Buries herself alive – but doesn't forget to powder her nose!

(H.I.59)

Smirnov, a man who 'calls a spade a spade', sees through Popova, and considers himself wise to all feminine wiles. But if Popova must be brought down to earth and shocked out of her 'romanticism', Smirnov must be tamed. No intrigue, no 'misunderstandings', are required: the source of the action lies in the characters and the clash of characters; equally, the source of the comedy lies in the clash between Popova's 'refinement' and Smirnov's 'vulgarity'. The worse he behaves, the greater her air of refinement, and vice versa. The exaggeration of these characteristic features was not Meyerhold's distortion of the play, but Chekhov's method of characterisation. The effect, though exaggerated, is nonetheless three-dimensional. Thus, although the conflict is set in motion by the fact that Popova is 'in no fit state to discuss money', while Smirnov, if he does not get the money, 'will be in a fit state to go bust with a capital B', the psychological motivation for the conflict arises exactly because of Popova's 'state' and Smirnov's use, so to speak, of 'capitals'.

Smirnov is, in fact, almost disarmingly aware of his own character: whereas Popova is full of guile, Smirnov is blunt to the point of rudeness, but, again, Chekhov allows the characters to reveal themselves. There is no exposition, in the conventional sense, of Smirnov's character – only self-revelation:

And people expect me to be cool and collected! I met the local excise man on my way here just now. 'My dear Smirnov,' says he, 'why are you always losing your temper?' But how can I help it, I ask you? I'm in desperate need of

money! Yesterday morning I left home at crack of dawn. I call on everyone who owes me money, but not a soul forks out. I'm dog-tired. I spend the night in some God-awful place – by the vodka barrel in a Jewish pot-house. Then I fetch up here, fifty miles from home, hoping to see the colour of my money, only to be fobbed off with this 'no fit state' stuff! How *can* I keep my temper?.
                                                                              (H.I.54)

Following the same tack in a monologue in Scene V, Smirnov also helps to create the off-stage dramatic world and the milieu of the play, and continues, comically, to reveal himself. The monologue itself, with Popova hurrying out to leave Smirnov on his own, is credibly motivated by the inevitable explosion of Smirnov's temper, but the relationship with the audience at this point is multifaceted. Chekhov's use of the artificial device of the monologue is interesting: on the one hand, an element of confidentiality with the audience is very much present in Smirnov's movement, attitude, and sometimes rhetorical questions; on the other hand, this outburst seems both natural and inevitable, given Smirnov's character and behaviour; but, in addition, Smirnov seems initially to continue his conversation with the absent Popova:

Well, what price that! 'In no fit state'! Her husband died seven months ago, if you please! Now have I got my interest to pay or not? I want a straight answer – yes or no? All right, your husband's dead, you're in no fit state and so on and so forth, and your blasted manager's hopped it. But what am I supposed to do? Fly away from my creditors by balloon, I take it! Or go and bash the old brain-box against a brick-wall? I call on Gruzdev[8] – not at home. Yaroshevich is in hiding. I have a real old slanging-match with Kuritsyn and almost chuck him out of the window. Mazutov has the belly-ache, and this creature's 'in no fit state'. Not one of the swine will pay. This is what comes of being too nice to them and behaving like some snivelling no-hoper or old woman. It doesn't pay to wear kid gloves with this lot! All right, just you wait – I'll give you something to remember me by! You don't make a monkey out of me, blast you! I'm staying here - going to stick around till she coughs up. Pah! I feel well and truly riled today. I'm shaking like a leaf, I'm so furious – choking I am. Phew, my God, I really think I'm going to pass out!
                                                                              (H.I.54–5)

It is the physical manifestation of the characters' emotional state in the farce-vaudevilles which gave Meyerhold his title: *33 Swoons*. In *The Bear*, in *The Proposal* and *The Anniversary* there are, in total, 33 occasions in which one character or another 'swoons'; situations, other people, or emotions cause a physical reaction which, invariably, is out of all proportion to cause. The discrepancy between the extreme physical reaction and the situation causing it, is a source of farce and slapstick but, as always with Chekhov, it too makes its own ironic point: the very discrepancy between cause and effect heightens the ridiculous in character and situation. This, too, relates to the 'hiding of the method – and showing it'. The audience thus accepts the straight farce (and correspondingly increased rhythm and tempo) of what is witnessed, but simultaneously recognises the ridiculous. In *The Bear*, Chekhov uses a 'swoon' to make *unconventional* the servant's reaction to the climactic mood around him:

SMIRNOV: (*jumping up*). You hold your tongue! Who do you think you're talking to? I'll carve you up in little pieces.
LUKA: (*clutching at his heart*). Heavens and saints above us! (*falls into an armchair*) Oh, I feel something terrible – fair took my breath away, it did.

and, as the tension builds:

I feel faint. Fetch water. (H.1.60)

In this way, the 'heroes' are made thoroughly unheroic, and the servant as human in his physical reactions as his masters. In the one-act plays this extreme physical reaction is primarily farcical, but in *Ivanov* or in the four last full-length plays, the physical state of many of the characters expresses a deeper psychological and sociological malaise. Thus, in *The Three Sisters*, for example, Andrey says to Chebutykin: 'I shan't play cards tonight, I'll just sit and watch. I feel a bit unwell. I get so out of breath, is there anything I can do for it, Doctor?'[9] The cure would be a different life-style and attitude. In *Uncle Vanya* the constant physical malaise of the characters says much about the way of life and the characters' ability or inability to cope with life. And, at other times, Chekhov conveys a character's inability to cope with reality not only by means of a physical *reaction* but also by an *action* expressive of an inner malaise: in *The Seagull*, for instance, Masha takes snuff and secret drinks as 'drugs' to insulate herself from reality; and similarly, in *The Cherry Orchard*, Gaev comforts and distracts himself with sweets and imaginary games of billiards. But where Chekhov retains an extreme physical reaction from his characters, it is not only to show a character's lack of a sense of proportion but develops in the later plays into a means of showing a character's inability to cope, and the effect is thus no longer necessarily farcical. In *The Three Sisters*, Olga feels faint and has to have a drink of water after Natasha has shouted at Anfisa; Olga cannot cope with unpleasantness, and reacts physically. Serious, or tragi-comic, techniques of the later plays may be seen as initially farcical in the earlier one-act plays.

This may be seen in *The Bear* where Smirnov's reaction to women expresses itself physically:

Talk to a woman – why, I'd rather sit on top of a powder magazine! Pah! It makes my flesh creep, I'm so fed up with her, her and that great trailing dress! Poetic creatures they call 'em! Why, the very sight of one gives me cramp in both legs, I get so aggravated.   (H.1.55)

Thus the constant request for water or vodka, the complaints of head-aches, cramps, pains in the heart, and a rage which makes Smirnov feel ill, all serve as a farcical 'running-gag' throughout the action of the play, but also relate to an extremity of behaviour and thinking which will have to be reversed: significantly, at the very moment when Smirnov stops feeling angry and becomes enamoured of Popova, all aches and pains are forgotten, and Popova's fury makes her completely forgetful of her role as the grieving widow. The characters' interaction first intensifies and then modifies their behaviour.

There are, therefore, two sources of fury in Smirnov (and of comedy in the play): his money and women. And the moment at which the one takes over from the other is psychologically accurate – Popova tries to use her sex as a means of getting rid of Smirnov:

POPOVA: Kindly don't raise your voice at me, sir – we're not in the stables.
SMIRNOV: I'm not discussing stables, I'm asking whether my interest falls due tomorrow. Yes or no?
POPOVA: You don't know how to treat a lady.   (H.1.57)

It is this – one of many challenges which Popova issues to Smirnov – which starts to increase the rhythm which climaxes in the duel, and which provokes Smirnov into exposing Popova's role-playing, into tearing down her pretence at refinement, and into exploding with fury against women. And the climax of Smirnov's outburst against women expresses itself in the most physical and farcical stage action: he 'clutches the back of a chair, which cracks and breaks'. This same stage action is repeated by Smirnov when he has reached the height of emotional con-fusion after refusing to fight the duel:

SMIRNOV: ...(*Shouts.*) Anyway, can I help it if I like you? (*Clutches the back of a chair, which cracks and breaks.*) Damn fragile stuff, furniture! I like you! Do you understand? I, er, I'm almost in love.   (H.1.63)

This, the kind of physical stage action accepted in slapstick and farce is, however, in keeping with Smirnov as a character – behaviour which is to be expected, and accepted, of a 'bear'.

The progression from comedy of situation to comedy of character is seen very clearly when Popova accuses Smirnov of not knowing how to treat a lady: what started as a situational comedy in which Smirnov simply wanted his money, increasingly develops into a clash between a man who is driven mad by women and considers them faithless, and a woman who is determined to remain faithful even in the face of her dead husband's infidelity. The conflict broadens out to generalise about men and women, and then focuses on one man, Smirnov, and one woman, Popova. In this way, Chekhov presents a shifting perspective which increases the audience's objective response to what is witnessed.

The form which Smirnov's outburst takes, however, is almost that of a dance: Smirnov starts by mimicking Popova, and proceeds to mimic and parody romantic love in general, but in such terms as vividly to suggest the accompanying movement:

'Silly, not very clever.' I don't know how to treat a lady, don't I? Madam, I've seen more women in my time than you have house-sparrows. I've fought three duels over women. There have been twenty-one women in my life. Twelve times it was me broke it off, the other nine got in first. Oh yes! Time was I made an ass of myself, slobbered, mooned around, bowed and scraped and practically crawled on my belly. I loved, I suffered, I sighed at the moon, I languished, I melted, I grew cold. I loved passionately, madly, in every conceivable fashion, damn me, burbling nineteen to the dozen about women's emancipation and wasting half my substance on the tender passion. But now – no thank you very much! I can't be fooled any more, I've had enough. Black eyes, passionate looks, crimson lips, dimpled cheeks, moonlight, 'Whispers, passion's bated breathing' – I don't give a tinker's cuss for the lot now, lady. Present company excepted, all women, large or small, are simpering, mincing, gossipy creatures. They're great haters. They're eyebrow-deep in lies. They're futile, they're trivial, they're cruel. (H.1.58)

In the midst of this tirade Smirnov, dancing about, breaks a chair, an action of which he seems totally unaware. And he ends up with a challenge to Popova:

You must know what women are like, seeing you've the rotten luck to be one. Tell me frankly, did you ever see a sincere, faithful, true woman? You know you didn't. Only the old and ugly ones are true and faithful. You'll never find a constant woman, not in a month of Sundays you won't, not once in a blue moon! (H.1.58)

Popova picks up the challenge immediately – she proves men's infidelity by telling Smirnov about Nikolai's deceit, and refutes the argument against women by telling of her own constancy. It is this which Smirnov explodes, with the result that after the two 'set speeches' by Smirnov and Popova, the situation and the clash of characters and attitudes reach an apparent impasse:

POPOVA: Just to be awkward, you won't get one single copeck. And you can leave me alone.

SMIRNOV: Not having the pleasure of being your husband or fiancé, I'll trouble you not to make a scene. (*Sits down.*) I don't like it!

POPOVA: (*choking with rage*) Do I see you sitting down?   (H.1.60)

Again, it is psychologically accurate that the clash should take on a renewed force after each has revealed much to the other about attitudes, previous experiences, and views of the opposite sex, but it is now that the insults and the tempo build, until Smirnov can bear the insults no longer:

SMIRNOV: Just because you look all romantic, you can get away with anything – is that your idea? This is duelling talk!

LUKA: Heavens and saints above us! Water!

SMIRNOV: Pistols at dawn!

POPOVA: Just because you have big fists and the lungs of an ox you needn't think I'm scared, see?...

SMIRNOV: We'll shoot it out! No one calls me names and gets away with it, weaker sex or no weaker sex.

POPOVA: (*trying to shout him down*). You coarse lout!

SMIRNOV: Why should it only be us men who answer for our insults? It's high time we dropped that silly idea. If women want equality, let them damn well have equality! I challenge you, madam!

POPOVA: Want to shoot it out, eh? Very well.

SMIRNOV: This very instant!

POPOVA: Most certainly! My husband left some pistols. I'll fetch them instantly (*Moves hurriedly off and comes back.*) I'll enjoy putting a bullet through that thick skull, damn your infernal cheek! (*Goes out.*)

SMIRNOV: I'll pot her like a sitting bird. I'm not one of your sentimental young puppies. She'll get no chivalry from me!   (H.1.61)

Ironically, in the heat of her fury, Popova is able to talk of her husband's pistols and the use she will make of them without a thought for the dead Nikolai, whereas at the beginning of the play the mere mention of Toby the horse brought tearful associations and the corresponding sentimentality which ensured that at every reference to Toby, Popova requested an extra bag of oats for the horse – oats provided, again ironically, by Smirnov. This was the cause of the debt. But by this time Popova has completely discarded her role as the grieving widow, and in the same moment Smirnov discovers the gentleman in himself. Smirnov starts to behave like a gentleman because Popova stops behaving like a lady:

SMIRNOV: There's a regular woman for you, something I do appreciate! A proper woman – not some namby-pamby, wishy-washy female, but a really red-hot bit of stuff, a regular pistol-packing little spitfire. A pity to kill her, really.   (H.1.62)

By the time Popova returns with the pistols, the situation has changed to that of dramatic irony: Popova does not know that Smirnov no longer wants to fight; that her acceptance of his challenge has made him reverse his opinion of her completely. This reversal of roles relates very clearly to the Chekhovian parody and reversal of dramatic conventions: first, a man and a woman fighting a duel; second, a duellist (Popova) who does not even know how to use a gun; and third, the eventual refusal by Smirnov to accept the challenge even in the face of insults from Popova when she accuses him of having 'cold feet' and having the 'wind up', insults which, if made by a man, would traditionally result in a fight to the death.

But in the interim, Smirnov has had to show Popova how to use her husband's 'Smith and Wessons, triple action with extractor, centre-fired',[10] and in the course of showing her, he no doubt has to have his arms round her, and becomes, as does the audience, fully aware of her physical proximity: 'Now, you hold a revolver like this. (*Aside.*) What eyes, what eyes! She's hot stuff all right!' This comic visual picture begins to prepare for the subsequent *dénouement*, but, both unconventionally and ironically, Popova does not acknowledge that she is in the arms of the man she hates; and the ostensible reason for being there is, in any case, to ensure equal ability to kill each other. There is a comic discrepancy between the nature and *ostensible* motive for the stage action done by Smirnov and the feelings which he brings to this stage action: a discrepancy between action and thought which, in turn, relates to the use of the aside and, ultimately, to subtext. The subtext becomes clear because of the dramatic irony. Irony, however, is increased by the very nature of that particular stage action: Smirnov, at home at last in a subject he understands as a man and as a retired lieutenant of artillery, can afford to be expansive as he shows 'the little woman' how a gun works. He achieves dominance by virtue of being a man in this situation, but, equally, is made vulnerable and susceptible by his proximity to Popova.

It is, however, still as a 'bear' that Smirnov proposes to Popova: he

clutches her hand so violently that she shrieks with pain (while she is
also still holding the revolver), and his words are the complete opposite
of romantic:

SMIRNOV: (*going up to her*). I'm so fed up with myself! Falling in love like a
schoolboy! Kneeling down! It's enough to give you the willies! (*Rudely.*)
I love you! Oh, it's just what the doctor ordered, this is! There's my interest
due in tomorrow, haymaking's upon us – and *you* have to come along!
(*Takes her by the waist.*) I'll never forgive myself.
POPOVA: Go away! You take your hands off me! I, er, hate you! We'll sh-
shoot it out! (*A prolonged kiss.*)   (H.1.64)

In a conventional vaudeville, the curtain would have descended after
the 'prolonged kiss', the *dénouement* has taken place, and everything
has been happily resolved, but Chekhov's ending of the play is quite
different. He parodies the convention of the 'interrupted love scene'
to end the play unconventionally with both an anti-climactic 'proportional statement' and a psychological curtain-line. The 'proportional
statement' is made by the prepared and motivated entry of Luka with
an axe, the gardener with a rake, the coachman with a pitchfork, and
some workmen with sundry sticks and staves; this 'army' is no longer
required, but it makes its own comment in contrast to the embracing
couple, a comment which is enhanced by the physical debris around
them from two broken chairs. Thus the visual makes its own superbly
comic statement. But Chekhov, having slowed the tempo with the
'prolonged kiss', ensures a slow ending – the *true dénouement*, so to
speak, which is also psychologically accurate and much more indicative
of the *real* Popova:

LUKA: (*seeing the couple kissing*) Mercy on us! (*Pause.*)
POPOVA: (*lowering her eyes*) Luka, tell them in the stables – Toby gets no oats
today.   (H.1.64)

Reality asserts itself.

The duel as such does not take place; yet, nonetheless, Smirnov and
Popova fight a duel throughout the whole play. This becomes evident
when looking at the structure of the play: it moves through a complex
succession of movements which could be compared to the 'parry' and
'riposte' of a fencing match; or, equally, the structure could be compared to a dance in which, in turn, Popova or Smirnov advances and
retreats. That the movement must be choreographed is made evident,
for example, towards the end of the play:

SMIRNOV: ...Take it or leave it. (*Gets up and hurries to the door.*)
POPOVA: Just a moment.
SMIRNOV: (*stops*) What is it?
POPOVA: Oh, never mind, just go away. But wait. No, go, go away. I hate
    you. Or no – don't go away. Oh, if you knew how furious I am! (*Throws
    the revolver on the table.*) My fingers are numb from holding this beastly
    thing. (*Tears a handkerchief in her anger.*) Why are you hanging about?
    Clear out!
SMIRNOV: Good-bye.
POPOVA: Yes, yes, go away! (*Shouts.*) Where are you going? Stop. Oh, go
    away then...   (H.1.64)

The rhythm and movement of the play are farcical, but farce never
detracts from the psychological validity of the characters. Thus, although the situation of the duel may be seen as improbable, the reality
of it is such that the appearance of the revolvers after the challenge is
inevitable. The entrances and exits also indicate the farcical nature of
the stage movement: does Luka, for example, always come from the
same place? These must be 'geographically' accurate given the dramatic
world and milieu which Chekhov creates, but the *use* made of entrances
and exits, of furniture, of the window in the room, all indicate the
farcical nature of stage business, and also extend their functional use to
make a credible dramatic world. Equally, the climax of a conventional
vaudeville, namely the 'prolonged kiss', is made anti-climactic by
Chekhov's very characteristic psychological curtain-line. Much is
implied about the future life of Smirnov and Popova in Popova's last
line. Throughout the play, in fact, the rhythm builds to a climax only
to become anti-climactic, as is evident in the number of times Smirnov
sits down, refusing to budge, or the number of times the argument
reaches an apparent impasse:

POPOVA: You'll get your money the day after tomorrow.
SMIRNOV: I don't want it the day after tomorrow, I want it now.
POPOVA: I can't pay you now, sorry.
SMIRNOV: And I can't wait till the day after tomorrow.
POPOVA: Can I help it if I've no money today?
SMIRNOV: So you can't pay then?
POPOVA: Exactly.
SMIRNOV: I see. And that's your last word, is it?
POPOVA: It is.
SMIRNOV: Your last word? You really mean it?
POPOVA: I do.   (H.1.54)

Thus, to sum up, the play *is* an amorous 'comedy-joke' similar in a number of crucial respects to the conventional farce-vaudevilles of the 1880s: a small cast, amorous entertainment (with a sudden transition), tension, brisk tempo, a happy ending, monologues, asides, running gags, a duel, a love triangle (of a kind), the observance of the unities, the division of the play into scenes according to the entrances and exits of each character,[11] and the use of farce and slapstick. But it is essentially a comedy of three-dimensional characters – without 'intrigue', without heroes and heroines, with the surprising appearing natural, with tension arising organically from the characters – and not the plot or intrigue, and with the use of comic techniques and forms ranging from pure slapstick to parody and irony. The inter-relationship of the visual with the verbal is equally complex.

This was the play, however, which was regarded by some critics on its first performance in 1888 as 'trivial', and to which the dramatic censor initially gave an adverse report:

The unfavourable impression produced by this highly peculiar theme is increased by the coarseness and impropriety of the tone throughout the play, so that I would have thought it quite unsuitable for performance on the stage.[12]

The Proposal (1888-1889)

The Proposal, written only a few months after *The Bear*, may at first glance seem a more conventional farce-vaudeville then its predecessor: there are more farcical scenes than in any other play by Chekhov, the situation of the play is suggested by its title, the cast size is small (a landowner, his daughter, and a neighbouring landowner), and the play ends with an engagement of marriage. Given the title and the list of characters, it would be a natural assumption for Chekhov's contemporary audience that the play must be an amorous vaudeville with a 'stock' situation and 'stock' characters. The 'stock' situation does not, however, materialise; Chekhov seems to extend the idea of *The Bear* in which *the* duel does not finally take place although the whole play is *a* duel, so that in *The Proposal*, Lomov, who has come to propose to Natasha, never actually does so, although at the end of the play the couple are engaged. In this way, Chekhov denies the event which belongs to the convention and presents instead the characters who themselves impede the event. In *The Proposal* it is, once again, evident that the characters of Chekhov's farce-vaudevilles are not created by or for the situation but create a situation simply by being themselves. The engagement of Lomov and Natasha starts off by design and ends, as it were, by accident, almost incidentally.

As in *The Bear*, it is possible to see where comedy of character takes over from comedy of situation or, to put it another way, where innovation takes over from convention: Lomov comes to propose, receives support (unimpeded by the usual obstacles) from his prospective father-in-law, and is left alone with Natasha. In his struggle to get the proposal off his chest, he mentions, fatally, an adjoining property: Oxpen Field. It is at this point that character takes over decisively from situation, and the clash begins:

LOMOV: I'll try to cut it short. Miss Chubukov, you are aware that I have long been privileged to know your family – since I was a boy, in fact. My dear departed aunt and her husband – from whom, as you are cognizant, I inherited the estate – always entertained the deepest respect for your father and dear departed mother. We Lomovs and Chubukovs have always been on the friendliest terms – you might say we've been pretty thick. And what's more, as you are also aware, we own closely adjoining properties. You may recall that my land at Oxpen Field is right next to your birch copse.

NATASHA: Sorry to butt in, but you refer to Oxpen Field as 'yours'? Surely you're not serious!

LOMOV: I am, madam.

NATASHA: Well, I like that! Oxpen Field is ours, it isn't yours.

LOMOV: You're wrong, my dear Miss Chubukov, that's my land. (H.I.71)

Oxpen Field, and the comparative merits and demerits of the dogs Tracker and Rover, both serve as the ostensible cause of the clash between Lomov and Natasha, but the real reason for the clash lies in the personality of the two characters: their respective personalities take over from the 'plot' of the proposal, and consistently thwart the very situation in which they are participants. But Chekhov also makes use of dramatic irony: Natasha does not know that Lomov has come to propose. Thus the audience's knowledge of a situation as yet unknown to Natasha allows of a degree of objectivity which throws the emphasis on behaviour, rather than on mystery of plot. By understanding the situation immediately, an audience is able to observe the characters' inter-relationship, and, implicitly, draw conclusions about the suitability of a match which in any case consistently fails to take place.

The title of the play is therefore the first of many 'ironies' in the play: 'the proposal' does not form the action of the play, whereas all the impediments to the proposal *are* central to the action; an amorous vaudeville, dependent on intrigue, does not take place – yet much of

the play *is* an amorous vaudeville, dependent on a comic misunderstanding (namely, Natasha's ignorance of Lomov's intentions). There is, in
fact, a crucial contradiction between the characters and their situation:
a discrepancy between behaviour and intention which makes *The
Proposal* by title, by structure, by situation, and by conventional criteria,
comically ironic. And the irony is achieved by Chekhov's particular
use of the conventional, a use which relates to parody on the one hand
and, on the other, to what Tolstoy called 'the lack of French nonsensical surprises'.

Thus the play does not move, as would a traditional vaudeville,
from 'complication' to 'unravelling', with intrigue preceding a *dénouement*; it is not structured through a series of incredible twists of plot –
it is motivated, in a sense credibly, by the characters. As Chekhov
wrote in a letter in the same year: 'One has to write nonsense in one-act
plays – that is their strength. Go on in such a way that the wife in earnest
wants to run away – she has become bored and wants new sensations;
he – in earnest – threatens to make a cuckold of her second husband.'[13]
From one point of view, it is incredible that a 'hefty and well-nourished'
man should collapse as frequently as does Lomov but Ivan Lomov is a
'hypochondriac', and this characteristic of Lomov's makes his collapses,
or swoons, both natural and inevitable. Thus, even in the list of characters preceding the play, Chekhov indicates the main feature of Lomov,
an indication which suggests the apparent contradiction in Lomov
between his physique and his temperament, a discrepancy between his
physical appearance and his nervous disposition: 'hefty and well-
nourished, but a hypochondriac'. The same technique may be found in
The Bear, in which Popova's widow's weeds contrast with her 'dimpled
cheeks', and the effect is much the same: an audience need have no real
fear of danger to Lomov's health; his hefty physique constantly makes a
visual comment on his hypochondriacal behaviour, and keeps even
the most extreme of 'swoons' in proportion, and well within the
bounds of comedy.

This method of characterising – through apparent contradictions –
may be seen, albeit in a more subtle form, in much of Chekhov's later
dramatic work: in *The Seagull*, Trigorin is a famous and successful
writer but, in Chekhov's view, 'he wears check trousers and his shoes
are in holes...and he does not even know how to smoke a cigar
properly';[14] in Act 2 of *The Cherry Orchard*, the governess Charlotte
Ivanovna wears a man's peaked hat, and sits with a shotgun in her lap,
and in the same play, Lopakhin 'waves his arms about' but, as Trofimov
says, he also has 'fine sensitive fingers, like an artist's'. These apparently

contradictory features of the visual appearance and of gesture relate, in
fact, to the contradictory nature of credible human beings, and it is this
kind of characterisation in-the-round which is normally related to
Chekhov's 'naturalism'; in the one-act plays, however, where this
feature of character is heightened and exaggerated, it may be seen in
terms of what Vakhtangov called 'broader realism'. A student of
Vakhtangov's, and the subsequent director of the Vakhtangov Theatre,
Ruben Simonov, wrote:

Chekhov's one-act plays afford the possibility of creating characters on the
basis of rather short text material...Plays with a number of acts portray the
development of the characters in a much slower tempo. The central characters
in a three- or four-act play show the beginning, growth, and conclusion of
action; in this way the characters are revealed gradually. The characters in a
one-act play must be immediately revealed by the actor and the regisseur; all
exposition must be omitted and the characters shown fully defined in both their
inner and outer design. Plays with several acts may be compared to a large river;
plays in one act to a rushing torrent.[15]

And earlier in the same book, describing Vakhtangov's production of
The Wedding:

At the basis of apparent eccentricity lies the truth of life. But whereas an actor
in dramatic presentation has three or four hours in which to reveal the character
and psychology of his hero, the actor-eccentric has at his disposal only five or
six minutes. In these he must live through a rich scenic life, filled with brilliant
events, and create an impressive living image. An actor-eccentric must go
through all the psychological transitions thoroughly in order to be convincing.
Where the dramatic actor has a number of pages of text, an actor-eccentric (in
vaudeville, for example) has just a few words – and sometimes no words – with
which to communicate to his audience a complex psychological state of mind.
    How does a talented actor-eccentric accomplish his peculiar scenic truth? He
does it by selecting the most typical and expressive details of that which he
wants to convey to the audience and building them up to the fullest scenic
expressiveness. Proportion and correlation between a canvas painted in oil and
a laconic, graphic design is similar to that between the dramatic actor and the
eccentric actor or clown. The exceptionally difficult art of an eccentric demands
extraordinary skill and certainly could not be considered a second-rate art.[16]

These words might well serve as directions to the actress playing the
part of Charlotte Ivanova in *The Cherry Orchard*, or to 'Waffles' in
Uncle Vanya, to Yepikhodov and Simeonov-Pishchik in The *Cherry
Orchard*, or to Shamrayev and Medvedenko in *The Seagull* – to all the
characters, in fact, who in the full-length plays might quite inappropri-

ately be regarded as 'minor' characters. It is, perhaps, a commonplace to say that there are no 'minor' characters in Chekhov's plays.

In Simonov's terms, however, given the brevity of the one-act plays, the approach of the 'actor-eccentric' might first and foremost be related to characters such as Smirnov and Popova, or Natasha, Chubukov and Lomov. And in *The Proposal* it could be argued that Chekhov retains certain short-cuts to characterisation which were traditional in vaudeville and to comedy as a whole: the use of 'meaningful' names. Thus Lomov's name may be translated as 'breaker', while Chubukov's name derives either from 'pipe' or from 'forelock'. In Chubukov's case, therefore, his name may be taken in several ways, possibly as a guide to his appearance or, if translated as 'forelock', he may be seen in opposition to Lomov 'the breaker', as a 'wedge'. In the case of neither Lomov nor Chubukov, however, is this an indication of 'type'; Chekhov also characterises immediately by the visual effect of Lomov and Chubukov and, again, this is largely achieved through the use of discrepancy and contrast. Lomov enters 'wearing evening dress and white gloves':

CHUBUKOV: (*going to meet him*). Why, it's Ivan Lomov – or do my eyes deceive me, old boy? Delighted. (*Shakes hands.*) I say, old bean, this is a surprise. How *are* you?

LOMOV: All right, thanks. And how might you be?

CHUBUKOV: Not so bad, dear boy. Good of you to ask and so on. Now, you simply must sit down. Never neglect the neighbours, old bean – what? But why so formal, old boy – the tails, the gloves and so on? Not going anywhere, are you, dear man?

LOMOV: Only coming here, my dear Chubukov.

CHUBUKOV: Then why the tails, my dear fellow? Why make such a great thing of it? (H.1.69)

The 'great thing' is the proposal, and Lomov had dressed in the most formal clothes he could think of, namely evening dress, even though it is lunchtime. There is, therefore, an immediate visual anachronism between Lomov and Chubukov,[17] and, crucially and comically, between Lomov and his bride-to-be: Natasha is wearing an apron:

NATASHA: Excuse my apron, I'm not dressed for visitors. We've been shelling peas – we're going to dry them. Why haven't you been over for so long? Do sit down. (*They sit.*) Will you have lunch?

LOMOV: Thanks, I've already had some.

NATASHA: Or a smoke? Here are some matches...But what's this I see? Evening dress, it seems. That *is* a surprise! Going dancing or something?

You're looking well, by the way – but why on earth go round in that get-
up? (H.1.71)

It is ironic that Lomov, who had clearly 'dressed up' in order to give
himself confidence and to formalise the 'great event', is, in fact, under-
mined by his appearance. The comic visual effect of Lomov in black
tails and white gloves in contrast to Natasha in her apron, is also
paralleled by the psychological effect: both Lomov and Natasha are at
a disadvantage because of what each is wearing. Lomov has 'over-
done', while Natasha is, correspondingly, 'under-done'. The effect,
then, is manifold: by showing Lomov inappropriately 'dressed to kill'
in a ridiculous light, the audience clearly keeps 'the great event' in
proportion, and is forced into an objective awareness both of Lomov
and of 'the proposal'; much is expressed about Lomov's personality
and his attitude through his physical appearance, and an audience is
forced – in the same 'frame', so to speak – to take stock of Lomov in
relation to Natasha; moreover, Natasha (dressed in her apron and
talking about shelling peas) may invite a domestic conversation, but
scarcely a romantic one. Turning up, without warning, at lunchtime
and dressed in evening clothes scarcely encourages a situation conducive
to a marriage proposal. Lomov makes his task more difficult (even
before any mention of Oxpen Field) and diffuses any 'romance' by
being excessive, and therefore ridiculous.

Chekhov's parody of a 'marriage proposal' is made evident when
Lomov's motives and attitude are expressed in his monologue (Scene 2)
immediately preceding Natasha's entrance:

LOMOV: I feel cold, I'm shaking like a leaf. Make up your mind, that's the great
thing. If you keep chewing things over, dithering on the brink, arguing the
toss and waiting for your ideal woman or true love to come along, you'll
never get hitched up. Brrr! I'm cold. Natasha's a good housewife. She's
not bad-looking and she's an educated girl – what more can you ask? But
I'm so jumpy, my ears have started buzzing. (*Drinks water.*) And get married
I must. In the first place, I'm thirty-five years old – a critical age, so to
speak. Secondly, I should lead a proper, regular life. I've heart trouble and
constant palpitations, I'm irritable and nervous as a kitten. See my right
eyelid twitch? But my nights are the worst thing... (H.1.70)

Lomov then continues to give a graphic description of his nights –
nights which, unless improved by the presence of a wife, would
almost certainly lead to the separation of the couple. This monologue
serves the usual purpose of exposition: an audience is informed about
Lomov's motivation for marriage, his view of his intended, and about

Lomov himself. What is not conventional, however, is the anti-romantic and unheroic posture of the prospective bridegroom: he is not in love with Natasha, but because she is a good housewife, 'not bad-looking' and 'an educated girl' he has finally, after much dithering, decided to take the plunge. In effect, however, what he really requires is a nurse or a nanny, not a young wife. Chekhov therefore uses the device of the monologue to expose Lomov's hypochondria, to prepare an audience for the physical reactions which Lomov has to any kind of situation, particularly emotional ones, and as a means of characterising this unprepossessing suitor.

It is interesting that when Natasha first enters she does not expect to see Lomov:

NATASHA: Oh, it's you. That's funny, Father said it was a dealer collecting some
   goods or something. Good morning, Mr Lomov. (H.1.70)

Had Lomov been passionately declaring his love for his intended, Natasha's opening remark might well have stopped him dead in his tracks; as it is, Chubukov's 'joke' in pretending to Natasha that a 'dealer' has come to collect goods is not acknowledged by the self-absorbed Lomov, but it does have an effect (albeit unconscious) on an audience. First, without realising it, Natasha 'deflates' Lomov and his purpose, by reducing his arrival to a mundane business; second, it indicates Chubukov's role in the background, a role which is not that of conventional vaudeville intriguer, nor of the parent placing obstacles in the path of a young couple, but that of a parent fully in support of the engagement who is just having a 'joke'. This 'joke' is, however, ironic: from Lomov's monologue, it is clear that in a way he *is* 'a dealer' who has come to collect 'goods', namely Natasha. This, the first comic misunderstanding in the play, sets in motion the major comic misunderstanding: it enables Natasha to enter without any knowledge of Lomov's presence or his intentions.

In fact, Chubukov's 'joke' about Lomov turns sour: Lomov is too much of a 'dealer' to avoid the fatal mention of their 'adjoining property', and from this Chekhov develops a theme to be found in Pushkin, Gogol, and Turgenev,[18] and often in the vaudeville – arguments over property leading to litigation between rival landowners:

LOMOV: But you have only to look at the deeds, my dear Miss Chubukov.
   Oxpen Field once *was* in dispute, I grant you, but it's mine now – that's
   common knowledge, and no argument about it. If I may explain, my
   aunt's grandmother made over that field rent free to your father's grandfather's labourers for their indefinite use in return for firing her bricks. Now,

your great-grandfather's people used the place rent free for forty years or
so, and came to look on it as their own. Then when the government land
settlement was brought out –

NATASHA: No, that's all wrong. My grandfather and great-grandfather both
claimed the land up to Burnt Swamp as theirs. So Oxpen Field was ours.
Why argue? That's what I can't see. This is really rather aggravating.

LOMOV: I'll show you the deeds, Miss Chubukov. (H.1.72)

The argument (over land with the unprepossessing names of 'Burnt
Swamp' and 'Oxpen Field') continues in a completely farcical manner;
long-deceased relatives on both sides are brought in as 'proof' or
justification (as Natasha says: 'Grandfather, grandmother, aunt – it
makes no sense to me. The field's ours and that's that'); and – perhaps
most revealing of all – both Natasha and Lomov separately claim that
the argument is over *principle*, not the land itself.

NATASHA:...I don't mind about the field – it's only the odd twelve acres,
worth the odd three hundred roubles. But it's so unfair...It's ours! Argue
till the cows come home, put on tail-coats by the dozen for all I care – it'll
still be ours, ours, ours! I'm not after your property, but I don't propose
losing mine either, and I don't care what you think!

LOMOV: My dear Miss Chubukov, it's not that I need that field – it's the
principle of the thing. If you want it, have it. Take it as a gift.

NATASHA: But it's mine to give *you* if I want – it's my property. (H.1.72–3)

The pointless argument builds in tempo and vehemence, until, in a
clear parody of the 'interrupted love scene', Chubukov is drawn by the
sound of the row. With his entrance, the rhythm drops slightly, but
only to reach renewed force in the argument now involving all three:
prospective suitor, would-be father-in-law, and the ferocious and un-
knowing bride-to-be. It is with Chubukov's entrance that the theme of
litigation comes to a head:

LOMOV: We'll see about that! I'll have the law on you!

CHUBUKOV: You will, will you? Then go right ahead, sir, and so forth, go
ahead and sue, sir! Oh, I know your sort! Just what you're angling for and
so on, isn't it – a court case, what? Quite the legal eagle, aren't you? Your
whole family's always been litigation-mad, every last one of 'em!

LOMOV: I'll thank you not to insult my family. We Lomovs have always been
honest, we've none of us been had up for embezzlement like your precious
uncle. (H.1.75)

With that, Lomov starts off a succession of insults – neatly reciprocated
by Chubukov – involving near and distant, living and deceased relatives

on both sides; the fury of the argument is such that each completely forgets the reason for Lomov's visit. The situation is not so much that of a comic misunderstanding as of an argument in which the 'heat' and subject causes both parties to forget what is important. Eventually the severity of Lomov's palpitations drives him away and Chubukov – again, ironically – shouts after him that he need never return to his house. The irony lies in the fact that seconds later Natasha, having at last learnt the real reason for Lomov's visit, hysterically sends her father to bring Lomov back. And the moment of truth comes not as an artificial, conventional revelation, but as a totally motivated and almost incidental comment:

CHUBUKOV: And this monstrosity, this blundering oaf, has the immortal rind to come here with his proposal and so on, what? A proposal! I ask you!
NATASHA: A proposal, did you say?
CHUBUKOV: Not half I did! He came here to propose to you!
NATASHA: Propose? To me? Then why didn't you say so before?   (H.1.76)

As it turns out, Natasha's knowledge of Lomov's intentions makes very little difference to her behaviour – Natasha behaves with as little self-control and discipline in the second argument, over the dogs Tracker and Rover, as she did in the argument over Oxpen Field. But perhaps the greatest irony in the play lies, as Vladimir Lakshin points out in his book *Tolstoy i Chekhov*,[19] in the fact that all property would, in any case, be shared and jointly owned after the marriage.

The greatest obstacle in the play is, therefore, the basic incompatibility of the characters; Natasha and Chubukov even argue about which of them was responsible for arguing with Lomov. And the subjects of the arguments – Oxpen Field, the two dogs, who started a row, and so on – are made deliberately absurd and petty both as expressive of the characters, and as a comment on them. Much the same technique and dramatic effect may be seen in Act 2 of *The Three Sisters*, in the argument between Chebutykin and Solyony:

CHEBUTYKIN: (*coming into the drawing-room with Irina*). They gave us real Caucasian food too – onion soup followed by a meat dish, a kind of *escalope*.
SOLYONY: A shallot isn't meat at all, it's a plant rather like an onion.
CHEBUTYKIN: You're wrong, my dear man. *Escalope* isn't an onion, it's a sort of grilled meat.
SOLYONY: Well, I'm telling you a shallot is an onion.
CHEBUTYKIN: Well, I'm telling you *escalope* is meat.
SOLYONY: Well, I'm telling you a shallot is an onion.

CHEBUTYKIN: Why should I argue with you? You've never been to the Caucasus or eaten *escalope*.
SOLYONY: I've never eaten them because I can't stand them. Shallots smell just like garlic. (H.3.104)

In this scene, the argument manufactured by Solony is not even over the same thing, the argument is a misunderstanding: Chebutykin fails to understand that Solyony is talking about *cheremsha*, not *chekhartma*, and they are not even listening to each other, Solyony arguing for the sake of it, Chebutykin reacting only out of irritation. And a few minutes later, in the same act, Solyony's latest source of argument, over whether there are one or two universities in Moscow, simply peters out when Andrey, characteristically, refuses to join in: 'Three if you like. So much the better.' In the later plays, such arguments over petty and unimportant matters are deeply expressive of character and clash of character but, perhaps more important, these 'flash-points' relate to Chekhov's method of expressing a way of life: often an argument is only the outward manifestation of a different subtextual tension, as in the argument in Act I of *Uncle Vanya* between Vanya and his mother Maria Vassilyevna over her pamphlets. In the later plays, as in many of the short stories, petty arguments spring out of boredom, unhappiness, dissatisfaction, and invariably mask something far from petty; in *The Three Sisters*, Solyony's posturing unhappiness and boredom result in the death of Tuzenbakh. The argument may be petty, but the way of life which breeds such pettiness is destructive.

It was perhaps with this pettiness and destructiveness in mind that Meyerhold determined on his interpretation and emphasis in his *Proposal* which formed part of *33 Swoons*, a production interpretation which must be understood in the context of its time, namely 1935:

The image created by Ilinsky [who played Lomov] does not fit into a vaudeville: the comic nervousness of Ilinsky's interpretation has grown to the scale of pathology. This is already a disease. One could say: a social disease. In Ilinsky's Lomov the spectator could see the Metrofanushka of Fonvizin's *The Minor* – but not the ignoramus of *that* period. That was a Metrofanushka who was bursting with health and strength; the future was standing before him. But now Metrofanushka has completed a historical circle...a degeneration, the finale. Now this Metrofanushka is of the period of decay, of the eve of the revolution, when - in all corners of the country, they chop down the cherry orchards. He is ill, incorrigibly sickly...whenever there is the smallest occurrence in his life - a trifle, a draught, unpleasantness – he has heart spasms - any moment he will die. This is the meaning of Lomov's hypochondria.[20]

According to Yuzovsky, the author of the above, Meyerhold's interpretation of Lomov was that of the down-trodden, pathetic 'little man',
an Akaky Akakeyevich, 'an unfortunate one, insulted and injured', a
'ludicrous person'. Thus Meyerhold interpreted Lomov not as a 'comic'
character but as a 'dramatic' character:

> this Lomov is, in fact, a lonely man of thirty-five, who has shut himself up on
> his estate, who has not known women, but is always thinking of them...this
> Akaky Akakeyevich element...This Lomov, is lonely, defenceless, and faint-
> hearted. When among people he wishes by his behaviour to hide these character-
> istics – he wears camouflage.[21]

Meyerhold expanded the significance of Lomov's evening dress, and
provided him with an everyday hat, in addition to his top-hat: when
wearing the top-hat, Lomov was the prospective suitor; when arguing
or 'swooning', Lomov wore his everyday hat: hats, gloves, and tails
were used not merely as 'props' but as physical extensions of Lomov's
mood and behaviour, as masks, and camouflage.

By all accounts,[22] Meyerhold's production of *The Proposal* was not
well received – in order to play Lomov dramatically, the fast tempo of
a vaudeville was lost; and although Meyerhold's interpretation of
Lomov was a strong one, it did not work well with Chekhov's Natasha.
But even in this less successful production, there is much to be learnt,
and in the extremity of this interpretation there is a crucial aspect which
should not be overlooked: Chekhov's play *is* farcical, but it is also
exposing a social milieu at a particular time, a time in which money,
mortgages, and the upkeep of the estates were an increasing pre-
occupation. Lomov and Chubukov, individualised and three-
dimensional, are also landowners (as are Smirnov and Popova in *The
Bear*); it is important to note that when Lomov is 'the suitor', he is at
his most nervous and agitated, but he has enough energy and strength
to protect 'his' property against Natasha. In fact, his nervousness is
initially attributed to only one thing by Chubukov:

LOMOV: ...I came to ask a favour, my dear Chubukov, if it's not too much
  bother. I have had the privilege of enlisting your help more than once, and
  you've always as it were – but I'm so nervous, sorry. I'll drink some water,
  my dear Chubukov. (*Drinks water.*)
CHUBUKOV: (*aside*). He's come to borrow money. Well, there's nothing doing!
  (*To him.*) What's the matter, my dear fellow?   (H.I.69)

Money, or the lack of it, forms either background or a major aspect of
most of Chekhov's plays – in *The Bear*, in *The Anniversary*, in *The*

4. *The Proposal*, from Meyerhold's *33 Swoons*, March 1935.
Igor Ilinsky as Lomov and Victor Gromov as Chubukov.

Wedding, in *On The High Road*, in the unfinished *Night Before the Trial*, *Ivanov*, *The Wood Demon* (and in *Uncle Vanya*), in *The Seagull*, *The Three Sisters*, and, of course, in *The Cherry Orchard*. In *The Proposal*, Chubukov's mistaken assumption is comic but it is also mean; and this meanness and greed is also very evident in Natasha's opening chatter:

It's lovely weather, but it rained so hard yesterday – the men were idle all day. How much hay have you cut? I've been rather greedy, you know – I mowed all mine, and now I'm none too happy in case it rots. I should have hung on.

(H.1.71)

In the same way, old grievances come out in the row, as when Natasha says: 'We lent you our threshing-machine last year, and couldn't get our own threshing done till November in consequence'. Or there is the new argument over the money paid for the two 'rival' dogs:

LOMOV: ...Do you know, I gave Mironov a hundred and twenty-five roubles for him?
NATASHA: Then you were had, Mr. Lomov.
LOMOV: He came very cheap if you ask me – he's a splendid dog.
NATASHA: Father only gave eighty-five roubles for Rover. And Rover's a jolly sight better dog than Tracker, you'll agree. (H.1.78)

There is much in *The Proposal* which is farcical, but there is also much which verges on the grotesque: Lomov's hypochondria motivates many of his physical complaints and physical reactions, but, even more than in *The Bear*, Chekhov again uses the extremity of physical reactions to 'deflate' his characters, and demonstrate their lack of a sense of proportion. Towards the end of the play, first Lomov, then Chubukov, and then Natasha collapse in a 'swoon', a comic visual picture of one after the other collapsing in a chair, which appears to reach a climax, only to become anti-climactic:

LOMOV: Oh, oh! My heart's bursting. My shoulder seems to have come off – where is the thing?[23] I'm dying. (*Falls into an armchair.*) Fetch a doctor. (*Faints.*)
CHUBUKOV: Why, you young booby! Hot air merchant! I think I'm going to faint. (*Drinks water.*) I feel unwell.
NATASHA: Calls himself a sportsman and can't even sit on a horse! (*To her father.*) Father, what's the matter with him? Father, have a look. (*Screeches.*) Mr. Lomov! He's dead!
CHUBUKOV: I feel faint. I can't breathe! Give me air![24]
NATASHA: He's dead. (*Tugs Lomov's sleeve.*) Mr Lomov, Mr Lomov! What

have we done? He's dead. (*Falls into an armchair.*) Fetch a doctor, a doctor!
(*Has hysterics.*)

CHUBUKOV: Oh! What's happened? What's the matter?

NATASHA: (*groans*) He's dead! Dead!

CHUBUKO: Who's dead? (*Glancing at Lomov.*) My God, you're right! Water!
A doctor! (*Holds a glass to Lomov's mouth.*) Drink! No, he's not drinking.
He must be dead, and so forth. Oh, misery, misery! Why don't I put a
bullet in my brain? Why did I never get round to cutting my throat? What
am I waiting for? Give me a knife! A pistol![25] (*Lomov makes a movement.*)
I think he's coming round. Drink some water! That's right.   (H.1.81)

The borderline between three-dimensional farce and the grotesque is a
narrow one.

It is in the anti-climactic aftermath of Lomov's 'return from the
grave' that the couple finally became engaged, and it is not Lomov
but Chubukov, again as a reversal of the 'stock parent' in a vaudeville,
who announces the engagement. The ending of the play is a complete
parody of the traditional finale of the vaudeville since the couple's
reconciliation only takes place when they are completely exhausted
from their quarrels and, in any case, after the engagement the rows
begin again with renewed vigour. The ending of the play not only
does not resolve the 'obstacles', but in fact emphasises the obstacles
even more clearly. In the sense that the couple *are* engaged, the play has
a happy ending, but equally it must be seen as an unhappy beginning.
Chekhov has written a comedy of character, not of situation: external
obstacles or difficult and unpleasant situations may be overcome, but
Lomov and Natasha do not suddenly change their nature. In this sense,
there is no *dénouement*, only a renewed outbreak of argument between
Lomov and Natasha; and the final irony is in Chubukov's direct comment and address to the audience: 'You can see those two are going to
live happily ever after! Champagne!' Any witness of this comedy is
only able to regard Lomov and Natasha as welcome to each other, an
objective assessment which comes from the balanced presentation of
all the characters and from their clearly expressed view of each other:
Lomov is a hypochrondriac, although well-fed and healthy; Natasha is
greedy, argumentative, and shrewish; Chubukov is bad-tempered and,
a nice reversal, was beaten by his wife.

The depth of characterisation is partly achieved by Chekhov's
particular use of speech peculiarities and individualised speech patterns
– Chubukov's catch-phrase is 'and so forth', and all of his speech is
larded with phrases like 'dear man', 'old boy', 'old bean', an individualised manner of speech which emphasizes Chubukov's *apparent* bluff

heartiness; Natasha is characterised by her frequent ability to speak her mind, and by short, sharp sentences, often composed of derogatory synonyms, while Lomov's speech is, of course, most characterised by the interruption of his own train of thought and argument by his physical ailments:

NATASHA: What a rotten, beastly, filthy thing to say.
CHUBUKOV: You're a thoroughly nasty, cantankerous, hypocritical piece of work, what? Yes, sir!
LOMOV: Ah, there's my hat. My heart –. Which way do I go? Where's the door? Oh, I think I'm dying. I can hardly drag one foot after another. (*Moves to the door.*)
CHUBUKOV: (*after him*) You need never set either of those feet in my house again, sir.
NATASHA: Go ahead and sue, we'll see what happens.   (H.I.75)

The play is full of phrases relating to hunting (although it clearly emerges that neither Lomov nor Chubukov are exactly 'sportsmen'), a requirement which Chekhov listed in his notes on *Things Most Frequently Encountered in Novels, Stories and Other Such Things*: 'an endless number of interjections, and attempts to use an appropriate technical term', and which he itemised as a requirement of the vaudeville: 'each character must possess individual features and idiosyncrasies and must speak in a language of his own'. It is, of course, partly the language which so strongly depicts and creates the milieu of the play.[26]

The structure of the play is also a parody: Lomov comes to propose – twice; Natasha and Lomov have a row – twice, and twice Chubukov's entrance parodies the 'interrupted love scene' and increases the ferocity of the argument; on each occasion, Lomov's 'swoon' results in an anti-climax. Thus, just as Beckett's *Waiting for Godot* requires two acts to make probable the continuation of another and another, so in *The Proposal* the 'ending' of the play serves to indicate the likely continuation of the action. The play is therefore appropriately structured according to the arguments which form the 'action': initiated by a comic misunderstanding, but subsequently carried by the momentum of the characters. In the 'repeat' action of the play (from Scene VI onwards), it is evident that these people can row even without a 'misunderstanding'. But Chekhov does introduce a new element of dramatic irony with Lomov's re-appearance: Natasha now knows Lomov's intentions, but he does not know that she knows!

The Proposal is, therefore, a fascinating 'mixture': Chekhov takes over the 'stock' situation of an 'amorous vaudeville', and parodies it;

he retains aspects such as the monologue and asides; the scene divisions and small cast of identifiable vaudeville figures, and the unity of time, place and action, but by substituting misunderstanding and character for intrigue and plot, and introducing the convention of 'rival land-owners', 'the proposal' becomes subsidiary to what, in effect, is closer to social satire.

A Tragic Role (1889)

By the time Chekhov wrote his one-act farce *A Tragic Role* in May 1889, he had already written *Platonov*, *On the High Road*, three versions of *Smoking is Bad for You*, *Swan Song* (*Calchas*), *Ivanov*, *The Bear*, *The Proposal*, and *Tatyana Repina*, and was in the middle of writing *The Wood Demon*:

Can you believe it? I've got the first act of *The Wood Demon* ready. It's turned out all right, though a bit long. I have a greater sense of my own strength than when I was writing *Ivanov*. The play will be ready by the beginning of June...Last night I remembered I'd promised Varlamov[27] to write a farce for him. Today I wrote it, and I've already sent it off. You see how fast I turn things out![28]

This letter to Suvorin was followed, two days later, by a letter to Leontyev, to whom Chekhov wrote:

A day or two ago I remembered promising Varlamov last winter to turn one of my novels [sic] into a play. I sat straight down and did so, making a pretty bad job of it. A novel on a stale and hackneyed theme produced a stale farce that falls flat. It's called *A Tragic Role*.[29]

Chekhov's diffident, not to say derogatory, view was not shared by contemporary audiences, the play was revived again and again in Chekhov's lifetime, but today it is virtually ignored by producers and dismissed as unworthy of analysis by critics. But although it cannot be claimed that *A Tragic Role* rates amongst the highest of Chekhov's dramatic works, there are a number of features of the play which relate crucially to an understanding of his dramatic method, and to the use he makes of stock situations and stock techniques.

The title of the play in itself brings translator and critic face to face with an important aspect of the play as a whole: like Molière's *Le Médecin malgré lui* (*A Doctor in Spite of Himself*), Chekhov's title conveys a meaning which a translator finds hard to capture. The play is normally referred to as *A Tragic Role*,[30] but a more literal translation is, in fact, like Molière's, *A Tragedian in Spite of Himself*. The title has also been translated as *The Reluctant Tragedian,* and in Eric Bentley's version as *Summer in the Country – Not a Farce But a Tragedy.* Thus the actual name of the play raises the question as to whether 'the role' is, in fact, a 'tragic' one, a question reinforced by the apparent disparity of the subtitle: Chekhov calls the play 'a farce'. But 'the reluctant tragedian' raises the question himself: reaching the end of his frenzied tirade, Tolkachov says, 'This isn't funny, it's downright tragic' or, to translate it another way, 'This isn't farce – it's tragedy.' In this play, Chekhov extends the meaning of the word 'farce' to encompass an attitude, an approach to life – a philosophy as well as a dramatic genre.

Chekhov's treatment of the 'hackneyed' situation of the henpecked, harassed, commuting husband is multifaceted: the play *is* a farce, and partly so by virtue of Tolkachov's extreme reaction to a commonplace situation; he insists on seeing himself as a tragic figure, but in a situation at which everyone laughs; at the same time, however, it is in fact the very banality of the situation which is driving him into a frenzy. There is, therefore, a conflict within the play between Tolkachov's situation and his reaction to it: he is an *unwilling* participant who none the less dramatises his role. Thus, whereas in *The Bear* or *The Proposal* the characters create their own situation and so the action of the play, the action of *A Tragic Role* is largely Tolkachov's reaction to his situation. Tolkachov's reaction is extreme and therefore comic; his insistence on seeing himself as a tragic figure is disproportionate and misplaced and therefore comic; the situation itself is as commonplace as somebody's 'mother-in-law', and therefore comic; but in the extremity of his reaction lies a real despair; in his 'martyrdom' to the mundane there is a serious protest; and in the very banality of the situation there is potential for tragedy. It is exactly the petty and trivial nature of the common-place which provokes Tolkachov into an assessment of his life – at the end of his tether, at the mercy of the mundane and the trivial, Tolkachov wants to find some meaning:

A family man? A martyr, more like – a complete drudge, a slave, a chattel, the lowest thing that crawls. Why don't I end it all – what am I waiting for, like some benighted idiot? I'm a regular doormat. What have I to live for? Eh? (*Jumps up.*) Come on, tell me what I have to live for, why this unbroken chain of moral and physical tortures? Certainly I can understand a man who sacrifices himself for an ideal, but to martyr yourself to women's petticoats, lampshades and that sort of damn tomfoolery – no, thank you very much. No, no, no! I've had enough! Enough, I tell you! (H.1.109)

As part of his tirade against his way of life, Tolkachov describes how at last, exhausted, he is able to go to bed:

Wonderful! Just shut your eyes and sleep. Nice and snug isn't it - like a dream come true? The children aren't screaming in the next room, the wife isn't there, and you've nothing on your conscience – what could be better? You drop off. Then, all of a sudden – bzzzzz! Gnats! (*Jumps up.*) Gnats! Damn and blast those bleeding gnats! (*Shakes his fist.*) Gnats! The Plagues of Egypt aren't in it – *or* the Spanish Inquisition! Buzz, buzz, buzz! There's this pathetic, mournful buzzing as if it were saying how sorry it was, but you wait till the nipper gets his fangs in – it means an hour's hard scratching. You smoke, you lash out, you shove your head under the blankets – but you're trapped. You end by giving yourself up like a lamb to the slaughter. (H.1.112.)

This completely realistic 'torment' of summer in the country be-comes, however, also an image of Tolkachov's situation: because gnats are basically harmless, a violent reaction to them may be seen as comically out of proportion; by being both harmless and common-place, gnats may be treated as a joke; but although not fatal, they first drive one into a frenzy, and then into passive exhaustion. The action of the play captures Tolkachov in such a frenzy, and possibly before passive exhaustion about his way of life finally sets in. Chekhov achieves this exactly by using the commonplace, the apparently harm-less, and the apparently undramatic. In Chekhov's terms, the majority of people are more likely to be 'martyrs' to lampshades, petticoats and gnats than to abstract ideas or dramatic actions:

Why write that someone boards a submarine and sails to the North Pole to seek some sort of reconciliation with people, and at the same time his beloved, with a dramatic wail, throws herself from a belfry? All that is false, and does not happen in reality. One must write simply: about how Peter Semeonovich married Maria Ivanovna. That is all.[31]

Part of what the play shows is the result of one such marriage; the play is an adaptation of a story written by Chekhov in 1887 and signifi-cantly titled: *One of Many*. The story describes the unhappy plight of a thoroughly married man who travels to town every day to work from his country cottage where his wife and children have moved for the summer. This 'hackneyed' situation has been treated by Chekhov in a number of short stories, in particular *Not Wanted*, *A Nest of Kulaks*, *Gone Astray*, or *The Grasshopper*. In *Not Wanted*, Chekhov describes a June evening at seven o'clock, and:

a crowd of dacha dwellers who had just come out of the train at the small station Khilkovo and were making their way towards the dacha colony, most of them fathers of families, burdened with shopping bags, briefcases and hat-boxes.

They all looked worn out, hungry and in a bad temper, as though the sunshine and the green grass meant nothing to them.

In the same story, Zaikin describes life in town once the family have moved to the country for the summer:

Back in town you have no furniture, no servants – everything is at the dacha. You feed on the devil knows what, have no tea to drink because there's no one to heat the samovar, you can't get a proper wash, and when you come out here, into the lap of nature, you have to walk from the station in the dust and heat... It's a miracle we're still alive.

And in *Gone Astray*, one such unhappy husband tries to get into the wrong dacha – they all look alike.

In *A Tragic Role* Chekhov retains the basic point of the story from which the play derives: the family man is over-burdened with demands from his wife and friends who take advantage of his daily commuting into town. In the story, *One of Many*, one of the burdens which he carries is a child's coffin, a 'prop' which Chekhov omitted from the stage adaptation not, as Magarshack explains, to 'preserve the decencies of the stage'; nor, as Bentley puts it, because 'a child's coffin on stage... would carry a higher charge of painful emotion than a farce can stand', but because Chekhov did not automatically lift the story from page to stage. He was clearly well aware of the physical limits of farce: in addition to all of Tolkachov's other burdens, it would be virtually impossible for any actor to carry a coffin as well; moreover, in stage terms, that particular 'prop' would be much cruder, much more grotesque as a visual statement than it is when merely described in a narrative; finally, its existence on stage would raise questions irrelevant to the action and point of the play. The actual list of Tolkachov's 'props' is, therefore, carefully contrived to suggest both credible purchases and yet objects of varying shapes, sizes, textures, and uses which immediately create, purely through visual effect, a farcical entrance:

Tolkachov comes in. He carries a glass lamp-globe, a child's bicycle, three hat-boxes, a large bundle of clothes, a shopping-bag full of beer and a lot of small parcels.

(H.1.109.)

Like a clown, Tolkachov enters balancing 'hostile' objects, all of which might well conspire to plague him: it is vital to this visual image that the objects should be commonplace – and yet potential hazards. Tolkachov's entrance introduces the audience into a world where the glass lamp-globe might break; the child's bicycle might trip him up; the hat boxes, piled one on top of the other, might slide off; the bottles of beer might burst; and the small parcels – of which there are many – might slip from under Tolkachov's arms and chin. The opening statement of the play, expressed purely through the visual, is an apparently commonplace one of a man over-burdened by daily objects: Tolkachov's entrance therefore operates on a literal, credible and comic level, and, simultaneously, as an image of his situation. A similar effect is found in *The Cherry Orchard* in which Yepikhodov, nicknamed Twenty-Two Calamities, lives in a world in which a new pair of boots, a billiard cue, even a glass of water, all conspire against him. Thus Tolkachov's burdens, like Yepikhodov's calamities, are farcical – and an image of a situation, a combination which may be seen, albeit in a more abstract context (and therefore perhaps as a more explicit image) in, for example, Lucky's first entrance in Beckett's *Waiting for Godot:*

Enter Pozzo and Lucky. Pozzo drives Lucky by means of a rope passed round his neck, so that Lucky is the first to appear, followed by the rope which is long enough to allow him to reach the middle of the stage before Pozzo appears. Lucky carries a heavy bag, a folding stool, a picnic basket and a greatcoat... Noise of Lucky falling with all his baggage.

The communication of meaning through a visual image is familiar to a twentieth-century audience, but the communication of meaning through a visual image within the context of a farce-vaudeville in 1889 clearly demonstrates Chekhov's unique extension of the farcical into the metaphorical. To Chekhov's contemporary audience, however, there was little particularly innovatory about the form: it relates clearly to the other two 'types' of farce-vaudeville popularised in the 1880s: the 'comic scene' and a version of the comic scene, the 'scene monologue'.

Thus whereas *The Bear* and *The Proposal* are 'amorous vaudevilles', *A Tragic Role* bears a clear generic resemblance both to the 'comic scene' – which employed more static action, the absence of an ending as such, and the portrayal of everyday life and everyday types – and to the 'scene monologue', which employed a comic situation narrated by a comic stereotyped character. But in particular, Chekhov employs the convention of the 'false monologue' in which other characters are present but do not interrupt or respond. Viewed in that way, it may be seen that Chekhov uses an artificial and conventional form in *A Tragic Role*, but it must also be seen that Tolkachov's monologue is, in fact, significantly modified and influenced by the 'control' presence of his friend Murashkin. Alexis Murashkin (whose name might be translated as 'Shivers') has a crucial function in the play which goes beyond the purely conventional one of reducing the artificiality of a monologue by providing a passive on-stage listener: Tolkachov has come to Murashkin to borrow a revolver in order to 'end it all'. Murashkin's presence thus serves as the ostensible motivation for Tolkachov's tirade – both Murashkin and the audience are recipients of Tolkachov's lengthy exposition of his situation – but Chekhov then reverses the conventional *dénouement* by means of Murashkin. The action of the play does not arise out of a comic misunderstanding which is then resolved; instead the comic misunderstanding comes at the end of the play and in fact *provides* the *dénouement* and, in effect, the anti-climax which virtually ends the play. This, in turn, is achieved by Chekhov's particular use of a form of comic misunderstanding: the 'conversation-of-the-deaf'. Murashkin, like the audience, has heard Tolkachov's frenzied exposition, but he has not listened to it, and therefore not taken it seriously:

TOLKACHOV: ...Look here, if you won't lend me a revolver, at least show a spot of fellow-feeling.

MURASHKIN: But I do feel for you.

TOLKACHOV: Yes, I can see how much you do. Well, good-bye. I'll get some sprats and salami, er, and I want some toothpaste too – and then to the station.

MURASHKIN: Whereabouts are you taking your holiday?

TOLKACHOV: At Corpse Creek.

MURASHKIN: (*joyfully*). Really? I say, you don't happen to know someone staying there called Olga Finberg?

TOLKACHOV: Yes. In fact she's a friend of ours.

MURASHKIN: You don't say! Well, I never! What a stroke of luck and how nice if you –

TOLKACHOV: Why, what is it?

MURASHKIN: My dear old boy, could you possibly do me a small favour, there's a good chap? Now, promise me you will.

TOLKACHOV: What is it?

MURASHKIN: Be a friend in need, old man – have a heart! Now, first give my regards to Olga and say I'm alive and well, and that I kiss her hand. And secondly, there's a little thing I want you to take her. She asked me to buy her a sewing-machine and there's no one to deliver it. You take it, old man. And you may as well take this cage with the canary while you're about it – only be careful or the door will break. What are you staring at?

TOLKACHOV: Sewing-machine –. Cage –. Canary – . Why not a whole bloody aviary?   (H.I.113.)

For Tolkachov, the irony of his friend's reaction is the last straw, but for the audience the effect of this ironic twist is mixed: on the one hand, Murashkin's attitude and response confirms the objective view that Tolkachov is over-reacting and self-dramatising but, simultaneously, Murashkin's failure to listen, and his casual response, justifies Tolkachov in his view that the situation is tragic, not farcical. In addition, **Murashkin** finally pushes his friend 'over the edge'. The dramatic effect of this, following immediately after Tolkachov's frantic monologue, is initially anti-climactic but then provides the climax on which the play ends: a climax which utilises a 'stock' technique but one usually used earlier in a play: the chase. The play ends as Murashkin frantically tries to get out of the way of the incensed Tolkachov. Again, the comedy is visual, farcical and psychologically apt: Murashkin is both literally and meta-phorically adding to Tolkachov's 'burden'. Murashkin therefore pro-vides a sense of proportion in a double-edged way: he points the extremity of Tolkachov's reaction but, by the inadequacy and even insensitivity of his response, he *justifies* Tolkachov's view of the situa-tion.

A further crucial feature of the play is the realism of the milieu depicted; Tolkachov – 'a family man, high up in the civil service' – exposes a whole way of life: the nature of his work in the office, the nature of life on the dacha surrounded by his immediate family (Sonya, Misha, Vlasin, his sister-in-law), Colonel Vikhrin's pregnant wife, and the French governess Mademoiselle Chanceau. He depicts the task of shopping in the city 'from draper's to chemist's, from chemist's to dressmaker's, from dressmaker's to sausage-shop, then back to the chemist's again'. Then there is the physical problem of carrying every-thing, the crowded train journey into the country with piles of pack-ages, the exhausted arrival, only to be greeted by the wife's request for social events such as a dance or – a nice ironic touch – a visit to an amateur performance of a play called *A Scandal in a Respectable Family*. This is followed by dancing, by gnats, and then by the wife practising songs with amateur tenors who 'sleep all day and spend their nights getting up amateur concerts'. And then the dash in the early morning mist for the train to town, and 'the whole ruddy rigmarole starts all over again'. It is not by chance that Chekhov called this particular place in the country Corpse Creek. Moreover, all this takes place in a heat wave which generates exhaustion and irritation, a 'naturalistic' element characteristic of much of Chekhov's dramatic work in which mood and behaviour are closely related to the weather and season, or the time of day or night.

Tolkachov's monologue serves, therefore, both as self-exposition and as the exposure of a way of life, an exposé which extends to other people who never appear on stage although they become very real to an audience. Tolkachov's wife, Mademoiselle Chanceau and her 'eighty-two' corset-size, the sister-in-law, the children and the Colonel are all graphically created through the nature of their requirements and demands; in this way, Chekhov creates off-stage characters and a credible off-stage dramatic world. In a similar way, the three-dimensionality of certain characters in the later plays is enhanced: in *The Three Sisters*, Natasha's admirer, Protopopov is heard, but not seen, a factor which does not inhibit an audience's awareness of the situation and of Natasha's behaviour; equally, Simeonov-Pishchik's life and character are made more real by his constant reference to his daughter, Dashenka, a character well-known by the end of the play, but one who never appears; the same is true of Vershinin's wife, and children. In *A Tragic Role*, the character of Murashkin, who *is* present on-stage, is presented in much the same light as the off-stage characters: by his demands and requirements, he joins the ranks of Tolkachov's tormentors.

The beginning and conclusion of the play are farcical, whilst the central part of the play – the 'false monologue' – is a satirical exposure of a way of life and a milieu, or, to put it another way, an indirect comedy of manners. Tolkachov is the 'stock' figure of the henpecked husband and frenzied commuter, but his state of mind is clearly communicated partly through the disproportionate physical reaction: Tolkachov wants to kill himself, dreams of crocodiles, and is made ill by his situation:

It's a rotten life, I can tell you – I wouldn't wish it on my worst enemy. It's made me ill, you know – I've asthma, I've heartburn, I'm always on edge, I've indigestion and these dizzy spells. I've become quite a psychopath, you know! (*Looks about him*). Keep this under your hat, but I feel like calling in one of our leading head-shrinkers. (H.1.112–13.)

The movement of the play follows his mood: from a suicidal Tolkachov to a murderous Tolkachov. But underneath this stereotyped figure in a commonplace situation is a human being struggling comically towards something more valuable – as Tolkachov puts it at the end of his monologue:

And you get no sympathy or pity, either, everyone takes it so much for granted. You even get laughed at. But I'm alive, aren't I? So I want a bit of life! This isn't funny, it's downright tragic. (H.1.113.)

Implicit in this play, as in many of Chekhov's short stories and in his dramatic works, is the sense that there is tragedy in the banal, the petty, but in that it *is* banal and petty, there is also farce.

The Anniversary (1891)

In his book on Chekhov, William Gerhardi writes:

Chekhov does not give us a cross-section of a lump of life, taken as it were, at random, by merely registering the irrelevant perceptions which make it up. Chekhov – because he is an artist as well as a psychologist – discriminates in his choice of those seeming irrevelancies which in literature go to the making of the illusion of real life...

Thus when he introduces an irrelevancy, it is always one of those seeming irrelevancies which are, in point of actual result, significant relevancies. For he charges each with several tasks. (*a*) To connote by its apparent irrelevancy the illusion of real life: it is so in real life, we think of one thing and then our thought goes off at a tangent. (*b*) To be in itself amusing, delightful, pathetic, tragic, or otherwise beautiful. (*c*) To be always significant, that is psychologically true, throwing additional light on the character as well as on his subjective existence. (*d*) To consolidate the form of the story by bringing in, if possible, the same apparent irrelevancy more than once – by making it characteristic of a person. And, above all (*e*), by emphasizing some irrelevancies at the expense of others to bring the reader to a point at which he can see where these more prominent irrelevancies...touch upon the fading threads of others in the background.[32]

The one-act farce *The Anniversary* (adapted from the short story written in 1887, *A Defenceless Creature*) relies for its comic action on a number of 'irrelevancies', some of which take the form of 'comic misunderstandings'.

In the midst of the hectic preparations for the anniversary celebrations of a private bank, the Chairman's wife, Tatyana Shipuchina, arrives in the bank fresh from the country, full of gossip and irrelevant information which distracts her husband and his elderly bank clerk; the 'action' is further interrupted by the arrival of a complete stranger – an old woman, Mrs Merchutkina – who has, in fact, come to the wrong address in the hope of getting money from the War Office medical department for her sacked and sick husband. This comic misunderstanding (which is partly achieved through the conventional 'conversation-of-the-deaf') results in such complete chaos that the clerk, Khirin, 'misunderstands' the Chairman's request, and tries to throw out the wrong woman, the Chairman's wife instead of Mrs Merchutkina. In this way, the farcical elements of the play (and the action) are set in motion by the arrival of the two women both of whom, by their interruption, create action seemingly irrelevant to the intended action of the play. This same technique may be seen in *The Proposal* in which Lomov's apparently irrelevant mention of Oxpen Field throws the intended action of 'the proposal'. The 'irrelevancies' of *The Proposal* become, in fact, the true action of the play, and in the same way in *The Anniversary* both Mrs Shipuchina and Mrs Merchutkina, by interrupting the 'action' of the play in effect create the real action. Part of the farce arises from the conflict between the intended action, namely the anniversary celebrations, and the resulting action, namely the interruptions. These interruptions also take the form of totally irrelevant information which simultaneously creates comedy and reveals character:

TATYANA: (*coming in after her husband*) We went to a party at the Berezhnitskys'. Katya was wearing a dear little blue silk frock with an open neck, and trimmed with fine lace. She does look nice with her hair up, and I arranged it myself. Her dress and hair were quite devastating!

SHIPUCHIN: (*who now has migraine*) Yes, yes, I'm sure. Someone may come in here at any moment.

MRS MERCHUTKINA: Sir!

SHIPUCHIN: (*despondently*) What now? What do you want?

MRS MERCHUTKINA: Sir! (*Points to Khirin.*) This man here, this creature – he taps his forehead at me and then on the table. You tell him to look into my case, but he sneers at me and makes nasty remarks. I'm a weak, defenceless woman, I am.

SHIPUCHIN: Very well, madam, I'll see about it. I'll take steps. Now do go, I'll deal with it later. (*Aside.*) My gout's coming on.

KHIRIN: (*goes up to Shipuchin, quietly*) Mr Shipuchin, let me send for the hall-porter and have her slung out on her ear. This beats everything.

SHIPUCHIN: (*terrified*) No, no! She'll only raise Cain and there are a lot of private apartments in this block.

MRS MERCHUTKINA: Sir!

KHIRIN: (*in a tearful voice*). But I have a speech to write. I shan't get it done in time. (*Goes back to the desk.*) I can't stand this.

MRS MERCHUTKINA: Please sir, when do I get my money? I need it at once.
(H.1.146.)

Much of *The Anniversary* is structured (as are the later full-length plays) by means of several different rhythms taking place simultaneously: Shipuchina trying to fill her husband in on family events and gossip; Mrs Merchutkina trying to get her money; Khirin trying to finish writing the speech in time, thwarted by his pet hate – women; and

Shipuchin himself trying to keep up appearances, maintain a formality, while expecting the delegation to arrive at any minute for the celebration. These different rhythms are composed of a mixture of the 'relevant' and the apparently 'irrelevant', and the apparently irrelevant rhythms in fact alter the action and, by so doing, become the relevant action of the play. Each of these different rhythms is completely expressive of one or other of the characters.

In the later full-length plays the same basic technique is used, but in such a way that the interruption or the interjection of the irrelevant does not alter the action: instead, it alters audience perception and sometimes stage mood. Such interruptions of the seemingly irrelevant become, in fact, relevant in their own right, are often a source of the comic, and – as in *The Anniversary* – simultaneously reveal character and thought-process. An example of this may be seen in Act 2 of *The Three Sisters* in which Fedotik and Rodé softly strum a guitar in the background; Vershinin, Tuzenbakh and Masha are talking; Irina is playing patience, and Chebutykin reads the paper:

MASHA: I feel that man should have a faith or be trying to find one, otherwise his life just doesn't make sense. Think of living without knowing why cranes fly, why children are born or why there are stars in the sky. Either you know what you're living for, or else the whole thing's a waste of time and means less than nothing. (*Pause.*)

VERSHININ: Still, I'm sorry I'm not young any more.

MASHA: As Gogol said, 'Life on this earth is no end of a bore, my friends.'

TUZENBAKH: What I say is, arguing with you is no end of a job, my friends. Oh, I give up.

CHEBUTYKIN: (*reading the newspaper*) Balzac got married in Berdichev. (*Irina sings softly.*)

CHEBUTYKIN: I really must put that down in my little book. (*Makes a note.*) Balzac got married in Berdichev. (*Carries on reading the newspaper.*)

IRINA: (*playing patience, thoughtfully*) Balzac got married in Berdichev.

(H.3.100.)

This interruption by Chebutykin of the seemingly irrelevant achieves several distinct results: first, it expresses the apparently random which creates 'a slice of life'; second, it is expressive of Chebutykin as a character; and third, juxtaposed with what has been said (yet maintaining the mood of the scene), it raises a question: if Balzac could be married in a place like Berdichev, then perhaps it is not the *place* which is significant, but the activity? As such, the dramatic technique here relates crucially to the 'action' of the play, to the discussion taking place, and to an audience, in that it shifts perspective and alters the focus and perception of the audience view. It takes the audience 'out' of the Prozorov household, out of the small garrison town – not 'to Moscow', but to a place like Berdichev. A further example may be seen in Act 4 of *Uncle Vanya* at the point just prior to his departure when Astrov accepts a glass of vodka from Marina:

MARINA: A little vodka then?
ASTROV: *(hesitantly)* Well, perhaps – *(Marina goes out.)*
ASTROV: *(after a pause)* My trace horse has gone a bit lame. I noticed it yester-
day when Petrushka was taking him to water.
VOYNITSKY: You'll have to get him reshod.
ASTROV: I'd better call at the blacksmiths' in Rozhdestvennoye. There's no-
thing else for it. *(Goes up to the map of Africa and looks at it.)* Down there in
Africa the heat must be quite something. Terrific!
VOYNITSKY: Very probably.   (H.3.66.)

The mention of Africa seems completely irrelevant, and is only prompted by what is, in fact, a stage 'prop', but again, it draws an audience back from the scene immediately witnessed to a wider world beyond; it reminds them of Vanya's aspirations and previous illusions, and it serves – comically – to express Astrov's awkwardness and embarrass-ment at this point of his departure: the inconsequential takes on a rele-vance and depth. In the later full-length plays, the inconsequential or the seemingly irrelevant may take many different forms: whether the form of a remark, music or a sound effect, reference to a stage object, an action, or the physical form of an entrance which 'interrupts' the action. This last may be seen in Act 2 of *The Cherry Orchard* where the unexpected arrival of the tramp vitally *affects* the play, but does not alter the action. The tramp's arrival is basically irrelevant to the dis-cussion preceding his entrance; he is seemingly irrelevant to the charac-ters' lives, but his entrance has a crucial effect on the meaning of the play, on the mood of the scene, and, again, on the audience's perception. Examples of such 'irrelevancies' may be found in all of Chekhov's later dramatic works.

These apparently random or irrelevant comments or actions are generally attributed to Chekhov's 'naturalism', but when seen in embryo, so to speak, and on a more overt level in the one-act plays, this technique may also be seen as a vital ingredient of Chekhov's farces. Thus in *The Anniversary* such interruptions and irrelevancies are only more overt because they do actually alter the action of the play and, given the resulting chaos, serve as an element of farce. But, as in the later plays, a multiple rhythmic structure is created, and character is revealed by the nature of the particular 'irrelevance'.

In both *The Anniversary* and, for example, *The Cherry Orchard*, the use of irrelevancies also results in, and relates to, the characters' failure or inability to communicate with each other:

ANYA: (*quietly embracing Varya*) Has he proposed, Varya? (*Varya shakes her head.*) But he does love you. Why can't you get it all settled? What are you both waiting for?

VARYA: I don't think anything will come of it. He's so busy he can't be bothered with me, he doesn't even notice me. Wretched man, I'm fed up with the sight of him. Everyone's talking about our wedding and congratulating us, when there's nothing in it at all actually and the whole thing's so vague. (*In a different tone of voice.*) You've got a brooch that looks like a bee or something.

ANYA: (*sadly*) Yes, Mother bought it. (*Goes to her room, now talking away happily like a child.*) Do you know, in Paris I went up in a balloon.   (H.3.149.)

From Varya's unhappiness, to a brooch, to a balloon in Paris – Anya is no longer listening to Varya, and each continues her own train of thought. In *The Anniversary*, Merchutkina resolutely fails to listen to anyone else and, following her own train of thought, introduces complete irrelevancies, meaningful to nobody but herself:

SHIPUCHIN:...As I've said already, madam, this is a bank – a private business establishment.

MRS MERCHUTKINA: Have mercy, kind sir. Think of yourself as my father. If the doctor's certificate isn't enough, I can bring a paper from the police too. Tell them to pay me the money.

SHIPUCHIN: (*sighs heavily*) Phew!

TATYANA: (*to Mrs Merchutkina*) I say, old girl, you're in the way, do you hear? This won't do, you know.

MRS MERCHUTKINA: Pretty lady, I've no one to stick up for me. Food and drink don't mean a thing, dearie, and I've had some coffee this morning, but it didn't go down well at all, it didn't.   (H.1.146–7.)

In the above scene from *The Cherry Orchard*, the context, the mood, and the effect are subtly different from the scene quoted from *The Anniversary*, but the technique is similar. And the technique is a well-known characteristic of comedy relating, in particular, to Gogol's 'comic illogic'. Thus 'speech flow through association', relying heavily on the apparently illogical or irrelevant, is used by Chekhov both as a source of the comic and as a means of creating 'a slice of life'. The comic convention becomes, in Chekhov's later dramatic work, a feature of realism which is different because of the context within which it is utilised.

This realism and the farce in *The Anniversary* emanate largely from the characterisation, and it is in the characterisation that further examples are found to justify Vakhtangov's 'broader realism': the characters in the play combine elements of 'stock' characterisation, of the three-dimensional, and of the grotesque. As in *The Bear* and *The Proposal*, certain characteristics are heightened and exaggerated. The use of 'stock' or 'type' characters relates to the harassed husband, Shipuchin, with his over-bearing young wife, Shipuchina; the elderly bank clerk, Khirin, who is a complete misogynist; and the old woman Merchutkina who, far from being 'a defenceless creature' is, in fact, a perfect pest. And as in the case of Lomov ('Breaker') in *The Proposal*, the names of the male characters may also relate to their distinctive features: Shipuchin may be translated as 'Hissing', and Khirin as 'Sickly'.

The Anniversary was the last of the three one-act Chekhov farces which formed Meyerhold's production *33 Swoons*, and as with *The Bear* and *The Proposal*, the interpretation was partly governed by certain distinctive features of the characters – Meyerhold isolated certain 'crazy features' of each character, and exaggerated them to create a grotesque farce:

The Anniversary in Meyerhold's programme carries Chekhov's title, but Meyerhold could daringly re-name it, and call it, for example, as follows: *A Mad Day or Chekhov's Anniversary*, or simply *A Mad Day* or even *Crazy People*. In Chekhov's vaudeville there walk about strange, odd people – in Meyerhold's production there run about lunatics. (Nine Swoons of the vaudeville – there are nine points where the madness reaches its climax.) The madness of each character or hero climbs to a crescendo until he completely loses consciousness, and falls flat on his back to the accompaniment of Strauss's music. In Chekhov's vaudeville they are simply funny people; Meyerhold exaggerates this comic feature. And so one has on stage crazy people. Every one of them has his/her special point of craziness: Shipuchin has gone mad over his grandeur; Merchutkina over the need to get her 'Twenty-four roubles, Thirty-six kopecks'; Khirin has his point of madness – suspicion, while Tatyana Alexeyevna has gone crazy through eroticism.[33]

This farce-vaudeville was turned, by Meyerhold, into a farce-grotesque, but although Meyerhold was himself subsequently highly critical of his own production and interpretation[34] it is not necessarily without valid justification from Chekhov's script. Thus Yuzovsky's description of Meyerhold's treatment of Khirin, for example, is revealing of the character as created by Chekhov:

About Khirin it is known that at home he chases his wife and sister-in-law with a knife. And that is sufficient. We have in front of us a lunatic who is looking around him suspiciously; he wraps himself in a shawl because he regards himself as ill, but this helps the actor in performance [Kel'berer] to keep his head bowed all the time as if suspecting, as if looking out for all kinds of tricks that may arise. It seems he talks to himself, he smiles a crazy smile; any moment – just wait – and he will do something crazy. In the play, Khirin shouts to Tatyana Shipuchina furiously: 'Clear out!' – in this performance he does this with obvious pleasure. He produces a revolver – which is not in Chekhov's play – and with a blissful smile he loads it bullet by bullet, and he does it slowly, enjoying himself. He chases the others present with the gun, and his eyes shine with joy. It is as if he has waited for this possibility for a long time . . . And if, suddenly, without any special reason he would have set fire to the bank, hardly anyone would have been surprised.[35]

Much of this may be seen as justified, if exaggeratedly so, by Khirin's own words in the opening monologue of the play. Khirin makes it clear that he is not writing Shipuchin's speech for him out of loyalty, or the desire to be helpful, but because he will gain by it:

KHIRIN: . . . He's promised to see I don't lose by it. If all goes well this afternoon and he manages to bamboozle his audience, he's promised me a gold medal and a three-hundred-rouble bonus. We shall see. (*Writes*) But if I get nothing for my pains, my lad, then you can watch out – I'm apt to fly off the handle! You put my back up, chum, and you'll find yourself in Queer Street, believe you me! (H.1.137)

Thus Khirin has a vested interest in ensuring that the proceedings do pass off satisfactorily; in addition, Khirin dislikes 'messes and muddles' which, in his terms, means the presence of women! By introducing Shipuchina and Merchutkina onto the scene, Chekhov has mixed 'a witch's brew': when an old misogynist meets a simpering, gossipy and flirtatious young woman, and an obstinate pest in the shape of an old woman, a clash is bound to occur. A situation will arise simply because of the interaction of these characters. And the possible result is carefully plotted in by Chekhov before the arrival of the women:

SHIPUCHIN: . . . Your wife was here this morning, complaining about you again – said you ran after her with a knife last night, and your sister-in-law too. Whatever next, Khirin! This won't do.
KHIRIN: (*sternly*) Mr Shipuchin, may I venture to ask you a favour on this anniversary occasion, if only out of consideration for the drudgery I do here? Be so good as to leave my family life alone, would you mind?
SHIPUCHIN: (*sighs*) You're quite impossible, Khirin. You're a very decent,

respectable fellow, but with women you're a regular Jack the Ripper. You are, you know, I can't see why you hate them so.   (H.1.138–9)

This sickly misogynist (or Jack the Ripper) is forced to witness the endless little kisses which Tatyana Shipuchina bestows on her husband, and much is comically revealed by his reaction, repeated several times: 'Khirin gives an angry cough', a brilliantly appropriate and economical sound which indicates both his hypochondria and his irritation. He is also forced to listen to Tatyana's gossip, her vanities, and her little song from *Eugene Onegin*, all while he is trying to finish Shipuchin's speech and meet a deadline. Merchutkina's arrival increases an explosive situation and, in effect, everything that the two women do and say only serves to motivate and justify Khirin's fears and fury. And to make matters worse, Tatyana starts to talk directly to him when Shipuchin's attention is taken up by Merchutkina, and her behaviour with Khirin is like a 'red flag to a bull':

TATYANA: (*to Khirin*) Well, I must begin at the beginning. Last week I suddenly get a letter from Mother. She writes that my sister Katya's had a proposal from a certain Grendilevsky – a very nice, modest young man, but with no means or position at all. Now, by rotten bad luck Katya was rather gone on him, believe it or not. So what's to be done? Mother writes and tells me to come at once and influence Katya.

KHIRIN: (*sternly*) Look here, you're putting me off. While you go on about Mother and Katya, I've lost my place and I'm all mixed up.

TATYANA: Well, it's not the end of the world! And you listen when a lady talks to you! Why so peeved today? Are you in love? (*Laughs.*)

SHIPUCHIN: (*to Mrs Merchutkina*) I say, look here, what's all this about? I can't make sense of it.

TATYANA: In love, eh? Aha – blushing, are we?   (H.1.142–3.)

Significantly – and dangerously – Khirin makes no reply, but his facial reaction, or the visually comic reaction which must follow, is such that seconds later Tatyana rather meekly and readily agrees to her husband's request to wait in the office outside. Ironically, however, Khirin seems to meet his match in Merchutkina – left by Shipuchin to deal with her, Khirin tries to frighten her into at last understanding that she has come to the wrong place:

KHIRIN: I don't think I've ever seen anything nastier in my life. Ugh, what a pain in the neck. (*Breathes heavily.*) I repeat, do you hear? If you won't clear out, I'll pulverize you, you old horror. I'm quite capable of crippling you for life, that's the sort of man I am. I'll stop at nothing.
     (H.1.145)

Merchutkina's response is both anti-climactic and virtually unanswerable:

MERCHUTKINA: You're all bark and no bite. You don't scare me, I know your sort.

Each thinks that the other is 'crackers', but when Mrs Merchutkina, having received some money, then starts asking for her husband's job to be returned, and when Tatyana returns still gossiping, Shipuchin can take no more; he appeals to Khirin to get rid of Mrs Merchutkina, and chaos (that crucial ingredient of farce) is the result. Either deliberately misunderstanding in order to get his revenge on Tatyana, or because he is too far gone in his rage to listen properly, Khirin first chases the wrong woman, and only then goes after Mrs Merchutkina. As a result, first one woman, and then the other 'swoons'. The extremity of Khirin's reaction is farcical, but it has been so carefully motivated that it becomes inevitable.

Until this moment, however, Shipuchin has tried to remain calm although – as so often with the characters of Chekhov's farce-vaudevilles – he is reacting by suffering increasing physical ailments. The play begins with Shipuchin feeling exhausted:

SHIPUCHIN:...I say, I'm getting as nervous as a kitten. I'm so on edge, I feel I'll burst into tears at the slightest provocation. (H.1.140.)

The provocation is, in fact, considerable: a few minutes of trying to cope with Mrs Merchutkina sends Shipuchin dizzy; coping with his wife, who is gossiping with the clerks in the outer office, brings on a migraine, and then his gout starts to come on. But his outward calm is for one crucial, comic, and psychologically accurate reason: he is desperate to keep up appearances. This factor, combined with his pretentiousness and vanity, is exactly what makes him – in terms of a comedy – ripe for deflation:

SHIPUCHIN: The clerks have just given me an album, and I hear the shareholders want to present me with an address and a silver tankard. (*Playing with his monocle.*) Very nice, or my name's not Shipuchin – no harm in it at all. A little ceremony's needed for the sake of the Bank's reputation, damn it. You're one of us, so you're in the know, of course. I wrote the address myself – and as for the tankard, well, I bought that too. Yes, and it set me back forty-five roubles to have the address bound, but there was nothing else for it. *They'd* never have thought of it. (*Looks around.*) What furniture and fittings! Not bad, eh? They call me fussy – say I only care about having my door-handles polished, my clerks turned out in smart neck-ties and a fat commissionaire standing at my front door. Not a bit of it, sirs. Those door-handles and that commissionaire aren't trifles. At home I can behave like some little suburban tyke – sleep and eat like a hog, drink like a fish –

...at home I can be a jumped-up little squirt with my own nasty little habits. But *here* everything must be on the grand scale. This is a bank, sir! Here every detail must impress and wear an air of solemnity, as you might say. (*Picks up a piece of paper from the floor and throws it on the fire.*) My great merit is simply that I've raised the Bank's prestige. Tone's a great thing. A great thing is tone, or my name's not Shipuchin.　　　　(H.1.139.)

This characteristic catch-phrase – 'or my name's not Shipuchin' – is one feature which Meyerhold emphasised; and, in addition to the monocle specified by Chekhov, Meyerhold also gave the actor playing Shipuchin (Chikul) 'a furcoat which hangs down from one shoulder which he holds with his other hand, and this gives him a special lightness, airiness, dandyism, chic'.[36] But the main feature which Meyerhold exaggerated was the image that Shipuchin has of himself as a 'firework': 'I'm hoping for a lot from this speech. It's a statement of faith – a firework display, rather. There's some pretty hot stuff in this, or my name's not Shipuchin.' The comic deflation, however, results in the firework 'hissing' but not taking off. Shipuchin's pretensions result in a final *tableau* which is contrary to everything for which he had hoped.

In his introduction to *The Oxford Chekhov* Hingley describes the women in the play as the chief culprits, implying what today might be called anti-feminism on Chekhov's part, but, in fact, both men are ripe for deflation: Shipuchin because 'Tone's a great thing' and because of his pretentiousness, and Khirin because he does not like 'messes and muddles' and also – given the structure and situation of a farce-vaude-ville – because the challenge of a misogynist must be met.

There is no doubt, however, that Tatyana meets this 'challenge': her entire conversation is about love, men, and romantic affairs, and – like her husband – she is very vain. Describing her train journey down to the country, Tatyana seems blissfully unaware that she is describing events which are not conventionally narrated to a husband:

TATYANA: ... There was this dark-haired young fellow sitting opposite me – not bad-looking, quite attractive, actually. Well, we got talking. A sailor came along and some student or other. (*Laughs.*) I told them I wasn't married. Oh, they were all over me! We chattered away till midnight – the dark young man told some screamingly funny stories and the sailor kept singing! I laughed till my sides ached. And when the sailor – oh, those sailors! – when it came out that I was called Tatyana, do you know what he sang? (*Sings in a bass voice.*)

> 'Onegin, how can I deny
> I'll love Tatyana till I die?'[37]

(*Roars with laughter. Khirin coughs angrily.*)   (H.I.141–2.)

Tatyana Shipuchina is vulgar, an outrageous flirt, and utterly insensitive to other people and her surroundings; dangerously, she tries her feminine charms on Khirin, and even when sent into the outer office to wait she distracts the clerks by flirting with them – as the stage direction reads: 'Tatyana's laughter is heard off-stage, followed by a man's laughter.' Her conversation is almost exclusively about men, their attentions to her, and her sister's love affair. But by means of Tatyana's ridiculous prattle, Chekhov – in her narrative – is in effect parodying 'romantic love' and a 'stock' situation from an amorous vaudeville. Describing how, finally, due to her influence, her sister Katya turned down young Grendilevsky, Tatyana continues:

TATYANA:...Katya and I are walking in the garden just before supper, when suddenly –. (*Excitedly.*) When suddenly we hear a shot! No, I can't talk about it calmly. (*Fans herself with her handkerchief.*) It's too much for me! (*Shipuchin sighs.*)

TATYANA: (*weeps*) We rush to the summer house, and there – there lies poor Grendilevsky with a pistol in his hand.

SHIPUCHIN: Oh, I can't stand this – can't stand it, I tell you! (*To Mrs Merchutkina.*) What more do you want?

MRS MERCHUTKINA: Please sir, can my husband have his job back?

TATYANA: (*weeping*) He shot himself straight through the heart, just here. Katya fainted, poor dear. And he got the fright of his life. He just lies there and asks us to send for the doctor. The doctor turns up quite soon and – and saves the poor boy.   (H.I.147.)

It is Tatyana's ridiculous hyperbole which creates the anti-climax to this melodramatic 'stock' situation of unrequited love and attempted suicide. Tatyana's probable accompanying mime, and her obvious enjoyment of this country drama both help to create the parody and reveal her character. Extending her 'point of craziness', namely love, Meyerhold produced all the scenes with Tatyana (played by Tyapkina) as 'some kind of completely exotic can-can.' In this, however valid as one feature of the character, Meyerhold's interpretation excluded other aspects. In the character of Tatyana, Chekhov creates a different type of misunderstanding: Tatyana is completely incapable of understanding that a married woman is expected to behave with propriety, and that the wife of the Bank's Chairman does not gossip about his business affairs. Her insensitivity and lack of awareness to situation and people is illustrated by her inability to leave: like Medvedenko in the last act of *The Seagull*, Tatyana several times states that she will 'only be a minute, and then leave', and – again like Medvedenko – consistently fails to go.[38] But whereas Medvedenko fails to leave because he is unhappily torn between leaving Masha or leaving the baby, Tatyana fails to go because she is too full of her own gossip, and too insensitive to realise when she is not wanted. She is incapable of understanding because she is incapable of listening. The convention of 'the conversation-of-the-deaf' has become a means of psychological characterisation.

It is this feature – perhaps above all others – which characterises Merchutkina: she is almost a physical embodiment of a 'comic misunderstanding', of the failure to communicate given a 'conversation-of-the-deaf'. In Meyerhold's production:

she appears unexpectedly, she 'arises' – a pale bird-like face, the eyes set fixedly on Shipuchin; the voice monotonous, colourless. She has got used to her own voice so she doesn't hear it herself. It seems to her that merely by her appearance, everyone will understand what she needs: that all understand, all know, all are preoccupied with that one and only thing – to give or not to give 'twenty-four roubles, thirty-six kopecks'.[39]

Ironically, given the title of the story from which the play derives, Mrs Merchutkina is not 'a defenceless creature': her total inability to listen insulates her from the world, and by remaining unmoved by Shipuchin's explanations, and Khirin's threats, she finally gets what she has come for, albeit to the wrong place, and from the wrong people:

SHIPUCHIN: I repeat, madam. Your husband was employed by the War Office medical department, but this is a bank, a private business.
MRS MERCHUTKINA: Quite so, quite so. I understand, mister. Then tell them to give me fifteen roubles, say. I don't mind waiting for the rest, sir.

(H.1.144)

The balance of sympathy for this character is carefully maintained by Chekhov: she is initially characterised as 'an old woman who wears an old-fashioned overcoat', and her speech is distinguished as of a lower social order, and as such, she conjures up images of 'the insulted and humiliated', endlessly sitting in the anteroom of some petty official, waiting for justice:

MRS MERCHUTKINA: Pity a helpless orphan, sir. I'm a weak, defenceless woman. Fair worried to death I am, what with lodgers to have the law on, my husband's affairs to handle, a house to run – and my son-in-law out of work as well. (H.1.144.)

But Merchutkina's defencelessness is qualified by the fact that she is going to have the law on her lodgers, that she *has* come to the wrong place, without her husband's knowledge, to get his money and job back, and that she does not listen to anything said to her. As far as she is concerned, she is 'not asking for what isn't mine', she has a medical certificate to prove her husband's illness, and, as she characteristically keeps repeating: 'I'm a weak, defenceless woman, I am.' Ironically, however, this comic misunderstanding is only deepened when Shi-puchin – out of exhaustion and despair – finally gives her the money: seemingly justified in her insistence and assumption that she has come to the right place, she starts a new plea: 'Please sir, can my husband have his job back?'

Significantly, Merchutkina gets her money through pestering, and not through justice. As she says: 'I've been in half a dozen different places already, mister, and they wouldn't even listen.' In this way, the comic misunderstanding has its serious side: the appeal of 'the little man' to an 'Excellency', the respect for 'authority' (even an inappropriate one) are crucial themes in Russian literature, whether in Gogol's *The Government Inspector* and *The Greatcoat*,[40] Dostoyevsky's *Poor Folk*, or Chekhov's short story, *The Death of a Government Clerk*. This same (misplaced) respect for authority may be seen in *The Wedding* in which 'a general' is invited simply because that adds tone and class to the event. Chekhov was therefore using a conventional theme or situation, and one which may be found in several vaudevilles of the period, but these 'comic scenes' of the conventional vaudeville used 'the little man' to laugh and sneer at him, while Chekhov treats such characters – whether Merchutkina or Nyukhin in *Smoking is Bad for You* – with objective, comic compassion. Merchutkina is irritating, a perfect pest, deaf to all reason, but she needs the money. Thus Chekhov's characterisation is completely devoid of sentimentality: Merchutkina's 'deafness' and self-pity create objectivity in an audience.

In one of his letters, Chekhov wrote that in the one-act 'miniature joke' – 'every character must be three-dimensional, and must speak his own language'.[41] The characterisation of *The Anniversary* is indeed three-dimensional, but it is also heightened and exaggerated: Chekhov creates a character 'in-the-round', but then singles out the main features and emphasises the basic and typical traits and 'speech peculiarities'.

The structure of *The Anniversary* is more complicated than that of *The Bear* or *The Proposal*: there are more characters all of equal importance, and the interaction of each character's different 'rhythm' provides the source of conflict and a multiple rhythmic structure which enables one to 'comment' on the other. In addition, it is the interaction of the characters which creates the comic misunderstandings and the chaos or confusion necessary to a farce-vaudeville. But the situation and the setting provide this interaction with an 'external' tension and time-limit: the anniversary celebration and its imminence motivates Shipuchin and Khirin in their actions and reactions. The setting, namely the Bank, is a public one in which formality is expected and respectability maintained; both Shipuchin's position and the nature of the setting are conveyed partly by other characters who, at regular intervals, come in and go out of Shipuchin's office – other characters who add to the realistic yet grotesque element in the play: 'While he [Shipuchin] is on stage, clerks come and go from time to time with papers for him to sign.' The 'off-stage' world of the Chairman's office is credibly created and maintained largely by off-stage sound effects and the to-ing and fro-ing of the clerks, while the setting of Shipuchin's office is given an individuality significant in its relevance to the action, characters and point of the play: 'The Chairman's office. A door, left, leading into the main office. Two desks. The furnishings have pretensions to extreme luxury: velvet-upholstered furniture, flowers, statues, carpets and a telephone.'

This visual pretentiousness is apparent at the opening of the play but, in addition, an immediate visual comic disparity is evident between the setting, and Khirin – in the midst of these 'posh' surroundings, Khirin wears felt boots, something which even Merchutkina notices and knows is not done: 'Sits around in the office with his felt boots on! Cheek! Where was you brought up?' But not content with that, Khirin has made no concession to the celebration, and his clothes are quite unsuitable even for a normal working day:

SHIPUCHIN: ...(*looking Khirin over*) My dear fellow, a shareholders' deputation may come in any moment, and here you are in those felt boots and that scarf and, er, that jacket thing – what a ghastly colour! You might have worn tails or at least a black frock-coat –

KHIRIN; My health matters more to me than your shareholders. I feel sore all over.

SHIPUCHIN: (*excitedly*) Well, you must admit you look an awful mess. You're spoiling the whole effect. (H.1.139)

The 'whole effect' is also spoilt by Tatyana when she enters 'wearing a mackintosh, with a travelling handbag slung over her shoulder'. This

provides one of the reasons for Shipuchin's desire to send her home:
'My dear, we're celebrating our anniversary today, and a shareholders'
deputation may turn up any moment. And you're not properly
dressed.' Merchutkina's entrance, however, provides a further visual
anachronism (and comic discrepancy): in her old-fashioned overcoat she
is immediately out of place in her surroundings. In this way, the conflict and the farce of the play are conveyed visually: the characters do
not fit their surroundings. Only Shipuchin, in his evening dress, is in
tune with the pretentiousness of the setting, and only at the end do
others enter who are appropriately dressed for this event: 'Enter a
deputation of five men, all in evening dress. . . '. These five men, dressed
in evening dress at noon,[42] reinstate the pretentious formality of this
celebration – but at the most critical, climactic and most farcical moment
in the play. The deflation (and the farce) are conveyed through the
visual clash between the pretentious and the comically inappropriate.
This technique may be seen in Chekhov's later dramatic work in, for
example, the treatment of Natasha in Act 1 of *The Three Sisters*, or in
Masha's black dress in Act 1 of *The Seagull* or – though to different effect
– in Charlotte Ivanovna's appearance in *The Cherry Orchard*.

The climax of the play – and the most farcical moment – is carefully
prepared by Chekhov, and used by him to explode the pretensions of
the anniversary celebrations and Shipuchin's façade. The technique
used – while credibly motivated – utilises a number of conventional
devices. First, the chase: the farcical situation of Khirin the misogynist
chasing a woman – and the wrong woman, namely Tatyana the flirt;
the confused husband joins in the chase to protect his wife; Khirin then
switches his enraged attentions to the old woman in her long overcoat;
Tatyana, trying to get out of Khirin's way, jumps on a chair and then –
feeling faint – collapses on to the sofa; while Merchutkina, also feeling
faint, collapses in Shipuchin's arms. The *tableau* which therefore meets
the eyes of the shareholders' deputation, and of the bank employees
who crowd in after them, is the frozen *tableau* of farce: Khirin frozen
in an attitude of ferocity, with his sleeves rolled up and in his felt boots;
Mrs Merchutkina in the arms of the Chairman who is apparently unaware that he has a strange old woman in his arms while his wife lies
groaning on the sofa. Inevitably, the office must be in some disarray
given the chase around the room.

This climactic *tableau* is held while one of the shareholders loudly
reads the address – bound in velvet – which had been so carefully prepared by Shipuchin, in a faltering attempt not to notice that anything
is amiss. The speech itself is a mixture of the pretentious and the ironic:

5. The final scene of *The Anniversary*, a film directed by Petrov, 1944, with V. O. Toporkov as Khirin.

the pretentiousness comes over in the style of the speech, and, comic-ally, in the totally inappropriate quotation from *Hamlet;* the irony comes from the comic disparity between what is seen and what is said. Thus the Shareholder's unfortunate mention of Shipuchin's 'natural tact', and his several times repeated phrase, 'the reputation of the Bank', creates a bizarre contrast to what the audience both on and off the stage are actually witnessing. This irony is further increased by Shipuchin's glassy-eyed reaction: in a complete daze, he utters a poetic verse of apparently comic irrelevance, from Krylov's *The Passers-by and the Geese.* 'Under the circumstances' the shareholders can only mumble that they will return later, and they retreat in embarrassment.

Thus the ludicrous formality of the celebratory event is reasserted in the play at the most farcical moment to create a natural climax – a climax which simultaneously serves as a deflatory device. It is significant that Chekhov did not end the play with the frozen *tableau:* by extending the play to include the Shareholder's speech, Chekhov underlines the pretentious, *and* slows the action down; by Shipuchin's dazed irrele-vancies, and the shareholders' and employees' embarrassed exit, a different tone is asserted. Thus the slower pace, the down-beat, the anti-climax, create a more thoughtful ending. The play comes to an end not with the usual conventional happy ending, but with what is undoubtedly a scandal.

This farce-vaudeville is not an 'amorous vaudeville' (although 'love' and 'romance' are parodied by means of both Tatyana and Khirin); it is not, of course, a 'scene-monologue' (although the play begins with Khirin's monologue); it is not simply 'a biting exposure of the private banks in Russia';[43] it is an innovatory 'comic scene of daily life' which is also in the tradition of Gogol: a satire on the pretentious, the petty, and the philistine. It combines comedy of situation and comedy of character, but the play is a comedy of the characters' own making.

The Night before the Trial (1890s)

The unfinished, posthumously published *The Night before the Trial* is not subtitled by Chekhov, but the situation, characterisation and dramatic techniques place the play clearly within the context of a farce-vaudeville, and the story of the same title, written in 1886, indicates the probable and farcical continuation of the play. With the exception of some of the little known or early parodies,[44] *The Night before the Trial* – although unfinished – is potentially one of Chekhov's most overt parodies: it utilises the most conventional, even traditional, comic situation, stock 'types', action and probable *dénouement*. It is, perhaps, for this reason that the play remained unfinished. Speculation is, of course, idle, but when the play is seen in the context of Chekhov's other work of the 1890s, it is probable that the play had out-grown its usefulness; it is, however, interesting for the light it throws on Chekhov's use – albeit unfinished – of traditional comic devices and situations.

The play relies for its comic plot on a succession of misunderstandings which arise from mistaken, and assumed, identity: a dissolute young man, Zaytsev, assumes the identity of a doctor in order to make love to a lovely young woman – apparently unaccompanied – whom he meets in the middle of the night in an inn, while a blizzard howls outside. The young lady is, however, accompanied by none other than her husband – an ugly old man – called Fred Gusev ('Goose'). Rapidly improvising a respectable 'motive' for his advances to the young wife, Zaytsev continues to play the part of a doctor, only to be asked by the old husband to examine the young wife, Zina. This Zaytsev does, and uses his medical disguise as a means of continuing his flirtation, aided by Zina herself. At the beginning of the play, however, Zaytsev tells the audience that he is on his way to town, to be tried at the assizes for 'attempted bigamy, forging my grandmother's will to the tune of not more than three hundred roubles, and the attempted murder of a billiards-marker'. And, as the original story makes clear, the prosecuting counsel turns out to be none other than Fred Gusev:

> As readers of this unfinished play can easily deduce for themselves, the dénouement would have involved Zaytsev facing Zina's husband as his prosecuting counsel in court next day. Such, at any rate, is the ending of Chekhov's short story with the same title, where the hero comments: 'Looking at him [the prosecutor], I remembered the bugs, little Zina and my diagnosis, whereupon a chill – nay a whole Arctic Ocean – ran down my spine.'[45]

In this way, presumably, the 'cuckolded husband' is able to get his revenge on the young imposter.

This is the only one of Chekhov's plays which uses the device of assumed identity to enable a character to practise a comic deception, but it is a device which goes back, through Molière, to the commedia dell'arte. This assumption of a 'respectable' identity was – equally traditionally – often utilised in order to make a cuckold of a husband, and this, in turn, was conventionally applied to the marital situation of an ugly old husband and a young, beautiful wife. Variations may be seen in Molière, whether in *Le Médecin malgré lui*, or in *Le Malade imaginaire*, or *L'Amour médecin*, or in the early play generally attributed to Molière, *Le Médecin volant*. Again, it was traditional for the 'respectable disguise' to be that of a doctor: first, because it allowed access to the young wife, which the husband would never normally permit, let alone encourage; secondly, because the joke was increased by the husband actually inviting the 'doctor' to examine his wife; and third, because (certainly in the case of, for example, Molière's *Monsieur de Pourceaugnac*), it motivates and justifies a parody of medical terminology and practice, a source of parody to which Chekhov, as a doctor himself, was not averse.[46]

All of these traditional sources of comedy are found in *The Night before the Trial*: 'stock' or 'type' characters, a 'stock' situation, and a greater emphasis on plot as such than on psychological depth of character. The stock characterisation may be seen in the figures of the charming scoundrel of a lover, the beautiful young wife, and the ugly old husband; the landlord of the inn scarcely figures in this fragment – unlike for example, Luka in *The Bear*, no attempt is made to create anything more than the functional with this character. It is, however, exactly in

Chekhov's particular use of the conventional that parody may be seen: Gusev is *excessively* ugly, while Zina is excessively young and beautiful; equally, Zaytsev has committed an excessive variety of crimes – thus the element of parody is contained in the 'excess' of all the conventionalised facets of the play.

Zaytsev's character is established partly by his opening monologue – a monologue which serves the usual purpose of exposition – and through it his attitude to women and his comically exaggerated mixture of crimes are revealed to an audience: 'It's here today, in jug tomorrow – and Siberia's frozen wastes in six months' time. Brrr.' The tone is light, and so is Zaytsev's casual and conventional solution to his problems: suicide.

> ZAYTSEV: . . . If the jury finds against me, I'll appeal to an old and trusty friend. Dear, loyal old pal! (*Gets a large pistol out of his suitcase.*) This is him! What a boy! I swapped him with Cheprakov for a couple of hounds. Isn't he lovely! Why, just shooting yourself with this would be a kind of enjoyment. (*Tenderly.*) Are you loaded, boy? (*In a reedy voice, as if answering for the pistol.*) I am that. (*In his own voice.*) I'll bet you'll go off with a bang – one hell of a ruddy great bang! (*In a reedy voice.*) One hell of a ruddy great bang! (*In his own voice.*) Ah, you dear, silly old thing. Well, lie down and go to sleep. (*Kisses the pistol and puts it in his suitcase.*)   (H.1.163)

The tone is such that no audience would take this threatened suicide in any way seriously: the parody, however, is evident in lines such as 'Why, just shooting yourself with this would be a kind of enjoyment'; through the emphasis on the size of the pistol, and through the 'characterisation' of the pistol by ventriloquism, all of which removes Zaytsev's threat from both depth motivation, and the realistic or serious consequences of suicide.

The use of ventriloquism in this play contrasts vividly with the use made of it – to totally different effect – in *The Cherry Orchard*. The governess, Charlotte Ivanovna, is renowned for her party tricks, but on several occasions Chekhov uses her tricks to express her unhappiness and loneliness, and thus ventriloquism as practised by Charlotte Ivanovna is one of the subtly appropriate means of communicating the psychological depth of this character:

> (*Lopakhin comes in. Charlotte quietly hums a tune.*)
> GAYEV: Charlotte's happy, she's singing.
> CHARLOTTE: (*picking up a bundle which looks like a swaddled baby*) Rock-a-bye, baby. (*A baby's cry is heard.*) Hush, my darling, my dear little boy. (*The cry

is heard again.) You poor little thing! (*Throws the bundle down.*) And please
will you find me another job? I can't go on like this.   (H.3.193)

In the characterisation of Charlotte Ivanovna, her comedy 'turns' serve
to mask her despair – comedy is used to comment on the serious. In
the case of Zaytsev, however, comedy is purely conventionalised, and
neither creates nor implies hidden, serious depths. This is also emphasised
by his actions, he kisses the pistol before 'putting it to bed', and readily
maintains the comic mood by immediately proceeding to do physical
jerks to warm himself up. Thus the monologue is in no way intro-
spective, self-revelatory, or disturbing – it serves as exposition of
situation, rather than revelation of character.

The frivolity of tone is continued when Zaytsev, hearing a noise,
realises that he has neighbours, and then muses that this might result in a
round of bridge, or, better still, a 'wayside romance' and 'an affair
better than any in Turgenev's novels'.[47] And he starts to remember a
previous affair at a post-house 'down Samara way' when, one night, 'The
door opens and . . .'. His reminiscences are interrupted by the entrance
of Zina, a comic coincidence in timing which, although absurd, is also
purely conventional. But the reason for Zina's disturbed night is not, as
it turns out, even remotely romantic: she has been bitten by bed-bugs!
Zaytsev, however, responds romantically; like a real gallant, he ven-
tures to offer his services as 'a gentleman and man of honour', wishes
to aid the lady in her distress, and offers help – an offer, made from the
bottom of his 'heart', which takes the prosaic form of insect-powder.
Sensing an affair, Zaytsev offers to put the powder down in her room,
and it is then that he starts to pretend that he is a doctor: 'From their
doctors and hairdressers ladies have no secrets.'[48] Zaytsev is confirmed
as a scoundrel and the 'villain' when he swears, on his word of honour,
that he really is a doctor; and equally 'villainous' is his – characteristically – excessive reaction to the discovery that Zina's husband is present.
The would-be lover turns the husband into the villain:

ZAYTSEV: . . . What a ghastly old frump! I'd bury him alive in insect-powder
   if I had my way. I'd like to beat the swine at cards and clean him out good
   and proper a dozen times over. Better still, I'd play him at billiards and
   accidentally fetch him one with a cue that would make him remember me
   for a whole week.   (H.1.166)

Zaytsev's contempt for the old man is increased when Gusev, accepting
that he is a doctor, asks him to examine his wife, and Zaytsev is quick
to take advantage of what is both gullibility and a very real concern

over Zina's health. In the true tradition of a farce-vaudeville and a comedy of situation, Zaytsev will, inevitably, receive his just deserts when he meets Gusev in court the next day.

The conventional nature of the characters is also evident – as so often in Chekhov's work – in their names: Zaytsev – a common name – means 'Hare', while Gusev – appropriately – is associated with 'Goose'. But in this case, the use of 'meaningful names' may also have another purpose: it introduces the element of the proverb, or fable. Relevant to Zaytsev's treatment of Gusev (and, no doubt, Gusev's treatment of Zaytsev the next day), is the Russian proverb: 'First catch your hare – and then cook him.' Equally relevant to the play is Krylov's famous fable *The Hare A-Hunting* in which the boastful hare is given a share of the spoils simply because his boasting is amusing, and the fable ends: 'We mock the boaster: all the same/In sharing up the spoils, he often gets his claim.' There is no evidence, however, that Chekhov necessarily had this fable in mind.

Gusev 'the goose' is characterised by Zaytsev with typical excess:

With that blob of a nose, those blue veins all over his face and that wart on his forehead, he – he has the nerve to be married to a woman like that! What right has he? It's disgusting! (H.1.166)

In this way, Gusev is made the epitome of the ugly old husband of the commedia dell' arte, while Zaytsev justifies the view of himself as a young fop:

And then people ask why I take such a jaundiced view of things. But how can you help being pessimistic under these conditions? (H.1.166)

With one stroke, Chekhov simultaneously maintains the comedy of Zaytsev's philosophy and morality, and satirises pessimism and a 'jaundiced view' of life, by providing a ridiculous motivation and justification for it. But the joke of the whole situation is continued by Gusev's zest in pushing Zina into Zaytsev's arms:

GUSEV: (*shouts*) Zina! Oh really, you are silly. (*To him.*) She's shy – quite the blushing violet, same as me. Modesty's all very well in its way, but why overdo things? What – stand on ceremony with your doctor when you're ill? That really is the limit. (H.1.167)

The joke is in the 'persuasion' by the husband – a 'stock' example of dramatic irony, but also in the fact that Zina is no more ill than any other traditional young lady in a similar situation (such as Lucinde in *L'Amour médecin*), and, finally, in what Gusev sees as Zina's 'modesty' and shyness: the husband is deceived not only by the wife's actions, but also by her character. A further source of the comic is Gusev's excessive respect for medicine, combined with an experienced lack of respect for certain doctors. It becomes clear that Zina has already carried on an affair with a certain Dr Shervetsov; Gusev, therefore, has cause for his jealousy, but still entertains no doubts as to Zaytsev's qualifications:

ZAYTSEV:...One more question – when do you cough more, on Tuesdays or on Thursdays?
ZINA: On Saturdays.
ZAYTSEV: I see. Let me take your pulse.
GUSEV: (*aside*) It looks as if there's been kissing – it's the Shervetsov business all over again. I can't make any sense of medicine. (*To his wife.*) Do be serious, Zina – you can't go on like this, you can't neglect your health. You must listen carefully to what the doctor tells you. Medicine's making great strides these days, great strides. (H.1.168)

Chekhov is satirising the inflated, exaggerated respect for medicine – a respect which was invariably divorced from the morality and worth of its practitioners. The 'Goose' therefore puts both Shervetsov's and Zaytsev's behaviour down to some strange mystery of medicine, and carries on ignoring 'the great strides' which 'medicine' has been making under his nose. Thus, only in a conventional farce situation of this kind is it acceptable that Gusev does not penetrate Zaytsev's improvised medical 'mumbo-jumbo'.

ZAYTSEV:...Your wife's in no danger as yet, but if she doesn't have proper treatment she may end up badly with a heart attack and inflammation of the brain. (H.1.168)

Gusev swallows this diagnosis without question, and then proceeds – unwittingly – to help Zaytsev improvise the cure:

ZAYTSEV: I'll write a prescription at once. (*Tears a sheet of paper out of the register, sits down and writes.*) Sic transit...two drams. Gloria mundi...one ounce. Aquae dest – ...two grains. Now, you take these powders, three a day.
GUSEV: In water or wine?
ZAYTSEV: Water.
GUSEV: Boiled?
ZAYTSEV: Boiled. (H.1.169)

Again, it was traditional for the 'mock doctor' to improvise in pidgin Latin in order to maintain the disguise, and gain respect, and – as in all such scenes – the 'Latin' is complete nonsense. The parody of medicine is obvious – as is the satire on its practitioners – but in that Chekhov uses conventional, even traditional, comic situations and forms, the play may be seen as, in fact, parodying a parody. And, in addition, Chekhov parodies those comedies, and farce-vaudevilles, which centre on the cuckolded husband and his young wife. Perhaps for this reason Gusev remains a 'stock' character, while very little is done with the character of Zina: she is twenty-two, attractive – and a flirt: 'My husband's coming now, I think. Yes, yes, he's coming. Why don't you speak? What are you waiting for? Come on, then – kiss me, can't you?' Zaytsev receives all the co-operation he requires from Zina, but she remains a character 'by function' rather than developed as an individual.

Chekhov employs the same setting as that of *On the High Road*, but once this is clearly established, once the bed-bugs have set the plot in motion, it plays very little part: true to the convention, the setting is not used for mood or atmosphere, but only to motivate the characters' transient relationship with the location. Equally conventional are the monologue and the extensive use of 'the aside', both of which – given the style of the play – are completely acceptable.

This unfinished comedy is strangely overt: the parody emerges through the exaggeration of the conventional, rather than by means of the 'counterbalancing' techniques which Chekhov employs in all the other farce-vaudevilles – techniques involving the parody, reversal, or extension of conventions. But it is, of course, impossible to draw any conclusions about what is an unfinished – and therefore unrevised – fragment. It is idle to speculate what the play might have become, but in its unfinished state, it demonstrates very clearly Chekhov's familiarity with conventional comedy techniques and situations; moreover, it serves as an interesting contrast to similar situations in Chekhov's dramatic work in which the 'stock' and the obvious are apparently established, only to be completely avoided subsequently. Thus, Dr Lvov in *Ivanov* treats Sara – but it is Ivanov who is unfaithful, not Sara and her doctor, or, in *Uncle Vanya*, both Astrov and Vanya are attracted by the young and beautiful wife of a garrulous old man, but everyone's expectations of infidelity are disappointed –

VOYNITSKY: ...she married him when he was already an old man and gave him her youth, her beauty, her freedom, her radiance. Whatever for? – Why?
ASTROV: Is she faithful to him?
VOYNITSKY: Yes, I'm sorry to say.
ASTROV: Why sorry?
VOYNITSKY: Because she's faithful in a way that's so thoroughly bogus. Oh,

it sounds impressive enough, but it just doesn't make sense. To be unfaithful to an elderly husband you can't stand, that's immoral. But if you make these pathetic efforts to stifle your own youth and the spark of life inside you, that isn't immoral at all.   (H.3.23)

Here the expectations of fidelity are given a new – philosophical - twist: convention can be stultifying, a sin against life rather than society. Equally, Chekhov reverses the situation of the cuckolded husband in his treatment of Andrey in *The Three Sisters*: Natasha's affair with Protopopov makes Andrey not a comic figure of fun, but a tragi-comic figure pretending not to see what is going on in front of him. Thus, what is treated as a joke and as farce in *The Night before the Trial*, may well have served as an experiment in situations and techniques which are reversed, modified, and then treated in an innovatory way in the later full-length plays. Perhaps relevant both to *The Night before the Trial*, and Chekhov's other dramatic works, is Strindberg's comment made in relation to *The Father* (1887):

A deceived husband is a comic figure in the eyes of the world, and especially to a theatre audience. He must show that he is aware of this, and that he too would laugh if only the man in question were someone other than himself. This is what is *modern* in my tragedy, and alas for me and the clown who acts it if he goes to town and plays an 1887 version of the Pirate King! No screams, no preachings! Subtle, calm, resigned! – the way a normally healthy spirit accepts his fate today.[49]

4

The dramatic studies

On the High Road (1885)

The action takes place at night in an inn on a high road. Among various tramps and scoundrels, who have come into the inn for a warm and a night's lodgings, is a gentleman who has gone to the bad and begs the barman to give him a drink on credit. It turns out in conversation that the gentleman took to drowning his sorrows after his wife had deserted him on their wedding day. In search of shelter from the bad weather a lady, in whom the unhappy drunk recognizes his faithless wife, happens to come into the inn. One of the customers brandishes an axe at her out of sympathy with the drunken squire, and the dramatic sketch ends with this attempted murder. In my opinion this gloomy, sordid play cannot be approved for performance.[1]

The above is the report by the dramatic censor, Keyzer von Nilkheim, on Chekhov's one-act play *On the High Road*, written and submitted to the censorship in 1885, and neither performed nor published during Chekhov's lifetime.[2] It is the second surviving play by Chekhov after *Platonov* (1880–1?), apart from the theatrical 'joke' *Dishonourable Tragedians and Leprous Dramatists*,[3] and like several of the plays which followed, it is an adaptation of a short story, *In Autumn*, written in 1883 when Chekhov was twenty-three. The differences, however, between the original story and the dramatic work are considerable, and relate to both characters and plot. Some features of the story remain: Chekhov took the essentials from the narrative and placed them in the stage directions; the characters of Bortsov, Tikhon and Kuzma remain unchanged, and their dialogue is virtually unaltered from story to play. But there are major additions: the group of travellers and pilgrims crammed into Tikhon's inn are presented as new characters and as individuals in the play - thus Savva, Nazarovna and Yefimovna or Fedya all become not only witnesses of the story, but participants in the action. And in addition to the introduction of new, individualised characters, Chekhov created a new emphasis on the expanded character of Merik,[4] the tramp-cum-robber whose part becomes central to the play. This, in turn, altered the plot itself: the short story *In Autumn* ends when Tikhon gives Bortsov a drink in exchange for a gold locket containing his wife's portrait; in the play, however, a meeting is staged between Bortsov and his faithless wife, and the curtain falls after an unsuccessful attempt by Merik to kill her. The changes and additions are from an atmospheric, evocative sketch of a rainy autumn evening, to a dramatic study.

A 'drama' in Russian literary terminology means 'a play of a serious nature' as distinct from a tragedy, and the seriousness of *On the High Road* is virtually unrelieved by humour. With very few exceptions, the characters are 'down-and-outs', beggars, tramps, or, as Merik says to them all: 'You might be a chain-gang having a night off.' It is the only one of Chekhov's plays which is set in 'the lower depths'; in a number of the later plays, this element is present, but not as the direct central action and setting. Instead, this social reality is usually described and decried by various characters, such as Astrov in *Uncle Vanya*:

A few weeks before Easter I went to Malitskoye. They had an epidemic there. Typhus. There were village people lying around all over the place in their huts. Filth, stench, smoke everywhere and calves on the floor mixed up with patients – little pigs as well. (H.3.20.)

or:

Our district still has the same old swamps and mosquitoes, the same terrible roads, the same poverty, typhus, diphtheria, the same fires breaking out all over the place. The point is, everything's gone downhill because people have found the struggle for existence too much for them. (H.3.48)

In the same play, a factory worker enters, looking for Dr Astrov who is needed at the local factory – the labourer's entrance is in strong contrast to the rest of the scene: Yeliena (Helen) sitting languidly on the swing, drinking tea, Telegin playing a polka on his guitar. Equally, a tramp enters suddenly in Act 2 of *The Cherry Orchard*:

(*The passer-by appears. He wears a shabby, white peaked cap and an overcoat. He is slightly drunk.*)
PASSER-BY: Excuse me asking, but am I right for the station this way?
GAYEV: Yes. Follow that road.
PASSER-BY: I'm uncommonly obliged to you. (*With a cough.*) Splendid weather this. (*Declaiming*) 'Brother, my suffering brother!' 'Come out to the Volga, you whose groans – .' (*To Varya.*) Miss, could you spare a few copecks for a starving Russian?

In Act 4 of *The Three Sisters*, two beggars enter – street musicians, about whom old Anfisa says: 'Poor wretches! You don't play music in the street on a full stomach.' And Anfisa herself – an old peasant woman of eighty-one – would have ended up begging on the streets, thrown out by Natasha, had she not gone to live with Olga.

But in these later plays, the beggars, tramps or workmen – or, for that matter, Trofimov's human beings looking 'from every cherry tree in the orchard, from every leaf and every trunk'[5] are significant intruders into the setting, though not the action; by seeming to come from a world beyond the estates or the Prozorov household, they make a crucial 'comment', and then recede into the distance like the telegraph poles in Act 2 of *The Cherry Orchard*. But in many of Chekhov's short stories, the poverty and savagery of his contemporary Russia is presented as the forefront of the action: *A Malefactor, Dreams, Peasants, In the Ravine, Rothschild's Fiddle, Sorrow, Misery, Vanka, I Want to Sleep, A Doctor's Visit, A Woman's Kingdom, A Father, The Old House*, and many others. It must, of course, be remembered that *On the High Road* was banned for performance; the censorship of plays was considerably more stringent than for literary or published works – a factor which resulted in some of Trofimov's speeches being cut by the censors before the play was approved for performance.

In *On the High Road*, Chekhov presents a cross-section of the 'down-and-outs': Savva, an old man, half-dead, is a pilgrim tramping from one holy place to another across the vastness of Russia; Nazarovna and Yefimovna, both over seventy, are two old women also tramping across Russia; Fedya, once a waiter, is now a factory-hand working at the local brick-works;[6] Kuzma, a former serf of Bortsov's, is a peasant, on his way to fetch a midwife for his wife; Yegor Merik has changed his name to avoid arrest – he is a tramp and a thief; others sheltering at the inn are coach-drivers, tramps, and pilgrims, while Simon Bortsov has come down in the world – he is an alcoholic, and penniless. Once a wealthy landowner,[7] he was, as Kuzma tells his engrossed audience in the inn, driven to drink by his wife's infidelity – on their wedding-day:

KUZMA: . . . Just as the ladies and gentlemen are going to sit down to the wedding breakfast, she ups and rushes off in a carriage. (*In a whisper.*) Dashes off to town to a lawyer-fellow who's her lover. How do you like that, eh? She certainly picks her moment! Killing's too good for her, I'd say.

MERIK: (*pensively*) I see. And what happened next?

KUZMA: He goes clean off his rocker. He went on the booze, as you see, and he's never looked back since, they say. First it was little ones, now he's got to pink elephants. Still loves her, he does. Look how he loves her. He's

walking all the way to town now just to have a peep at her, I reckon.
Then he'll come back. (H.1.27)

Bortsov's story is repeated some twelve years later in *Uncle Vanya* –
Telegin, an impoverished landowner, suffered a similar experience,
but the dramatic treatment is radically different:

TELEGIN: (*in a tearful voice*). Vanya, I hate it when you talk like that. Well,
really. Anyone who betrays a wife or husband could easily be unreliable
enough to betray his country as well.

VOYNITSKY: (*with annoyance*). Turn the tap off, Waffles.

TELEGIN: No, let me go on, Vanya. The day after we were married my wife
ran away with another man because of my unprepossessing appearance.
Since then I've always done my duty. I still love her, I'm still faithful to
her, I help her as much as I can and I've spent all I had on educating her
children by this other man. I've lost my happiness, but I've kept my pride.
What about her, though? She's no longer young, she's lost her looks – as
was bound to happen sooner or later – and her lover is dead. So what has
she got left? (H.3.23)

Both Bortsov and Telegin have gone down in the world, lost their land
and money, and therefore their independence, but whereas Bortsov has
gone to pieces, become a drunk and a beggar, and was duped out of his
money, Telegin still has, as he says, his pride and dignity. Sensitive to
other people's attitude to him, Telegin is upset when a shopkeeper in
the village calls him 'a sponger' (Act 4); and while Bortsov lost his
money out of weakness, Telegin gave his money to his wife and her
children as a deliberate act of goodness. His attitude to his life and other
people may be simplistic, but the compassion and humility of this
character comes over very clearly. Telegin, or Waffles, as he is called,
is characterised as a tragi-comic figure in three-dimensional depths, and
he is completely credible as a result. His story, his attitude to life, and
his situation are dramatised by means of understatement, through what
is implied and indicated, not through over-statement. Bortsov, on the
other hand, is very much a character belonging to Chekhov's earliest
period of dramatic writing, the period of *Platonov*: both the character
of Bortsov and his story are made overtly dramatic, not to say melodramatic, and demonstrate (as do *Platonov* and *The Wood Demon*) the
process Chekhov went through as a playwright before he was able to
write sardonically about the *untruth* involved in a story of 'high drama',
like the woman who 'with a dramatic wail, throws herself from
a belfry'.[8] It was at the time of writing *The Wood Demon* (1889–90)
that Chekhov wrote:

The demand is made that the hero and the heroine [of a play] should be dramatically effective. But in life people do not shoot themselves, or hang themselves or fall in love, or deliver themselves of clever sayings every minute. They spend most of their time eating, drinking, running after women or men, talking nonsense. It is therefore necessary that this should be shown on the stage.[9]

An important factor in the treatment of Bortsov, however, is the extent to which his situation is a result of his own foolishness and weakness. But in this early dramatic work by Chekhov, it is not three-dimensional characterisation through self-revelation which creates the objective balance, it is the rather overt exposition (though motivated) of Kuzma, Bortsov's former serf:

KUZMA: Well, friends, the next thing that helped to ruin him was his brother-in-law, his sister's husband. He takes it into his head to back this brother-in-law, a bank loan to the tune of thirty thousand. The brother-in-law's a regular shark – the swine knows which side his bread's buttered on, of course, and he don't bat an eyelid. Borrows the money, but don't feel obliged to pay it back. So the master pays up all thirty thousand. (*Sighs.*) A fool and his money are soon parted. His wife has children by this lawyer-man.[10] Brother-in-law buys an estate near Poltava, and our friend crawls round like an idiot from one low dive to another a-moaning and a-groaning to the likes of us: 'I've lost my faith, friends. I don't trust no one now!'

And then Kuzma continues:

Sheer weakness, I call it. We've all got our troubles nagging at us, but that don't mean we have to drown 'em in drink, do it? Take our village elder, now. His wife entertains the schoolmaster in broad daylight and spends her husband's money on booze, while her old man goes round with a grin on his face. He has got a bit thin, though.   (H.1.28)

Kuzma's description of the village elder – going around with a grin, but getting thin – is indicative of what was later to become a major characteristic of Chekhov's dramatic technique; in Act 4 of *The Seagull*, Medvedenko desperately tries to maintain the façade that all is well between himself and Masha; in *The Three Sisters*, Andrey pretends ignorance of Natasha's affair with Protopopov, but (an interesting reversal) he is getting stout.

IRINA: ...everyone's laughing at him and he's the only one who doesn't know or see what's going on. And when everyone rushed off to the fire just now, there was he sitting in his room not taking the slightest notice and just playing his violin.   (H.3.118–19)

Under Natasha's influence and through his own weakness, Andrey mortgages the house (although it belongs to the sisters as well as to him) to pay his gambling debts; and in the same play, Kulygin puts on a false beard and moustache in a gauche attempt to cheer Masha up after Vershinin's departure – he knows that his wife loves Vershinin, but clumsily and ineptly he plays the clown in an effort to help her. This aspect of Chekhov's technique is also evident in his advice to Stanislavsky on how to play Astrov in the last act of *Uncle Vanya:* 'Astrov whistles! Whistles! Understand? Uncle Vanya weeps, but Astrov whistles.' Equally, Chekhov's advice to his wife when she played Masha in *The Three Sisters* was: 'People who have been unhappy for a long time, and grown used to it, don't get beyond whistling and are often wrapped up in their thoughts.'[11] Thus Chekhov's later method was to imply despair or unhappiness through understatement and implication, and where a character seems overtly 'dramatic' in later Chekhov plays, it generally means that a character (even Vanya) is self-dramatising, and meant to be seen as such. In *On the High Road*, however, comparatively little is implied, and less is understated. Thus Bortsov does not reveal *himself* as 'excessive' or foolish – this is done, as part of exposition, by Kuzma. Equally, an audience is not made critically aware of Bortsov through the juxtaposition of the serious and the comic – critical awareness comes largely from what Kuzma says of him: 'It all comes from being so feeble. And spoilt.'

Kuzma has little respect for 'the fool' who was parted from his money, who falls for a flighty, giddy young woman: 'The gentry like that kind – think they're real clever, when none of us peasants would give 'em house room.' And he has even less respect for one who, unlike the village elder, runs away from reality by becoming a drunk – the peasants and the tramps have greater problems. This outspoken contempt (though tinged with compassion) for the excessive behaviour of an impoverished landowner is, no doubt, one of the reasons why the play was banned, but it is important to note that in his later dramatic work Chekhov presents excessive or melodramatic behaviour in order to expose the melodramatic: 'form' is used to make a comment on the 'content'. An example of this may be seen in Konstantin's suicide attempt in *The Seagull* – Chekhov uses a melodramatic convention, but in the discrepancy between cause and effect, in the extremity of Konstantin's action and reaction, and in his self-dramatisation, the 'melodrama' is exposed for what it is. This later innovatory use of melodrama to expose the melodramatic, of the excessive to expose the ridiculous, is not found in the early plays such as *Platonov* or *On the*

High Road, but Chekhov's awareness of the melodramatic and his· attitude to it is very evident in his short parody-joke written in 1884 (the year before *On the High Road*), *Dishonourable Tragedians and Leprous Dramatists.*[12]

In the story of Bortsov there is the traditional story of a man brought to ruin by a woman, but instead of the conventional joke, or romantic story, or threatened ruination of a cuckolded husband, Chekhov shows a man *literally* brought to ruin. Kuzma's audience in the inn listen to the story engrossed, waiting for the next instalment as if it were a fiction, but because it is the real story of a man in front of them, Tikhon gives Bortsov a free drink, and Merik gives Bortsov his sleeping place. Merik's attitude is strongly contrasted with Bortsov's: Merik, unlike Bortsov, recognises that his own affair with a woman 'weren't love, it were all a fraud'; again, unlike Bortsov, Merik – a thief, a tramp, and an outcast wanted by the police – has a greater awareness of reality, and the ability to face that reality. Like his forerunner, Ossip, in *Platonov*, Merik voices a feeling of dissatisfaction with life, a protest against the existing morals and customs, which is provoked by Tikhon's refusal earlier in the play, to give Bortsov a free drink:

MERIK: Why don't you preach at him, you pious old women! And you, Tikhon, why don't you kick him out? He hasn't paid for his night's lodging, has he? Get rid of him, chuck him out on his ear! People are that cruel nowadays, there's no gentleness and kindness in them. A lot of brutes, they are! If they see a drowning man, they shout: 'Go on then – drown. We've no time to watch – we've got our work to do.' As for throwing him a rope, not a chance! Ropes cost money. (H.1.22)

Again, such a speech was no doubt a reason for the censor's verdict of 'gloomy' and 'sordid'. But Merik's energy, his broader vision, and his outspoken denunciation of superstition, hypocrisy and meanness, make him a vivid, powerful and significant character in the play, albeit perhaps a romanticised one. Merik is not a 'Robin Hood', but he is really one of the only characters in the play with red blood in his veins. As the ending shows, he is just as desperate as the others in the inn, but he is not eaten up with dreams and illusions. Thus, Fedya – the factory worker – paints an idyllic picture of the Kuban District[13] where Merik is planning to go, but Merik rejects Fedya's dream of the Kuban District, and of 'luck':

MERIK: Luck? Luck walks behind your back, you don't see it. Bite your elbow and you may glimpse it. It's all foolishness. (H.1.19)

Whether it is old Savva hoping to tramp to Jerusalem, or Bortsov lying in a drunken stupor in the dark and gazing at the portrait of his faithless wife, or Fedya dreaming of the Kuban,[14] escape through dream or illusion is no solution – a characteristic leitmotif of Chekhov's work, both literary and dramatic. Merik lives for the moment, not for a distant dream which he knows will be illusory, but for every day as it comes, even if it means going to Siberia as a convict. The play increasingly becomes Merik's play, not Bortsov's, and the melodramatic culmination of the action is the clash, not between Bortsov and his wife, but between Merik and Bortsov's wife.

The ending of the play – the addition to the original story – is both contrived and melodramatic. Chekhov relies heavily on the kind of coincidence to be found in either farce-vaudeville or melodrama, but which is unconvincing in a 'dramatic study'. The crowd in the inn have settled down for the night when suddenly there is banging on the door; a coachman, Denis, enters and asks for a rope to mend a broken spring in a carriage; his lady passenger comes in to warm herself and, in the dark, is seated next to Bortsov. It is his wife. Recognising her, Bortsov collapses at her feet; Maria tries to get away but is stopped by Merik who, in a fury, tries to kill her with his axe – but misses. The last few lines of the play indicate the tone of the final scene:

BORTSOV: (*clutches the air with his hands*) Mary: Where are you, Mary?
NAZAROVNA: My God, my God, you've made my heart bleed, you murderess. What a dreadful night!
MERIK: (*dropping the hand which holds the axe*). Did I kill her or not?
TIKHON: You're in the clear, praise the lord.
MERIK: I didn't kill her, so – (*Staggers to his place.*) So I'm not to die through a stolen axe. (*Falls on his coat and sobs.*) I'm so fed up, so damn miserable – aren't you sorry for me, all of you? (H.1.33)

Given the characterisation of Merik, his last lines are effective, but the treatment of Bortsov is melodramatic; so too is the contrived and coincidental arrival of Mary, whose carriage happens to break down at the very inn where Bortsov is sheltering; Merik's violent reaction is insufficiently motivated – even given his sympathy for and identification with Bortsov's situation; equally unlikely, however, is the fact that Merik, swinging an axe in a confined and crowded space, misses Mary and injures no one. The failure of this murder attempt (although making its own dramatic point) is scarcely credible: whereas Vanya's attempt and failure to shoot Serebryakov three times in a confined space is a tragi-comic reversal of a stock situation, Merik's failure in the context of this dramatic study is contrived and unlikely.

The setting of the play, and the use made of it, is also a mixture of the dramatically effective and realistic – and the melodramatic:

Tikhon's inn. Right, the bar; shelves containing bottles. At the back of the stage, a door opening on the road, with a dirty red lantern hanging above it on the outside. The floor and benches by the walls are jammed with pilgrims and travellers. Many are sleeping in a sitting position for lack of room. It is late at night. As the curtain rises there is a clap of thunder, and a flash of lightning is seen through the open door. (H.1.13)

An accordion, played by Fedya, is heard quietly, and the atmosphere is strongly evoked through the visual and through sound effects. The opening statement of a flash of lightning and a clap of thunder, however, mars what in later Chekhov becomes a much more economical and contrapuntal use of the visual and aural. Again, it is the excess of effects which introduces the melodramatic element: an opening curtain followed almost simultaneously by thunder and lightning is a stock-in-trade of a melodrama. In the stage directions of this early play, however, are all the elements later to be used by Chekhov in evoking atmosphere, mood, and place – the effects of the weather, time of night, and the external off-stage dramatic world on the characters in the play.

The play, therefore, demonstrates very clearly avenues of content and technique which were to be refined, pared down, or altered in Chekhov's later plays. The characterisation and motivation are still sketchy (Maria is not really characterised at all); the plot is at times contrived and even melodramatic, but the atmosphere, some of the dramatic techniques, and several thematic points are extremely powerful and effective. And at least one of the themes was to become a leitmotif in many of Chekhov's plays – a leitmotif summarised by Kornei Chukovsky as: 'the struggle between human will and the lack of will power'.[15] The play relies heavily on such conventional elements as obvious exposition, coincidence, attempted murder, the ruination of man through woman's infidelity, or a thief almost with a 'heart of gold', but the play was also sufficiently innovatory and politically dangerous to be denied performance by the censorship, and subsequent to this play, Chekhov was to by-pass the hazards of censorship by implying, rather than overtly depicting, the conditions of the characters of 'the lower depths'.

A number of critics mention the play – in passing – as Chekhov's most 'naturalistic' play: Magarshack, for example, calls it 'the only purely naturalistic play' ever written by Chekhov. But closer examination of the play illustrates the elements which Chekhov discarded in his later work as being 'untruthful' or incredible – this, his first one-act 'dramatic study', is, in fact, not 'naturalistic', but, like *Platonov* which preceded it, marred by melodrama, excess and over-seriousness. Chekhov's subsequent realisation of the play's faults is, of course, evidenced in the work which followed, but also in his refusal to include the play in his *Collected Works* (1902); and in the nature of the suggestions which he made to the young Maxim Gorky for avoiding the faults from which he himself had learnt. On 22 October 1901, Chekhov wrote to Gorky about Gorky's new play, *The Philistines*:

And so I read only three acts, but I think it is enough to judge the play by. It is, as I expected, very good, done in the Gorky manner, original and very interesting. But if I were to begin to talk of its faults, I have noticed thus far only one, a defect as unalterable as red hair in a red-haired person – namely, the conservatism of its form. You introduce new, original people and make them sing new songs to old, outworn tunes.[16]

Chekhov never returned to the 'lower depths' setting of *On the High Road* (with the exception of the unfinished *The Night before the Trial* in which, in fact, the inn is less sordid and the characters of a different class background); he never again wrote a play in which the tramps and down-and-outs are constantly in the forefront of the action – partly, no doubt, because of the problems of censorship; equally, he never again wrote a play – whether one-act or full-length – which is unrelieved by humour, and of all the plays which were to follow, only *Tatyana Repina*, *Swan Song* and *The Three Sisters* are subtitled 'dramas', and none of them are devoid of strong comic elements.

Swan Song (Calchas) (1887-1888)

In Chekhov's *A Dreary Story* (*From An Old Man's Notebooks*), written in 1889, letters are exchanged between the old Professor of Medicine and his young ward, Katya, who has gone to work with a theatre company full of enthusiasm for the theatre and her new work as an actress. Like Nina in *The Seagull*, Katya's idealism is rapidly tempered by reality:

– Katya wrote to me that her comrades did not attend rehearsals and never knew their parts. The absurdity of the plays produced, and the behaviour of the actors on the stage, showed that each of them felt the utmost contempt for the audience. In the interests of box-office receipts, which was the sole topic of conversation, actresses demeaned themselves by singing *chansonnettes*, and tragic actors sang couplets in which deceived husbands and the pregnancy of unfaithful wives was made fun of. It was quite a wonder that provincial theatres still survived, and that they could continue in such a meagre and corrupt vein.

In reply, I sent Katya a long, and, I'm afraid, an extremely tedious letter. Among other things I wrote: 'I have often had talks with old actors, high-minded people who have been good enough to bestow their affections on me. From conversation with them I could see that their work is ruled not so much by their own minds and wills as by the fashion and mood prevailing among audiences. The best of them, in their time, have had to act in tragedies and operettas, in Parisian farces, and in pantomime, and in every case they believed themselves to be following the right path, and doing good. So you see the root of the evil must be sought for not in the actors, but deeper, in art itself, and in the attitude of society towards art.'

This letter of mine only irritated Katya. 'We are talking at cross purposes,' she replied. 'I did not write to you about high-minded people who bestowed their affections upon you, but about a band of rotters with nothing high-souled about them. They are a horde of savages, only in the theatre because unable to find employment anywhere else, and only calling themselves actors out of insolence. Not a single talented person, but any amount of mediocrities, drunkards, schemers, and backbiters. I can never tell you how bitter it is to me that the art I love so much should have fallen into the hands of people I detest.'

This disagreement between the Professor and Katya over whether the actor is a high-minded participant in a 'sacred art', or merely the mediocre 'tool' of a debased entertainment, is a subject of concern and source of debate in a number of Chekhov's works, whether in early short stories (such as *Stage Manager Under the Sofa, The Jeune premier, A Cure for Drunkenness, Boots* (1885), *An Actor's End* (1886), *Calchas* (1886)), or in the second one-act play which Chekhov wrote, the drama *Swan Song (Calchas)*, or in the full-length comedy *The Seagull*, written in 1896.

This – a contemporary debate – arose out of the disparity between the idea of theatre as a 'moral institution' and the contemporary reality of theatre practice. In *A Dreary Story, Swan Song* and *The Seagull*, Chekhov uses this disparity to explore also a wider issue: the gulf between the ideal and the reality, or the romanticised and the actual. Thus, Katya in *A Dreary Story* initially explained to the Professor that:

The theatre is a force uniting within itself all the arts, and actors are missionaries. No art or science exercises such a powerful and unequivocal influence on the human spirit as the stage, and it is not for nothing that even the most mediocre actor is more popular than the greatest scientist or artist. And no other public activities give such enjoyment and satisfaction as acting gives to actors.

Within two years, Katya's 'rainbow-hued hopes' have turned into total disillusionment – a disillusionment which has also been brought about by an unhappy love affair, and the loss of her child. In this, Katya's story is, subsequently, paralleled by Nina's experience in *The Seagull*, but while Katya's realisation and recognition of reality crushes her, Nina 'endures'. Nina too has worshipped 'a sacred art', has romanticised the lives of actors and writers (and courted fame), but when she returns after a two-year interval in Act 4, her life as an actress is sordid, and concerned with the struggle for survival, not creative art:

So you're a writer now, you're a writer and I'm an actress, we've got caught up in this hectic whirl. I used to be as happy as a child and woke up singing in the morning, I loved you and dreamed of being famous. But now – I have to go to Yelets early tomorrow morning, third class, along with the peasants. And when I get there I shall be pestered with the attentions of the more educated local businessmen. It's a rough life. (H.2.278–9)

Konstantin, who cannot himself face reality and so arranges life in abstract images, condemns Arkadina, the 'establishment' actress, for believing in 'the myth': 'She adores the stage. Serving humanity in the sacred cause of art, that's how she thinks of it.' But Arkadina, as a famous and successful actress, has insulated herself against reality – whether the realities of theatre practice, or the realities of life. As such, she will not even face the fact that she is ageing, and has an adult son. Nina, as a young unknown provincial actress, travels third-class, but Arkadina travels first-class. This point is also brought out in Chekhov's story *A Cure for Drunkenness*: a fairly well-known actor arrives by train in a provincial town, and as he is respectfully greeted by the theatre manager at the station, he steps out of a first-class carriage, but, in fact, he has travelled first-class only for the last stage of his journey. This concern for appearances is shown as futile when the actor is exposed as an alcoholic; equally, Arkadina's need to keep up appearances to the detriment of her son exposes her selfishness – yet this selfishness is in the name of the 'sacred art'.

In *Swan Song*, however, the old comic actor Svetlovidov declares that he has no illusions about 'the sacred art':

I remember how I acted that same night. It was a vulgar, slapstick part, and I could feel the scales fall from my eyes as I played it. I saw then that there's no such thing as 'sacred art', that the whole thing's just a phoney racket – saw myself a slave, a toy for people's idle moments, a buffoon, a man of straw. (H.1.42)

And he continues, ignoring Nikita the prompter:

Then my eyes were opened, but the vision cost me dear, Nikita. After that affair – with the girl – I began drifting aimlessly, living from hand to mouth with no thought for the morrow. I took cheap slapstick parts and hammed them. I was a corrupting influence. But I'd been a true artist, you know, I was really good! I buried my talent, cheapened it. I spoke in an affected voice, I lost my dignity as a human being. This black pit swallowed me up and gobbled me down. I never felt like this before. But when I woke up tonight, I looked back – and I've sixty-eight years behind me. I've only just seen what old age means.

(H.1.42)

The action of *Swan Song* is concerned with the moment of realisation – the moment one night in an empty theatre when an old actor faces the realities of his professional work, and an old man faces the realities of his life. Chekhov uses the device of 'meaningful names' to bring out the point: the name Svetlovidov literally means 'seeing the light'. The point may also possibly be made by Svetlovidov's costume and thus the part he had played that night: the part of Calchas, a seer or prophet. The stage directions specify that Svetlovidov enters 'in the stage costume of Calchas', and he himself refers to his 'damnfool costume', but no specific mention is made of the play in which Svetlovidov had performed that night – his Benefit Night. Unless an adaptor had written a 'new' play in which the character Calchas appears, the supposition must be that Svetlovidov had played Calchas in Shakespeare's *Troilus and Cressida* – a small part, in which the character appears as the traitor requesting his reward.[17] Elsewhere, the character does not appear on the stage, but is referred to in Homer's *Iliad*, and in *The Agamemnon* in which he is the official Greek army seer on the Trojan expedition. Thus, without pushing conjecture and hypothesis too far, Svetlovidov's role and costume carry the – albeit literary – implications of a traitor to the cause, and – most likely – of a prophet, a seer. As a stage image, however, this is neither immediate, nor quite clear.

This literary allusion, though, is carried over by Chekhov from the short story *Calchas* from which the play is adapted, and which was written in 1886. The first mention of the play comes in a much-quoted letter which Chekhov wrote to Maria Kiselyova, the daughter of the director of the Imperial Theatres in Moscow. This letter of 14 January 1887 is not, however, frequently quoted because of its reference to the writing of *Swan Song*, but because of the insight it gives into Chekhov's thinking about literature and the role of a writer. Replying to specific questions raised by Kiselyova, Chekhov makes several crucial points:

Literature is accepted as an art because it depicts life as it actually is. Its aim is the truth, unconditional and honest... But the writer is not a pastry chef, he is not a cosmetician and not an entertainer. He is a man bound by contract to his sense of duty and to his conscience. Once he undertakes this task, it is too late for excuses, and no matter how horrified, he must do battle with his squeamishness and sully his imagination with the grime of life. He is just like any ordinary reporter. What would you say if a newspaper reporter as a result of squeamishness or a desire to please his readers were to limit his descriptions to honest city fathers, high-minded ladies, and virtuous railroadmen?...

Writers are men of their time, and so, like the rest of the public, they must submit to the external conditions of life in society...To write in...scornful, condescending accents about little people just because they're little does the human heart scant honour. The lower ranks are just as indispensible in literature as they are in the army; that's what your head tells you, and your heart should tell you even more.

And then Chekhov concludes this letter with a reference to *Swan Song:*

I've written a four-page play. It will take fifteen to twenty minutes to perform, the shortest drama on earth. Korsh's famous actor Davydov will act in it. It will be published in *The Season* and will therefore make the rounds. It's much better as a rule to write short works than long ones: fewer pretensions and more success...What else could you ask for? My play took me an hour and five minutes to write.[18]

The play was first performed at Korsh's Theatre in Moscow on 19 February 1888 (as a minor item on the bill) some three months after the first performance of *Ivanov* also at Korsh's Theatre, in which Davydov played the leading role. It was in this season, 1888–9, that a number of Chekhov's dramatic works were crucially interwoven with his involvement in theatre practice: *Ivanov* was first produced in Moscow in November 1887 and then in Petersburg at the Alexandrinsky in January 1889; *Swan Song* was produced in Moscow in February 1888 and then again in Moscow, at the Maly Theatre, in October of the same year; in December 1888, Chekhov saw the Petersburg production of Suvorin's play, *Tatyana Repina*, and in January 1889, he worked on the Moscow Maly production of Suvorin's play; in March of 1889, Chekhov wrote a kind of one-act 'reply' to Suvorin's *Tatyana Repina*, and from 1888 to 1890, he was planning, writing, and re-writing, the full-length comedy *The Wood Demon*. And it was the leading actor of the Maly Theatre, A. P. Lensky (with whom Chekhov was to work on the Moscow production of Suvorin's play) who decided to do the second Moscow production of *Swan Song*. As a result of Lensky's request, Chekhov had to submit the play for approval to the Theatrical and Literary Committee of the Imperial Theatres: 'The play has no merit, I attach no importance to it at all, but the fact is that Lensky is absolutely set on playing it on a small stage. It's not so much my request as Lensky's.'[19]

Nonetheless, Chekhov clearly considered the play to have sufficient merit to warrant some important revisions – revisions which increasingly justified the subtitle of the play as 'a dramatic study'. First, sending the play to Lensky after approval was received for performance, Chekhov wrote that he had changed the title of the play:

I have changed the title of *Calchas* to *Swan Song*. It's a long, bitter-sweet title, but I could not think of another one, however hard I tried.[20]

By November 1888, Chekhov had expanded the play beyond the point at which the original short story and the first dramatic version had ended: the story and first version end as the prompter leads a wasted and unhappy man off into the wings; in the later version, however, the action continues as Svetlovidov, remembering his early talent and potential, quotes extracts from Pushkin's *Boris Godunov*, and from *King Lear*, *Hamlet* and *Othello*, and for a while forgets his old age and wasted life. Thus Chekhov alters and extends the whole mood of the play, and enables Svetlovidov to rethink – albeit temporarily – his earlier contempt for 'the sacred art', and to distinguish between great art and theatre practice:

SVETLOVIDOV:...There's no such thing as old age, that's all stuff and nonsense. (*Roars with happy laughter.*) So why the tears? Why so down in the mouth, you dear, silly fellow? Now this won't do, it really won't. Really, old chap, you mustn't look like that – what good does it do? There, there. (*Embraces him with tears in his eyes.*) You mustn't cry. Where art and genius are there's no room for old age, loneliness and illness – why, death itself loses half its sting. (*Weeps.*) Ah, well, Nikita, we've made our last bow. I'm no great actor, just a squeezed lemon, a miserable nonentity, a rusty old nail. And you're just an old stage hack, a prompter. Come on. (*They start to move off.*) I'm no real good – in a serious play I could just about manage a member of Fortinbras's suite, and for that I'm too old.   (H.1.44–5)

Svetlovidov moves from a view close to Katya's disillusioned attitude in *A Dreary Story*, to one closer to the Professor's view of actors' work as 'ruled not so much by their own minds and wills as by the fashion and mood prevailing among audiences', in which a distinction must be made between what *is* 'a sacred art' and what is daily done in the name of that art. But Svetlovidov's realisation of the difference between 'art' and the 'phoney racket' opens up, in turn, a tragic gulf in his life: the gulf between what he has done and what he could have done. And having realised this, it is now too late. Svetlovidov is too old, and the tragedy lies in exactly that: the realisation has come too late in his life.

A similar realisation comes to Vanya in *Uncle Vanya* – brought to a head by Serebryakov's wish to sell the estate in Act 3, Vanya has wasted his life for the Professor of Art, Serebryakov:

VANYA: For twenty-five years I've been cooped up in this place with this mother of mine. All our thoughts and feelings were for you alone. In the daytime we talked of you and your writings, we were proud of you and worshipped the very sound of your name. And we wasted our nights reading books and journals that I now utterly despise... We thought of you as a superior being and we knew your articles by heart. But now my eyes have been opened. Everything's perfectly clear. You write about art, but you haven't the faintest idea what art is all about. Your entire works, which once meant so much to me, aren't worth a brass farthing. You've made fools of us all... You've ruined my life! I've not lived, not lived, I tell you! Thanks to you the best years of my life have been thrown down the drain. You are my worst enemy!... My life's ruined. I'm gifted, intelligent, courageous. If I'd had a normal life I might have been a Schopenhauer or a Dostoyevsky. (H.3.54–5)

As so often in Chekhov's plays, emotional intensity is qualified by an excessive and therefore comic, deflatory touch: it is unlikely that Vanya would have been a Schopenhauer or a Dostoyevsky, or that Svetlovidov would have been a great actor, but this does not diminish the tragedy of a wasted or cheated life. In Vanya is the desperate realisation that life has passed him by, and that all that he had believed in was a sham: the Professor of Art knows nothing about art. Vanya's realisation is partly that he has sacrificed himself to an illusion; equally, Svetlovidov's realisation is that he has devoted forty-five years of his life to the second-rate: he has not played Boris Godunov, or Lear, or Hamlet, or Othello, or Chatsky in *Woe from Wit*. He was a comic actor, not a tragic actor: 'in a serious play I could just about manage a member of Fortinbras's suite.' It is in this that the 'bitter-sweet' quality of the play lies: the comic actor gains insight into tragedy, but will only play it in an empty theatre late at night. Thus the old actor distinguishes between the cheat and the sham of the second-rate, and real art and genius, but only after he has given his life to the sham; and the old man recognises that 'if you are good enough, Nikita, being old doesn't count', but, as he says himself, 'I'm no real good.' The play captures a moment towards the end of a life of a comic actor – a moment of realisation and self-knowledge which comes too late. The title 'Swan Song' captures the bitter-sweet duality of the play: Svetlovidov rises to new heights, but for the first and last time.

It was no doubt to emphasise the 'bitter' element in the play, the waste of a life, and the realisation which comes too late, that Chekhov's final revision[21] – which was made after he had written *The Seagull* and *Uncle Vanya* – was to increase Svetlovidov's age from fifty-eight to sixty-eight, and thus the duration of his stage career from thirty-five to forty-five years. In this way, Svetlovidov's insight really does come too late in his life.

The play is the next 'drama' Chekhov wrote after *On the High Road* (1885), and was written after two versions of *Smoking is Bad for You* had already been completed (in 1886 and 1887); *Swan Song* has been variously called 'a tear-jerker'[22] and 'a vaudeville', but although it contains certain of the conventional elements of the farce-vaudeville, it should more properly be seen in terms of Chekhov's own subtitle: a dramatic study in one act. Thus where the 'drama' of *On the High Road* is marred by melodrama, by unchecked emotional intensity and excess, the 'drama' of *Swan Song* is controlled partly by comedy, and partly also by a number of elements which are in fact devices to provoke thought and objectivity on the part of the audience – devices which could almost be called 'distancing' techniques in Brecht's sense of the term.

The first of such devices may be seen in the setting itself:

The empty stage of a second-class provincial theatre. Right, a row of roughly-made unpainted doors leading to the dressing-rooms. The left and back of the stage are cluttered up with litter and rubbish. There is an overturned stool in mid-stage. Night. Dark.

(H.1.39)

As in *On the High Road*, the emphasis on atmosphere is considerable, an emphasis which is comparatively lacking in *The Bear* or *A Tragic Role;* and there are few places with as much atmosphere as an empty theatre late at night. Thus the opening of the play is purely visual and atmospheric: Chekhov powerfully evokes the desolation of an empty theatre, of the litter and rubbish on the stage; the sordid reality of a second-rate provincial theatre open to the eyes of an 'audience'. What an audience is shown, therefore, is the reverse of what an audience normally sees or expects to see: instead of a lit scene with characters on stage and the 'workings' of a stage and theatre hidden from view by a setting, an audience is shown darkness, a stage bare of actors and setting, and the dirty, naked reality of an area normally used to create illusion. But like all empty theatres it is both peopled with memories and echoes, and waiting in a kind of suspended animation: exactly because it is an empty stage, an audience views it with expectancy – something is going to happen. In this way, Chekhov, purely through visual statement and the atmosphere, works on an audience's natural assumptions and associations, and thus creates suspense by showing a reality which is not normally perceived by an audience. But by stripping the stage of its normal trappings, by exposing a sordid reality, Chekhov enables an audience to see for itself what lies behind the illusory façade of theatre; the visual image contains much of the meaning of the play even before Svetlovidov's entrance. And it is with Svetlovidov's entrance that an audience's expectations – though not conventional assumptions – are rewarded; but instead of a blaze of lights, and the reassuring activity of a peopled stage, what an audience receives is the exact reverse: the dim and flickering light of a single candle up-stage which comes increasingly nearer – and 'laughter in the dark'. The stage directions read:

Svetlovidov, in the stage costume of Calchas, comes out of a dressing-room carrying a candle, and roars with laughter.   (H.I.39)

Thus the play begins with an image of its meaning – and an image of Svetlovidov's situation: alone, apparently forgotten, and revealed as 'a man' before an audience which normally sees 'an actor'.

Svetlovidov's laughter, however, also relieves the tension, as does his expositionary opening sentence: 'This is the limit, it really is too much – falling asleep in my dressing-room.' But he then introduces a point which is reiterated several times in the course of the play – a point which creates an immediate awareness on the part of an audience, an awareness of its own identity and 'role'. Svetlovidov, continuing his opening lines, says: 'The play ended hours ago, the audience went home – and there's me snoring away without a care in the world.' A little later, Svetlovidov moves down-stage and peers out front:

I say, I've been on the stage for forty-five years, but this must be the first time I've seen a theatre in the middle of the night, the very first time. You know, it's weird, damn it. (*Goes up to the footlights.*) Can't see a thing. Well, I can just make out the prompter's box and that other box over there – the one with the letter on it – and that music-stand. The rest is darkness, a bottomless black pit like a tomb: the haunt of Death itself.   (H.I.39–40)

In Beckett's *Endgame*, Clov puts the telescope to his eye and, peering at the audience, says: 'I see...a multitude...in transports...of joy. (*Pause.*) That's what I call a magnifier.' The result of this is laughter; equally, in *Waiting for Godot*, Estragon advances 'to front, facing auditorium', and says: 'Inspiring prospects'; and later Vladimir refers to the audience as 'that bog' and again the reaction from an audience is laughter, but the laughter emanates from an audience's recognition of its own presence and its own role; it arises from an audience's recognition of its responsibility and participation in 'theatre', and – apparently paradoxically – it comes from an audience's identification with the situation on the stage. By extending the 'stage situation' into the auditorium, the spectator is made a participant in the same situation – no longer a passive *voyeur* of an illusion taking place at a safe distance. Thus, by denying the presence of an audience, Svetlovidov makes the audience intensely aware of its own presence; by referring to the audience as 'a bottomless pit', Svetlovidov provokes the audience into an awareness of its own individual identity, and – a little later in the play – Svetlovidov also provokes the audience into an awareness of its own culpability:

The audience has left and gone to bed, and it's forgotten the old clown...

What's become of it all, where have those days gone to? God, I just looked into this black pit and it all came back to me! It's swallowed forty-five years of my life, this pit has – and what a life! (H.1.41)

In this way, the audience is also made responsible for theatre and actors – as the Professor in *A Dreary Story* writes to Katya: 'the root of the evil must be sought for not in the actors, but deeper, in art itself, and in the attitude of society towards art.' Svetlovidov's 'accusation' of the audience is continued when he describes himself as 'a toy for people's idle moments', and says:

It was then I took the public's measure. Applause, bouquets, wild enthusiasm – I've never believed in 'em since. Yes, Nikita, these people cheer me, they pay a rouble for my photograph, but to them I'm just a stranger, I'm just so much dirt – an old whore, practically! They scrape up acquaintance with me to make themselves feel important, but not one of them would sink to letting me marry his sister or daughter. I don't trust 'em. (*Sinks on to the stool.*) Don't trust 'em. (H.1.42)

Invariably, an audience would take this personally, would be provoked into an assessment of its responsibilities, expectations and attitudes.

Thus Chekhov's use of theatre in this play is multifaceted, but reveals a technique and approach which are characteristic of his later dramatic form: he creates illusion by appearing to expose illusion, or, to put it another way, illusion is created by the apparent exposure of reality. An audience listening to Svetlovidov *is* present in the auditorium and watching *Swan Song*, in which an actor is playing the part of an actor. And a twentieth century audience might well interpret *Swan Song* in the light of both Brecht and Beckett: as in Brecht's plays, the workings of theatre are revealed by Chekhov to make an audience think, to create objectivity about reality through the apparent exposure of stage illusion; like Beckett, Chekhov's use of theatre in this play becomes an image of a situation, a metaphor in which actors and audience alike are participants.

It must, of course, be remembered that Chekhov was familiar with a classical precedent[23] for making an audience aware of itself within the context of a play, a precedent which made an audience part of the play, participant and not only spectator: in *The Government Inspector* Gogol breaks through 'the fourth wall' at the end of the play, when the Mayor learns the truth about Khlestakov:

He'll tell his dirty little tale all over Russia. I shall be a laughing-stock. Some inky little scribbler'll put us all in a play, yes, every one of you! That'll hurt, I promise you! He won't spare us – rank, position, appearance, anything to make an audience snigger, it'll all go in! (*He suddenly turns on the audience.*) What do you think you're laughing at, eh?! You're laughing at yourselves, do you know that?

And the motto of the play is: 'Don't blame the mirror if your mug is twisted.' In *Swan Song*, however, Chekhov uses dramatic irony: the effect is achieved through a *denial* of the audience's presence – the audience is never explicitly accused by an acknowledgement of its presence in the theatre.

The innovatory features of the play, must, though, be seen in the context of certain conventions which Chekhov retains and employs. The play is divided, by the common method, into two scenes, the second scene commencing with Nikita's entrance. But, more significantly, the structure of the play utilises two basic 'types' of farce-vaudeville: the monologue, and a version of the 'false monologue'. The monologue, which forms Scene i of the play, serves the usual function of exposition: Svetlovidov thus informs 'the audience' that he has fallen asleep, drunk after his Benefit night; that he has been locked into the 'empty' theatre late at night, and that George and Peter – whom he had paid to look after him – have either fallen asleep somewhere, or left. The monologue also serves, however, to reveal Svetlovidov's character in addition to his situation, and this is partly achieved through his internal dialogue – he talks to himself, but partly through the use of the third person:

The old codger gets drunk, but what has he to celebrate? He hasn't the foggiest! God, I've got back-ache, the old head-piece is splitting, I'm shivering all over, and I have this dark, cold feeling, as if I was in a cellar. If you won't spare your health, you might at least remember you're too old for this caper, you silly old so-and-so. (*Pause.*) Old age – whether you try to wriggle out of it or make the best of it or just act the fool, the fact is your life's over. Sixty-eight years down the drain, damn it! Gone with the wind! The cup's drained, there's just a bit left at the bottom: the dregs. That's the way of it, that's how it is, old man. Like it or not, it's time you rehearsed for the part you play in your coffin.   (H.1.39)

Svetlovidov, sitting alone on a little stool in the middle of a darkened empty stage with the candle flickering beside him, also – through his monologue – sustains and extends the atmosphere and mood of the opening visual statement; he thus simultaneously reveals his character, providing a comic self-portrait, and increases the air of expectancy and tension leading to Nikita's entrance:

It's cold, there's a piercing draught from the auditorium. Just the place to call up spirits! It's eerie, blast it, it sends shudders down my spine. (*Shouts.*) George! Peter! Hell, where are you? But why do I talk of hell, God help me? Oh, why can't you stop drinking and using bad language, for God's sake, seeing you're old and it's time you were pushing up the daisies? At sixty-eight people go to church, they get ready to die, but you–. Oh Lord, you and your bad language and your drunken gargoyle's face and this damn fool costume! What a sight! I'll go and change quickly. It's all so eerie. Why, if I stayed here all night, I'd die of fright at this rate.   (H.1.40)

It is at this point that the atmosphere and expectancy build to a climax, but only to result, in fact, in a characteristically comic anti-climax:

(*Makes for his dressing-room. At that moment Nikita, wearing a white dressing-gown, appears from the furthest dressing-room at the back of the stage.*)

Scene ii

SVETLOVIDOV: (*seeing Nikita, gives a terrified shriek and staggers back*). Who are you? What are you after? Who do you want? (*Stamps.*) Who are you?

NIKITA: It's me, sir.

SVETLOVIDOV: Who's me?

NIKITA: (*slowly approaching him*). It's me. Nikita, the prompter. It's me, Mr Svetlovidov, sir.

SVETLOVIDOV: (*collapses helplessly on the stool, breathes hard and shudders all over*) God, who is it? Is it you – you, Nikita? W-w-what are you doing here?

NIKITA: I always spend the night here in the dressing-rooms, sir, only please don't tell the manager. I've nowhere else to sleep, and that's God's truth.
(H.1.40)

The ghostly apparition in the white dressing-gown turns out to be none other than the old prompter, but the comedy of Nikita's entrance is qualified by another change of mood: old Nikita is, in fact, worse off than Svetlovidov – he has nowhere else to go at night, and is always alone in the empty theatre at night. His only home is, quite literally, this second-rate provincial theatre. Nikita's situation, therefore, reinforces everything that 'the audience' learns about the reality of working in the theatre, but, unlike Svetlovidov, Nikita, who is only a prompter, 'an old stage hack', has no Benefit night, no home, and not even the applause which an actor may find sustaining. And he is terrified that the manager might discover that he is sleeping in the theatre each night. But, in contrast to Svetlovidov, Nikita is without self-pity. It is with Nikita's entrance that Chekhov's version of the 'false monologue' begins: Nikita the prompter actually serves the function of a prompter in the play. Svetlovidov uses him as his audience and, picking up cues from Nikita, launches into memories, reminiscences, or maudlin complaints:

NIKITA: I've nowhere else to sleep, and that's God's truth.
SVETLOVIDOV: So it's you, Nikita. Hell, I had sixteen curtain-calls, three bunches of flowers and a lot of other things...I'm old, Nikita. Sixty-eight, I am. I'm ill. I feel faint and weary. (*Leans over the prompter's hand and weeps.*) Don't leave me, Nikita. I'm old and weak and I've got to die. I'm frightened, so terribly frightened.
NIKITA: (*gently and respectfully*) It's time you went home, Mr Svetlovidov, sir.
SVETLOVIDOV: I won't go. I haven't got any home – haven't got one, I tell you.
NIKITA: Goodness me, the gentleman's forgotten where he lives!   (H.1.40–1)

The play is not a 'tear-jerker': Nikita's lack of self-pity contrasts vividly with Svetlovidov; the balance of Svetlovidov's characterisation is carefully maintained, and sentiment is avoided by the audience's knowledge that Svetlovidov is drunk, and thus feeling ill, maudlin, and full of self-pity. In addition, Svetlovidov may be seen as self-absorbed and selfish – he does not listen to what Nikita says about his own situation, and it is only at the end of the play that Svetlovidov treats Nikita as an old, spent man like himself. And, with Nikita as his audience, there are times when Svetlovidov is quite obviously self-dramatising and 'acting', as when he begins to recount the story of an old love affair:

She was elegant, graceful as a young poplar, innocent, unspoilt. And she seemed all ablaze like the sun on a May morning. Those blue eyes, that magic smile could banish the darkest night. The ocean waves dash themselves against the cliffs, but against the waves of her hair the very cliffs, icebergs and snow avalanches might dash themselves to no avail.   (H.1.41–2)

Svetlovidov's self-dramatisation and exaggeration maintain the 'bitter-sweet' quality of the play – a sentimental response from 'the audience' is avoided by objective awareness of Svetlovidov's own sentimentality and self-pity:

I've only just seen what old age means. The show is over. (*Sobs.*) You can ring down the curtain. (H.1.42)

In this way the balance of sympathy is carefully maintained: objective understanding of Svetlovidov's and Nikita's situation is achieved through comedy, contrast, and, in the case of Svetlovidov, through three-dimensional, balanced characterisation; and, as so often in Chekhov's later dramatic work, sentiment is used only to expose the sentimental. The play is not, therefore, a tragedy, or a 'tear-jerker'; it is not a comedy or a farce-vaudeville in the conventional sense – but, as Chekhov describes it, it is 'a dramatic study' in which comedy and tragedy combine to form a tragi-comedy and the 'bitter-sweet' quality to which Chekhov refers.

In *The Seagull*, the debate about theatre and art is also a debate about motivation and endurance in life, as Dr Dorn says in Act 1: 'a work of art must express a clear, precise idea. You must know why you write, or else – if you take this picturesque path without knowing where you're going you'll lose your way and your gifts will destroy you' (H.2.246). Life, like literature, requires motivation and purpose – an aim. In play after play, although treated in different ways, Chekhov captures the moment of realisation, the moment in which characters either face reality, and 'endure', like Nina, or Vanya and Sonya; or insulate themselves from reality, like Arkadina, or Serebryakov; or, ridiculously, run away from reality at an early age – like Konstantin Treplev or people who 'do a Tatyana Repina'.

Although differently treated, *A Dreary Story*, *The Seagull*, *Uncle Vanya*, and *Swan Song* explore art or literature or theatre as a metaphor for life: romanticism and illusions are exposed, and reality is revealed. At the end of *Swan Song*, two old men leave an empty stage in a deserted theatre; through the exposure of the illusory, reality has been revealed. In *Swan Song*, Chekhov uses the stage as both the literal and metaphorical setting of the play.

Tatyana Repina (1889)

In the winter of 1881, a performance of Ostrovsky's history play *Vasilisa Melentieva* was given at the Kharkov Dramatic Theatre. The performance was nearing the end, and had reached the point in the play where Vasilisa Melentieva – the wife of Ivan the Terrible – poisons herself on stage. Suddenly the curtain was lowered and the performance remained unfinished: the famous actress, E. P. Kadmina, playing the part of Vasilisa, had substituted the theatrical death scene for reality, by literally taking poison and committing suicide at the very moment required by her role. As the press subsequently reported, Kadmina had loved 'Officer T—', a nobleman who considered marriage with an actress to be beneath him. After a lengthy affair, he had parted from Kadmina and decided to marry a rich widow. Hearing about the proposed marriage, Kadmina sent Officer T— and his fiancée theatre tickets for her performance in *Vasilisa Melentieva*, and swallowed poison on stage.

The real-life 'drama' of Kadmina's death made a considerable impression on contemporary society, and became source material for several major and minor writers: in 1882, Turgenev wrote a romance, *Clara Milich*, in which Clara, a young actress, commits suicide when rejected by her lover but after her death 'takes possession of him'; in 1883, V. Kunitskin wrote *The Singer's Husband* on the same subject;[24] in 1884 a drama by Fyodorov-Solovtsov, *Evlampia Ramina*, was based on Kadmina's story; in 1886 A. S. Suvorin, Chekhov's publisher and friend, wrote a comedy called *Tatyana Repina*, and in 1889 Chekhov wrote a drama in one act which he named after Suvorin's play, and which was, in fact, written as a private joke between Chekhov and Suvorin, Chekhov's one-act drama being a continuation, or a 'fifth' act, of Suvorin's comedy: it is set in a cathedral during the wedding ceremony of Sabinin (Repina's ex-lover), and his bride, Olenina.

This one-act drama by Chekhov has, however, created considerable controversy amongst critics and historians; as one such critic, E. S. Smirnova-Chikina, puts it: 'Up to the present time, the play presents one of the riddles of the writer's literary heritage.'[25] The controversy centres on the seriousness and the nature of Chekhov's intent in writing the play: published for the first time as late as 1924 by his brother, M. P. Chekhov,[26] the play is regarded as either a parody of Suvorin's play,[27] or as a serious stage in Chekhov's development as a writer of dramas. In fact, these two critical views are not necessarily mutually exclusive: it was exactly through the parody and reworking of certain stock techniques and conventions of the farce-vaudeville (as in *The Proposal*), or the parody of melodrama conventions (as in the little-known sketch *Dishonourable Tragedians and Leprous Dramatists*)[28] that Chekhov developed as an innovator, not so much as a writer of dramas, but rather one who consistently erased the division between comedy and drama. Thus whether or not the play *is* a parody of Suvorin's work or – as one critic argues – a parody on the work of the French writer 'Gip',[29] or a specific reworking of Suvorin's content and form for a particular philosophical and dramatic reason, the play must be seen as important for what it reveals of Chekhov's experimentation, his attitude to the contemporary theatre, and his reaction to conventional dramatic forms.

Suvorin's play was initially called *The Hunt for Women*, then changed to *Men and Women*, and finally titled after the leading part in the play, the actress, Tatyana Repina. Perhaps surprisingly, given the subject and source of the play, it is subtitled 'a comedy'. But, as one critic put it, Suvorin built the dramatic mood on 'loud vulgar effects in the style of a French melodrama. Not without cause did his contemporaries compare his *Tatyana Repina* with *The Lady of the Camellias*.'[30] Suvorin's version seems to suffer from many of the clichés and conventions of numerous plays of the period:

there is a shattering effect in the last entrance of the fourth act: the poisoned Repina has just finished playing her part of Vasilisa Melentieva; the acting was inspiringly beautiful; she has conquered the whole audience with her sincerity – including her rival Olenina and the traitorous Sabinin – and now, in dreadful torment, she is dying back-stage. But out in the auditorium the audience is calling emphatically: 'Repina! Repina!' There is a crowd round the door of her dressing-room and suddenly, from amongst them, comes the shattered Sabinin who rushes to the dying Repina, falls on his knees in front of her, and begs forgiveness: 'Forgive me, forgive...I have behaved badly...Like the lowest of the low!...Forgive me!' Asked not to add to her agony by staying, Sabinin submits – but his last words are filled with despair:'This is all my doing ...I've done all this! I wish somebody would kill me...!' This kind of reaction and motivation is conventionally the turning-point in a similar series of events – when the weak-willed hero wants to build his personal well-being on the destruction of another's life, the author makes him appear at the tragic end of his victim in order to bring out his feeling of repentance with even greater strength.[31]

It is in this final scene that the similarity with *The Lady of the Camellias* may be seen: as Marguerite Gautier dies of consumption, Armand falls at her feet and begs for forgiveness.

The play was produced in the 1888–9 season both in Petersburg and in Moscow; at the Alexandrinsky Theatre in Petersburg, where the title role was played by no less an actress than Maria Savina, with the famous actors Davydov and Dalmatov also in the cast; and at the Moscow Maly Theatre where the almost equally famous Yermolova played Tatyana Repina. And it was Chekhov, in Moscow at the time, who helped to supervise the production and who wrote regularly to Suvorin about difficulties with the actors and faults in the play. Many of these faults were exposed by the newspaper criticisms and reviews of the play, criticisms ranging from 'its light literary style' to 'the absence of typical or characteristic language', and 'the absence of psychological details.'[32] The generally derogatory view of the play, and the consistent and critical comments which Chekhov made about it, make it most unlikely that Chekhov wrote his one-act play as 'a compliment' to Suvorin, a view put forward by Hingley.[33] Several of the reviews of both the Petersburg and Moscow productions are worth quoting because of the insight they offer on the faults of the play, and the similarity of Chekhov's views:

The characterisation...is done by Suvorin in an extremely simplified manner: each one of the characters has an extensive soliloquy in which he draws a picture of himself... When all the characters have 'read' to the audience a few light and slight articles by Mr Suvorin, and as many leading articles from *Novoe Vremya*,[34] the first act is finished... The third act is quite superfluous, the fourth act must also be shortened...and then what would be left but a scenic play unimaginatively put together with a slightly humorous plot and a melodramatic finish.[35]

The paper *Novosti* of 12 December 1888 wrote that *Tatyana Repina* was neither more nor less than 'a slight *feuilleton* in a contemporary style... a dramatised short little play in four acts',[36] and stressed the trite and coarse nature of the scenic effects of which, the critic noted, the last act was particularly full. And the *Peterburgskie Vedomosti* considered Suvorin only 'a mediocrity' who rises to a play of words such as 'pivoneer' instead of 'pioneer', to 'anecdotes about a financial bigwig and similar pearls of wit...which did not collect a single round of applause – not even from the Sunday Alexandrinsky Theatre public'.[37] Yet another Petersburg paper wrote that: 'the characters and the relationships...and the whole course of the dramatic action appears completely incomprehensible, unexplained and unmotivated'.[38]

The Moscow press was less savage in criticising the play partly because 'the dissatisfaction with the old dramatic subjects and methods, and the search for new forms were, obviously, felt much more strongly in Petersburg than in Moscow, where Krylov was sitting in state in the dramatic committee.'[39] But partly also because criticism of the play was modified by the critics' respect for Yermolova's acting as Repina:

the fear of death gripped the public, there were fainting fits in the boxes, and hysterical cries in the stalls. . . Bedlam broke out in the auditorium, the perform-ance was interrupted and it was necessary to lower the curtain.[40]

A few critics, however, specifically underlined the fact that this reaction was caused by the acting, and not the play: 'Yes. . .They applauded there, they shouted, only. . .dear friend, it was not meant for you!' the critic Lupus mocked Suvorin in *Teatr i Zhizn*.[41] But of all the news-paper reviews, it was the *Russkie Vedomosti* which gave the most serious and searching analysis of the play: praising the fact that Yermolova was given such an acting vehicle, and stating that the idea of the play was interesting, it nonetheless concluded that the part of Repina was of 'a purely journalistic character',[42] and that:

the author filled the play with journalistic monologues and with stories on the zemstvos, law courts, the police, the state, the family, talent, the theatre, children, people.[43]

A considerable number of these monologues on every conceivable subject were 'tirades' spoken by a character called Adashev, a character whom Chekhov totally omitted from his one-act 'continuation' of Suvorin's play. Adashev's function in the play is, in fact, only that of 'author' or 'speech-maker', a 'philosopher' who aroused Chekhov's irritation. In one of his most outspoken comments to Suvorin on the play, Chekhov wrote that neither Adashev nor anyone else should pronounce long monologues on the necessity of living – in front of someone who is dying of poison, and therefore suffering from dreadful stomach pains. And it must be remembered that three years earlier, in a letter to his brother Alexander, Chekhov had listed the 'ingredients' necessary to a story, one of which was 'the absence of lengthy verbiage of a political-social-economic nature'; and in 1887, Chekhov had also listed the requirements of stage-craft, one clear requirement being 'no long speeches'. A further requirement on Chekhov's list was that 'each character must possess individual features and idiosyncrasies, and must speak in a language of his own'. Chekhov was extremely critical of Suvorin's play for this reason: the characters lacked individuality.

Thus, in one letter to Suvorin, Chekhov wrote that in his *Tatyana Repina* there is 'much that is good and original, which is new in dramatic literature, but also much that is bad (for instance, the language)',[44] and in another letter, written on 30 May 1888, Chekhov clarified his view of the play, its characterisation and language, in no uncertain terms:

As to your play, I try in vain to see why you speak so ill of it. Its defects do not spring from your not being sufficiently talented, or from your not having great enough powers of observation, but from the nature of your creative ability. You are more inclined to austere creation, which was developed in you by extensive reading of classical models, and by your love for these models. Imagine your *Tatyana* written in verse, and you will see that its defects will take on a different aspect. If it were written in verse, nobody would notice that all its characters speak one and the same language, nobody would reproach your characters for uttering nothing but philosophy, and for '*feuilleton*-izing' in the classic form – all this would blend with the classic tone as smoke blends with air – and one would not observe in your *Tatyana* the absence of the commonplace language and the everyday petty actions that the modern drama must provide in plenty... Give your characters Latin names, attire them in togas, and you will get the same thing: the defects of your play are irremediable because they are organic. Console yourself with the thought that they are the product of your positive traits and that if you were to make a gift of them to other playwrights, Krylov or Tikhonov for example, their plays would become more interesting and more intelligent.

Chekhov's criticism, although couched with a characteristic intent not to hurt, is nonetheless very clear and outspoken, and his reference to Krylov and Tikhonov is telling: he had a low opinion of the work of Victor Krylov, and, although he corresponded with Vladimir Tikhonov, he had little time for Tikhonov's comedies which enjoyed a temporary popularity in the 1880s.

Chekhov's view that the 'defects...are irremediable because they are organic' was also shared by Nemirovich-Danchenko, who pointed out the faults of Suvorin's play and stated that the monologues:

not only do not emanate from the characters' positions, but also do not assist the development of the action, and do not even relate to the characters' personalities, or help to reveal or describe those personalities. The monologues are all written in the same – incidentally, beautiful, – purely *feuilleton* language.[45]

Given the generally unfavourable reaction to the play, and Chekhov's own deeply critical attitude, Chekhov could scarcely have written his one-act play as a compliment to Suvorin; in fact, his play is written rather more like a 'reply' to Suvorin's play, a 'reply' involving a number of points which Chekhov raised in his letters when describing particular problems of the play. Some of these problems emerged from Chekhov's involvement on Suvorin's behalf in the Moscow Maly Theatre's production of the play;[46] and his criticism of the play deepened as he increasingly discovered the difference between the play as 'literature' and the play 'in performance', and the requirements of stagecraft necessary to take a play from page to stage. Working with the actor Lensky (who played Adashev), Chekhov saw that the actor's considerable ability could not make a weak play into a good one: 'He [Lensky] is angry that in his speeches there is too little movement',[47] Chekhov wrote to Suvorin; and in December 1888, in another letter to Suvorin, he expressed his concern over the structure of the play:

The first act of your Repina has been constructed in such a way that I am quite confused...I am still not yet quite clear about whether your play is any good or not. In its architecture there is something which I do not understand.

And Chekhov was equally critical of Suvorin's excess:

There is in you too much that is superfluous, too much suspicion towards yourself, over-conscientiousness; you are tying your own hands and that means you are not free or sovereign...For instance, out of fear that you are not sufficiently exact, and that you will not be understood, you find it necessary to motivate every situation and every move. Repina says: 'I have poisoned myself', but this is not enough for you – you force her to say two or three unnecessary sentences and so you sacrifice truth to your over-conscientiousness.[48]

Thus Chekhov's criticism of the play was far-reaching: the language, the characterisation, the structure, its superficial journalese, its light literary (as opposed to dramatic) form, and a basic, organic lack of artistic truth. Some years later (in a letter to Gorky written in 1899) Chekhov was to warn of excess and over-writing. The brunt of Chekhov's criticism relates, in fact, to the form of Suvorin's play; he makes comparatively little mention of the *content* and the social and political comments and monologues in the play, but much of what he wrote about the excess in the play relates also to the content. Thus, in another letter, Chekhov implicitly criticised Suvorin's anti-semitism in the presentation of the Jewish intriguer, Sonnenstein (a character retained in Chekhov's one-act play, but presented in a mild – if comic – way), and he wrote to Suvorin that there was no need for Tatyana to use the word 'damned' all the time: 'the damned offender' or 'damned Jew'. And in the same letter, Chekhov wrote that Repina's speech lacks even one 'rich sentence', or, to put it another way, was constructed crudely and excessively.[49]

Chekhov's comments on Suvorin's play extend over the year 1888–9,[50] the period of the Alexandrinsky's production of *Ivanov* (which was taking place at the same time as the Moscow production of Suvorin's play), and the period in which he started work on *The Wood Demon*, a play which he had, initially, considered writing in collaboration with Suvorin. This was the period in which Chekhov was at his most explicit about his exploration of theatre forms and conventions, and dramatic theory and practice. His letters to Suvorin, to Pleshcheyev, to Shcheglov, or to his brother, were consistently concerned with problems of dramatic form, and with the conventional and innovatory in dramatic writing. On 11 September 1888, Chekhov makes an interesting and identical (though probably coincidental) use of the same phrase as that used by Strindberg in his Preface to *Miss Julie*, by writing: 'All I am doing now is pouring new wine into old bottles.'[51]

By the time Chekhov wrote his one-act *Tatyana Repina*, he had already written an extremely witty 'joke' satirising both melodrama, and Suvorin. Written in 1884, *Dishonourable Tragedians and Leprous Dramatists*[52] includes the following 'dig' at Suvorin's sermonising:

Thunder and lightning. The calendar of Alexsei Suvorin (the provincial secretary) lies on this very spot and foretells, with the impartiality of a bailiff, the collision of the earth with the sun, the destruction of the universe, and the increased prices of pharmaceutical goods.

And only a few weeks after finishing his *Tatyana Repina*, Chekhov wrote another sketch, *A Forced Declaration*,[53] which is both a parody and a satire of, among other things, 'stock' situations, and techniques of melodrama. Thus Chekhov's own use of 'stock' theatre techniques and popular forms of theatre – whether farce-vaudeville or melodrama – is also a means to an end: he uses parody not only as a dispassionate critical weapon, but also as a means of making something 'natural' and 'credible' out of the 'artificial' and 'stock'. In, for example, the sketch *A Forced Declaration*, parody is used to expose the ridiculous and, simultaneously, to expose the ill-treatment of horses; equally, in his 'drama' *Tatyana Repina*, Chekhov retains most of the characters, a consistent setting following the end of Suvorin's play and the previous plot, all in order to expose its defects by contrast, and also, crucially, to communicate a different attitude to the situation. Thus, referring to Chekhov's 'witty parody on Suvorin's *Tatyana Repina*', one critic writes:

Chekhov's play is a contrast, contrary to it, giving it a silly appearance and robbing it of artistic verity. The originality of Chekhov's parody consists in the fact that he did not exaggerate the defects of Suvorin's language, and did not introduce even longer monologues. He totally rejected Suvorin's method of creating the characters' speech, and gave them his own. He laughs at the melodramatic content which had charmed Suvorin by giving it a silly outcome.[54]

Chekhov's play describes Sabinin's marriage to Repina's rival, Olenina; the play is set in the cathedral, and stages the marriage ceremony; the majority of Suvorin's characters are retained, with the exception of Adashev, and the addition of Kuzma, the Cathedral caretaker, and a mysterious Woman in Black, a woman whom Sabinin sees as the reincarnation of Repina who has come to the wedding to haunt him. By taking over Suvorin's play and writing an additional act, a continuation of the plot but in his own style, Chekhov offers both an implicit critique of Suvorin's play – a 'reply' – and a radically different philosophy in terms of the content. This difference in attitude to the content is evident in the fact that whereas Suvorin called his play 'a comedy', Chekhov quite deliberately called his *Tatyana Repiňa* 'a drama', and the reason for this is perhaps best expressed by Chekhov himself in a letter to Suvorin of 23 December 1888:

I would know that to people who have dedicated themselves to the study of life I am just as necessary as a star is to an astronomer. And I would then put my back into the work, and I would know for the sake of what I would be working. But at present I, you...et al. resemble maniacs writing books and plays for their personal pleasure. Personal pleasure is, of course, a good thing; one feels that while one is writing – but afterwards? However...there, I'm closing the valve. In a word, I feel hurt about Tatyana Repina, and I feel pity not because the heroine poisoned herself but because she lived her allotted years, died a martyr's death, and was depicted for no reason whatsoever and without any benefit to people.[55]

Quite explicitly, Chekhov makes it clear that his compassion was directed to the manner of Repina's living, not to the way in which she died: her life was wasted, and particularly so given that the story was not depicted in such a way as to teach other people something valuable. There *is* a moral in this, and it is, perhaps, for this reason that Chekhov's Woman in Black is presented critically (satirically is, perhaps, to put it too strongly) by means of her own excessive and exaggerated attitude and behaviour and in contrast to the view held by Father Alexis. Thus, at the end of the play, melodrama is used to expose the melodramatic:

WOMEN IN BLACK: I've taken poison – because I hate him. He insulted – . So why is he so happy? My God! (*Shouts.*) Save me, save me! (*Sinks to the floor.*) Everyone should take poison, everyone! There's no justice in this world!

FATHER ALEXIS: (*in horror*) What blasphemy! O God, what blasphemy!

WOMAN IN BLACK: Because I hate him. We should all poison ourselves. (*Groans and rolls on the floor.*) She's in her grave and he, he – the wrong done to a woman is a wrong done to God. A woman has been destroyed.

FATHER ALEXIS: What blasphemy against religion! (*Throws up his arms.*) What blasphemy against life!

WOMAN IN BLACK: (*tears all her clothes and shouts*) Save me! Save me!

(H.I.102–3)

The Woman in Black is not a very good advertisement for her own philosophy: the characteristic technique of disparity between what is heard and what is seen, her obvious agony, and her reiterated (though contradictory) wish to survive, all expose the dangerous and the ridiculous in suicidal gestures, or in 'doing a Tatyana Repina'. Chekhov is implicitly as critical of those 'doing a Tatyana Repina' as he was of those 'being Hamlet', and the view that everyone should take poison is made ridiculous. This is brought out very clearly earlier in the play:

VOICE: 'Yes, some doctor's wife – in the hotel.'

DEACON: And for the Most Holy Orthodox Patriarchs of eternal memory –

VOICES: 'That's the fourth one to do a Tatyana Repina and poison herself. How do you explain these poisonings, old man?' 'Sheer neuroticism, what else?' 'Are they copying each other, do you think?'...

VOICES: 'Suicide's catching.' 'There are so many neurotic females about these days, it's something awful!'...   (H.I.93)

and:

VOICES: 'Tatyana's death has poisoned the air. Our ladies have all caught the disease, their grievances have driven them mad.' 'Even the air in church is poisoned. Can you feel the tension?'   (H.I.94)

Equally, Father Alexis' view of blasphemy against life is a characteristic leitmotif of a number of Chekhov's plays. Referring to Konstantin's suicide attempt in *The Seagull*, Chekhov commented: 'a failure who runs away from life is not the subject of a tragedy'. In the farce-vaudevilles, the constant threat of suicide is ridiculed, as in Zaytsev's 'solution' in *The Night before the Trial*; but it is in *Uncle Vanya* that Chekhov, using the 'stock' device of a suicide attempt, makes it much more credible (and moving) that Vanya does *not* kill himself – living is harder than dying. Thus Vanya's 'theatricality' is used, in effect, to increase the reality of his situation and despair:

VOYNITSKY: Please give me something. (*Pointing to his heart.*) I've a burning feeling here.

ASTROV: (*shouts angrily*) Oh, shut up! (*More gently.*) Those who live a century or two after us and despise us for leading lives so stupid and tasteless, perhaps they'll find a way to be happy, but as for us – . There's only one hope for you and me, that when we're resting in our graves we may have visions. Even pleasant ones perhaps. (*Sighs.*) Yes, my dear fellow. In our whole district there were only two decent, civilized people – you and I. But ten years or so of this contemptible, parochial existence have completely got us down. This filthy atmosphere has poisoned our blood and we've become as second-rate as the rest of them. (*Vigorously.*) Anyhow, don't you try and talk your way out of it. You give me back what you took.

VOYNITSKY: I didn't take anything.

ASTROV: You took a small bottle of morphia out of my medical case. (*Pause.*) Look here, if you're so terribly keen on doing yourself in, why not go into the woods and blow your brains out there? But do give me back that morphia or people will start talking and putting two and two together and they'll end up thinking I gave it to you. It'll be quite bad enough having to do the post mortem. You don't suppose that will be exactly fun, do you?

(*Sonya comes in.*)

VOYNITSKY: Leave me alone.

ASTROV: (*to Sonya*) Sonya, your uncle has taken a bottle of morphia from my case and he won't give it back. Tell him that this is – well, not particularly bright of him. Besides, I'm in a hurry, I ought to be off.

SONYA: Uncle Vanya, did you take the morphia? (*Pause.*)

ASTROV: He took it all right.

SONYA: Give it back. Why frighten us like this? (*Affectionately.*) Give it back, Uncle Vanya. I daresay I'm no less unhappy than you, but I don't give way to despair. I put up with things patiently and that's how I mean to go on till my life comes to its natural end. You must be patient as well. (*Pause.*) Give it back. (*Kisses his hands.*) Uncle, darling Uncle, do give it back. (*Weeps.*) You're kind, you'll have pity on us and give it back. You must be patient, Uncle. Please.

VOYNITSKY: (*gets the bottle from the table drawer and give it to Astrov*) There you are, take it. (*To Sonya.*) But we must hurry up and start work, we must do something quickly, or else I just can't carry on.   (H.3.61–2)

Enduring, facing reality and not running away from life – themes reiterated in numerous of Chekhov's works, both literary and dramatic. It is significant that the most pessimistic view in *Tatyana Repina* is put by Kuzma, the caretaker, who has no thought of suicide:

ACOLYTE: . . . It's a smart wedding. (*Puts on a fur coat.*) These people know how to live.

KUZMA: It's all so pointless. No sense in it.

ACOLYTE: What?

KUZMA: Take this wedding. We marry them, christen them and bury them every day and there ain't no sense in it at all.

ACOLYTE: Then what exactly would you like to do?

KUZMA: Nothing. Nothing at all. What's the point? They sing, burn incense, recite the liturgy – but God don't listen. Forty years I've worked here and never heard God's voice. Where God is, I just don't know. There's no point in anything.

ACOLYTE: Well, yes. (*Puts on his galoshes.*) 'It's talk like this that makes your head go round.' (*Moves off with squeaking galoshes.*) Cheerio! (*Goes out.*)

KUZMA: (*on his own*) We buried a local squire this afternoon, we've just had a wedding, and we've a christening tomorrow morning. Where will it all end? What use is it to anyone? None, it's just pointless. (H.1.101–2)

Kuzma's function is largely to provide a sense of proportion: first, by going on living although having no aim or point; second, by the context which he provides for the whole action of the play – the everlasting and inescapable reality of a life-cycle, namely, birth, marriage and death. But Chekhov also provides another 'proportional' statement: the Acolyte's squeaking boots (like Yepikhodov's in *The Cherry Orchard*) deflate Kuzma's philosophising by comic juxtaposition. Equally, Father Ivan sighs over his life, about the girl he had married, as he says: 'Oh, what a life, when you come to look at it.' Such comments, expressed informally, almost casually, form a striking contrast to Suvorin's histrionics, and to the melodramatic extremes which follow from the Woman in Black. It is not accidental that these views are expressed after the ceremony is over, and the priests are making ready to go home: the situation is now informal, the 'focus' on a small group for a longer period of time than in the previous part of the play.

The contrast with Suvorin's play exists on every level: whereas Suvorin's play is composed of lengthy, unmotivated and high-flown monologues, Chekhov's characters speak in short sentences, in ordinary speech, with the dialogue constructed out of interjections, irrelevancies, association of ideas, and rapid responses. Individuals are picked out as if by a camera panning across a crowd, pausing, and then passing on, or cutting rapidly:

KOTELNIKOV: These crowns are heavy. My hands feel numb already.

VOLGIN: Never mind, I'll take over soon. Who's that stinking of cheap scent? That's what I'd like to know.

ASSISTANT PROSECUTOR: It's Kotelnikov.

KOTELNIKOV: That's a lie.

VOLGIN: Shush!

FATHER IVAN: O Lord our God, crown them with glory and honour. O Lord our God, crown them with glory and honour. O Lord our God, crown them with glory and honour.

MRS KOKOSHKIN: (*to her husband*) Doesn't Vera look nice today? I've been admiring her. And she isn't a bit nervous.

KOKOSHKIN: She's used to it. It is her second wedding, after all.

MRS KOKOSHKIN: Well, that's true enough. (*Sighs.*) I do hope she'll be happy, she has such a kind heart.

ACOLYTE: (*coming into the middle of the church*) The prokimenon of the Epistle, tone viii. Thou hast set upon their heads crowns of precious stones: they asked life of thee, and thou gavest it them.

BISHOP'S CHOIR: (*singing*) Thou has set upon their heads –

KOTELNIKOV: I wish I could have a smoke. (H.1.88–9)

In this way, the structure of the play is created partly by Chekhov's increasingly frequent use of juxtaposition – the solemnity of the wedding ritual, the prayers and the singing of the choir are juxtaposed throughout the play with the joking and chatting public and – as so often in Chekhov's plays – one is used to comment, sometimes comically, on the other:

ACOLYTE: This is a great mystery: but I speak concerning Christ and the church. Nevertheless let every one of you in particular so love his wife even as himself; and the wife see that she reverence her husband...

VOICES: 'Hear that, Natalya? "Let the wife reverence her husband."' 'Oh, you leave me alone!' (*Laughter.*)... (H.1.90)

In addition, such interjections 'individualise' members of the crowd, their relationships, and, at times, their characters.

The duration of the action is the duration of the wedding ceremony and its aftermath, which Sabinin and other members of the congregation constantly complain is taking too long. The dramatic tension, therefore, is created and established by the ceremony, by the duration of the action, by the heat and lack of air, and by the crowd 'jammed in like sardines'. It is motivated that Sabinin and Vera Olenina should feel faint and dizzy, and that someone in the crowd should collapse: the Woman in Black. In this atmosphere, feeling physically weak and with a guilty conscience, it is credible that Sabinin thinks that he recognises the Woman in Black:

SABININ: I say, Kotelnikov.

KOTELNIKOV: What is it?

SABININ: Nothing. Oh, God, Tatyana Repina's here. She's here, I tell you!

KOTELNIKOV: You must be crazy.

SABININ: That woman in black – it's her. I recognized her, saw her.

KOTELNIKOV: There's no resemblance. She's just another brunette, that's all.

SABININ: For God's sake – I can hardly stand. It's her. (H.1.94)

In this aspect of the play, Chekhov is very much closer to Turgenev's version of Kadmina's story in *Clara Milich* than to Suvorin: the dead actress haunts the faithless lover and 'embodies' a guilty conscience, but Chekhov effectively provides what could be called a satirical joke at Sabinin's expense. Thinking that he has 'seen' Repina, Sabinin wants absurdly to rush off to the cemetery as soon as the wedding is over, and then desperately wants to hold a requiem service; but as soon as the ceremony is finally over, Sabinin forgets all about his fears and does nothing. Moreover, as the end of the play makes clear, the Woman in Black is *not* Repina's ghost, or the embodiment of guilt, simply another woman who has 'done a Tatyana Repina'. As a result, the reader experiences a sense of anti-climax, which is, simultaneously, a climax, but one which, in turn, becomes anti-climactic through absurdity. Thus, on the one hand Chekhov indicates a psychological state and disturbance in Sabinin and motivates it by the past and by the present physical tensions, while on the other hand he debunks superstition and, given the contemporary influence of Tatyana Repina's (Kadmina's) death, effectively explodes a 'myth'.

The characterisation is, in itself, a means of making a particular philosophical statement: Sabinin and Olenina are presented through the eyes of the congregation, as well as by their own presence on stage; but they are more like the leading actors of a performance enacted before an audience. Thus Chekhov's cathedral is turned into a performance space, the wedding into a public ritual, and the characters into a mixture of actors and audience; as a result, the reader is given a constantly shifting perspective which then governs the objective view of the whole scene, and which enables him to see the comic in juxtaposition with the dramatic, and those moments where the 'dramatic' is, in fact, quite deliberately shown as 'melodramatic'.

Thus Chekhov uses Suvorin's play (the previous action and the characters), but makes a completely different play out of it, with a different philosophical attitude. If the play had simply been a straightforward parody, then the logical end of this 'additional act' would have been analogous to Suvorin's most dramatic effect in the final scene which defines the composition of the play: the Woman in Black would die in the cathedral in full view of the crowd, cursing Sabinin. Chekhov is not, therefore parodying Suvorin's comedy so much as reworking it, almost replying to it and to the contemporary fixation on 'doing a Tatyana Repina'. As is evident from his farce-vaudevilles and from *A Forced Declaration* written only a few weeks later, Chekhov often made both critical and innovatory use of the very conventions and assumptions which he was satirising.

The play was written to be read, not performed, and given the portrayal of a church ritual on stage it would, in any case, never have received approval from the censor; it was written, as Chekhov put it when he sent it to Suvorin, as 'a very cheap and useless present', but 'one which I alone can give'.[56] But it must be seen as more than a mere curiosity; it provides a significant example of Chekhov's reworking of contemporary theatre practices; it illustrates the thin dividing-line in his work between parody, satire, and criticism, and it provides an example of Chekhov's attitude to the melodramatic on the stage – and in life.

5

A play in one act

The Wedding (1889–1890)

The Wedding, the only one-act dramatic work which Chekhov sub-titled 'a play',[1] is the most frightening of all his works for the theatre. It is frightening because of the mood and atmosphere, the situation and personalities of the characters, and, in particular, because of the milieu of the play. As Gorky wrote:

No one understood as clearly and finely as Anton Chekhov the tragedy of life's trivialities, no one before him showed men with such merciless truth the terrible and shameful picture of their life in the dim chaos of bourgeois everyday existence.

His enemy was banality; he fought it all his life long; he ridiculed it, drawing it with a pointed and unimpassioned pen, finding the mustiness of banality even where at the first glance everything seemed to be arranged very nicely, comfortably, and even brilliantly...[2]

The setting of *The Wedding* is 'a large, brilliantly lit room'; the situation, a wedding celebration, is normally thought to be a happy one, but the effect of the play is achieved partly through Chekhov's reversal of the conventional and the expected, and partly through the virtually unrelieved depiction of *poshlost* in the play. The Russian word *poshlost* is untranslatable by any single word, but it encompasses philistinism, the petty, the trivial, the mundane, and the banal: indicative of human behaviour and attitudes, it becomes a social disease and thus also a spiritual disease. The characters of *The Wedding* are *poshly* people, and thus the world of the play provides an exposure of philistinism and pettiness. As such, *The Wedding* goes beyond the farcical to the satirical grotesque. The mood of the play, and the resulting effect, may best be summed up by Vakhtangov's view of *The Wedding* as depicting 'a feast in time of plague':

Let naturalism in the theater die...I would like to direct *The Seagull* theatrically, as Chekhov wrote it. I want to present Pushkin's *Feast in Time of Plague*[3] and Chekhov's *A Wedding* in one evening. In *A Wedding* there is 'a feast in time of plague'.[4]

Chekhov's hatred of philistinism and the banal is evident from innumerable short stories, and from other one-act plays, such as *The Anniversary* or *A Tragic Role*, and may be seen colouring the presentation of a character such as Natasha in *The Three Sisters*, 'a petite-bourgeoise'. But in no other dramatic work by Chekhov is philistinism depicted as mercilessly as in *The Wedding:*

Anton Pavlovich in his early stories was already able to reveal in the dim sea of banality its tragic humour; one has only to read his 'humorous' stories with attention to see what a lot of cruel and disgusting things, behind the humorous words and situations, had been observed by the author with sorrow and were concealed by him.[5]

It is from several early stories that *The Wedding* derives: Chekhov combined and extended several elements from different early short stories, thus heightening and sharpening the effect of any one of them. From the short story *The Wedding Season*, written in November 1881, Chekhov took the character of the Greek confectioner Kharlampy Dymba. The first part of the story *A Marriage of Convenience*, written in 1884, was lifted almost verbatim to provide the quarrels over electricity, the dowry, and debts, which create a major part of the conflict and pettiness of the play. From the same story Chekhov took over the central characters: Yat, the telegraphist (called Mr Blinchikov – 'Pancake' – in the story); the bridegroom, Aplombov; the parents of the bride; and the bride herself, Dashenka, 'on whose face are inscribed all the virtues save one – the power of thought'. In the same year, 1884, Chekhov contributed two satirical articles to the humorous weekly, *Fragments*, on the lower middle class custom of hiring a general for a wedding in order to provide 'tone' and 'class', and 'without which no shopkeeper's wedding is complete'. And it was from another short story, written in December of that year and called *A Wedding with a General*, that the 'second part' of the play derives: the arrival of Revunov-Karaulov as 'the general' and the comic-grotesque misunderstandings which follow from this pretentious and yet revealing custom.

The subject of quarrels and disputes over the marriage dowry is also, however, treated in other short stories by Chekhov, in *The Cook's Wedding*, *Suitor and Papa*, *A Happy Ending*, *A Slander*, *A Blunder*, and several others, but – like disputes between rival landowners – it may also be seen as a traditional source of conflict and social satire in Gogol, in Ostrovsky, and in Dostoyevsky.

In Gogol's famous play, *Marriage*, written in 1833, the dowry figures large in the minds of the prospective suitors. In Act 1, scene i, the matchmaker Fyokla gives the unwilling suitor, Podkolyosin (whose name might be literally translated as 'Under-a-wheel'), a description – which tails off into characteristic Gogolian 'comic irrelevancies' – of the property which forms part of the dowry:

PODKOLYOSIN: About the dowry? Tell me again about the dowry.
FYOKLA: The dowry! Well there's the property in the Moskovsky District – a stone-built house – two storeys high – a real fine investment. The corn-chandler pays 700 for the shop alone. And there's the beer-cellar – that attracts a lot of people too. Two wooden outbuildings – well, one of them's all wood but the other has a stone foundation; each one brings in 400 roubles. Then there's the market garden in the suburbs at Viborg. It's been let for three years now to a cabbage-merchant – and such a sober man he is, too; never touches a drop, and he has three sons.[6]

The suitors have an inventory which one of them, Yaichnitsa ('Omelette'), checks off very carefully:

Anyhow, let's have another look at the inventory. (*Reads.*) Two-storey stone house. (*Raises his eyes and looks around the room*) Yes! (*Goes on reading*) 'Two outbuildings, one on a stone foundation; one all wooden' – well, wood's not much good. 'A light carriage, a double sledge hand-carved, with a large carpet and a small one' – maybe only good for firewood. Though the old woman assured me it was fine quality – all right, let's suppose it is fine quality. 'Two dozen silver spoons.' Of course, you need silver spoons in a house. 'Two fox fur coats.' Hm. 'Four large feather beds and two small ones.' (*Significantly compresses his lips.*) 'Six silk dresses and six cotton dresses, two nightcaps, two...' This is a frivolous item. 'Linen, napkins...' She can please herself about them. Although, one's got to check up on everything. Nowadays, they'll promise you houses and carriages and when you're married all you'll find is feather beds.[7]

And in Act 2, scene i, Podkolyosin's friend, Kochkaryov, tries to reduce the ranks of rival suitors by lying to Yaichnitsa, first about the young lady's sanity and then about the dowry:

YAICHNITSA: Has she been queer for long?
KOCHKARYOV: Ever since she was a child.
YAICHNITSA: Of course it would be better if she had more sense, but in any

case, a silly woman will do as well – as long as the other items in the inventory are in good order.

KOCHKARYOV: But she's got no dowry.

YAICHNITSA: How can that be – what about the stone house?

KOCHKARYOV: They only say it's stone, but if you only knew how it's built. The walls are only finished off with brick, but inside there's all kinds of rubbish – sweepings off the floor, bits of wood, old shavings.

YAICHNITSA: You don't say!

KOCHKARYOV: Well, of course. Don't you know how they build houses nowadays? 'As long as they're good enough to get a mortgage on.'

YAICHNITSA: But this house isn't mortgaged.

KOCHKARYOV: Who told you that? That's just the point – it's not only mortgaged, but they haven't even paid the interest for the last two years.[8]

In 1851, Ostrovsky wrote a five-act play, *The Poor Bride* (*Bednaya nevesta*), concerning 'a girl without a dowry', and in 1878 he wrote the play actually titled *The Girl without a Dowry* (*Bespredannitsa*); Turgenev also included the subject of 'the dowry' in *A Month in the Country*, but it is in Dostoyevsky's story, *A Disgraceful Affair*[9] (*Skverny anekdot*), written in 1862, that the most interesting comparison may be made with *The Wedding*. The same theme – a general at a wedding – receives characteristically different treatment in Dostoyevsky's story: a high Tsarist official with liberal ideals pays a well-intentioned but patronising visit to the wedding celebration of one of his subordinates, a visit which ends in a disastrous wedding-night for the unfortunate bridegroom, Pseldonymov, and in degradation and humiliation for State Councillor Ivan Ilyitch Pralinsky. The story shows what happens when a *real* general turns up, uninvited, at the wedding of a subordinate: the results are both grotesque and ironic.

Comparing Chekhov's *The Wedding* with Dostoyevsky's *A Disgraceful Affair*, Ruben Simonov writes:

There are two plays[10] created by two great Russian writers, Chekhov and Dostoevsky, on the same theme – a general at a wedding. The same plot is used, but the plays are completely different in both the essence of the basic idea and its realization. Chekhov's *A Wedding* is imbued with a subtle and, at times, bitter humour; the one-act play by Dostoevsky, *A Nasty Joke* [*A Disgraceful Affair*], is written with a cruel, sarcastic, and merciless pen. In this play, Ivan Ilyich Pralinsky, a general, is forced to walk home because his driver is delayed. Passing the house of one of his subordinates, Pralinsky decides to make the small functionary happy by attending his wedding. From that moment, a chain of incredible events begins. On the threshold of the functionary's house, the General treads upon a dish of brawn placed in a passageway to cool off. That is the beginning of the mishaps and the bad luck of the General. With his usual consistency Dostoevsky unfolds the gradual downfall of the General from the heights of his grandeur. Dostoevsky misses no detail, not one characteristic trait, not one chance to horsewhip the General in a most painful manner. He brings Pralinsky to a 'nasty joke', putting him deadly drunk on the bed of the newly-weds, and thus forcing the bride and groom to spend their first night on chairs.[11] We are in complete accord with the manner in which Dostoevsky deals with his high-ranking nonentity. The petty small officials – the host, hostess, and their guests at the wedding – were treated by Dostoevsky with the same intense, biting, and implacable condemnation. The result is an irreparable, black picture of human degradation.

A Nasty Joke needs for its scenic embodiment a sharp, grotesque form, similar to the expressive art of Goya. For the scenic embodiment of Chekhov's *A Wedding*, a remarkable Russian painter, Fedotov... would be the right person.[12]

In both Dostoyevsky's story and Chekhov's, the 'wedding dowry' is clearly the motivation for the wedding, but in *A Disgraceful Affair* the pathetic and miserable bridegroom, Pseldonymov, is totally unable to stand up for himself:

The old man himself offered her hand to Pseldonymov. Poverty-stricken though the latter was, he still asked for a little time to reflect. He and his mother considered the proposal for quite a while. However, the house was to be transferred to the bride's name, and though it was wooden, one-storied and drab, all the same it was worth something. On top of that the old man was giving four hundred roubles – it was not so easy to save so much.[13]

The father-in-law, Mlekopitayev, encouraged the match because he was sick of all the women in the house, to spite them because he knew they disapproved of the match, and because he wanted Pseldonymov under his thumb 'because I am his benefactor'. To test his docility, Mlekopitayev regularly forced his son-in-law to dance the *Kazachok* in front of him. But after the wedding feast, surrounded by the broken chairs of the temporary wedding-bed, and the rubbish left by the guests on the stained and dirty floor, Pseldonymov sat on his own and realised:

that although Mlekopitayev had given fifty roubles towards the wedding expenses – which had been spent to the last kopeck – he had not thought to let them have the four hundred roubles promised as dowry, nor even made further mention of them. Even the house had not been officially transferred to his name.[14]

In contrast, Chekhov's bridegroom in *The Wedding* is not spineless and pathetic, or one of Dostoyevsky's 'insulted and humiliated'; true to his name, and his profession of pawnbroker, Aplombov states:

No one makes a monkey out of me. I've brought your daughter happiness, but if I don't get those tickets today I'll make her wish she'd never been born – as I'm a man of honour! (H.1.119)

Obviously, Aplombov is *not* a man of honour, and is not going to bring Dasha happiness; he is an appraiser, a calculator determined to get what he thinks of as his due. The lottery tickets (which have, in fact, already been pawned by Mrs Zhigalov, his mother-in-law), 'certain household utilities', and a general's presence at the wedding celebration, are all part of the dowry; it is only later that the rest of the dowry is described in such a way as to leave an audience in no doubt of the motivation for marriage, and of the values of all those involved in the wedding. One of the guests is the unfortunate Yat, the telegraphist, who had 'gone around' with Dasha before her marriage to Aplombov, and it is Yat's presence at the wedding which serves as an irritant to Aplombov, but also to everyone else. He consistently says the very things calculated to cause a row but, in doing so, he reveals much of the truth:

YAT:...I've always wished Dasha a good husband with all my heart. They don't grow on trees these days, Mrs Zhigalov, good husbands don't. Nowadays everyone's out for what he can get, they all want to marry for money.

APLOMBOV: That's an insinuation!

YAT: (*taking fright*) No harm intended, I'm sure. I wasn't speaking of present company, it was just, er, a general remark. Oh, for heaven's sake – everyone knows you're marrying for love. It's not as if the dowry was up to much!

MRS ZHIGALOV: Oh, isn't it? You mind your Ps and Qs, young man. Besides a thousand roubles in cash, we're giving three lady's coats, a bed and all the furniture. You'll not find many dowries to match that!

YAT: I meant no harm. Certainly the furniture's nice, and, er, so are the coats, of course. I was merely concerned with this gent being offended on account of my insinuations.

MRS ZHIGALOV: Then don't *make* any. We ask you to the wedding out of regard for your mother and father, and now we get all these remarks! If you knew Mr Aplombov was marrying for money, why not say so before? (H.1.123–4)

But the fact is that Aplombov *did* marry for money: the marriage is in no way a love match, or a romantic affair – it is a bargain, a financial arrangement, or a business deal which, by its very nature, is deeply expressive of the petty materialistic values and attitudes of the characters. Everything can be bought, whether a husband – or a general! But even the 'buying' of a general is not a straightforward deal. Andrey

Nyunin is a friend of the family and has been entrusted with twenty-five roubles to 'hire' a general, but Nyunin, an insurance clerk, plays a fraudulent trick in not hiring a *real* general and in pocketing the money for himself. Unaware that Nyunin has passed him off as a general, Revunov-Karaulov has come to the wedding out of kindness and finds himself accused of the very pretence which Nyunin has set up and of which the guests assume him guilty; moreover, the old man is accused of taking money under false pretences. The pretences and the pretensions are those of all the wedding guests and not of the deaf, doddery old man.

It is in this atmosphere, however, of the marketed and the marketable, 'of that blind alley, that airless atmosphere of the petty Philistine environment of old Russia',[15] that a conventionally happy event, a wedding, takes place. Chekhov reverses an audience's assumptions of the conventional. There is, therefore, a grotesque and ironic disparity between the event and the characters' reactions to it. Celebration and joy are completely absent. In the earlier farce-vaudevilles, whether in *The Proposal* or in *The Bear*, or the later farce-vaudeville, *The Anniversary*, the discrepancy between cause and effect is put to comic use to expose the ridiculous, but in *The Wedding* the discrepancy between the celebratory gathering and characters' behaviour and values is frightening – not only because it is conventionally inappropriate, but also because it makes something joyless and sordid out of a normally happier event. This discrepancy is also, simultaneously, revealing of motives and attitudes which would otherwise remain hidden: the characters reveal themselves and each other. In *The Anniversary*, the pretentiousness of Shipuchin's office helps to reveal the disparity between characters and setting; in *The Wedding*, it is the juxtaposition of setting and music with dialogue and gesture which reveals the disparity between cause and effect, and, in addition, provides the most complex structure of all of Chekhov's one-act plays. It is this structure, however, which is similarly utilised, although extended, in later plays such as *The Three Sisters* or *The Cherry Orchard*.

In *The Bear*, Luka factually but unfavourably compares Popova with the cat, and thus puts Popova'a attitudinising in proportion; in *Swan Song*, Svetlovidov is drunk and maudlin, and this enables an audience to keep the 'pathos' in proportion; in *The Anniversary*, Mrs Shipuchina is heard off-stage laughing and joking with the clerks, which serves to reinforce an audience's awareness of the setting, of her character and behaviour, and the effect on Shipuchin and Khirin; in *Tatyana Repina*, the solemnity of the wedding service is juxtaposed with the laughing and chatting crowd, and thus one comments on the other; but in *The Wedding* it is the physical nature of the setting which serves as a means of juxtaposition. Chekhov creates an *off-stage* focus of sound which is juxtaposed with the on-stage focus of action. By moving, at different but significant points in the play, from 'close up' to 'long shot' within the single 'frame'. Chekhov creates a double rhythm of action in which one source of action comments on or heightens the effect of the other. This, however, is motivated quite simply by the setting, and by the use made of it:

A large, brilliantly lit room. A big table laid for supper with tail-coated waiters fussing round it. A band plays the last figure of a quadrille off-stage. (H.1.119)

For this wedding reception, the dancing takes place off-stage, but at the opening of the play the audience hears the brisk sound of a quadrille before seeing any of the main characters: a social event is established with the opening of the play, and only then, gradually, some of the guests.

(*Mrs Zmeyukin, Yat and The Best Man cross the stage.*)
MRS ZMEYUKIN: No, no, no!
YAT: (*following her*) Oh come on, have a heart.
MRS ZMEYUKIN: No, no, no!
BEST MAN: (*hurrying after them*) This won't do, you two. Where do you think you're off to? What about the dancing? *Grand-rond, seel voo play*!
(*They go out. Mrs Zhigalov and Aplombov come in.*)
MRS ZHIGALOV: Don't bother me with this stuff – you go and dance instead.
APLOMBOV: I'm not spinning round like a top, thank you. Me spin? No sir, I'm no Spinoza! I'm a solid citizen, a pillar of society, and I'm not amused by such idle pursuits. But the dancing's neither here nor there. I'm sorry, Mother, but some things you do have me baffled. Take the dowry, for instance. (H.1.119)

It is only when the context of the wedding has been established, the apparent gaiety and merriment expected at a wedding celebration, that the characters are seen working against their setting and creating an atmosphere both contrary to the music of the quadrille and heightening it. But the first, brief, entrances also create the *type* of social event which is witnessed: Mrs Zmeyukin, in a bright crimson dress, coquettishly escaping from Yat who is earnestly playing the Don Juan, both of whom are followed by the Best Man – the Master of Ceremonies who, from the beginning, has a hopeless task. Equally, it is the off-stage action of the dance which allows them to enter and exit within seconds, while simultaneously conveying characteristic attitudes and functions. Thus, until the moment in the play when all the guests are seated at the supper-table, it is the off-stage action which dictates the rhythm of the play: characters 'drop behind' or leave the dancing to converse on-stage to the often opposing rhythm of the off-stage music. Thus Aplombov's discussion with Mrs Zhigalov about the dowry takes place 'over' the *grand-rond* off-stage; equally, Aplombov's unpleasant threat over the dowry is inter-cut by the merrymaking which this time intrudes on-stage:

APLOMBOV: So you don't like hearing a few home truths ,eh? Just as I thought. Then behave yourself. That's all I ask, behave properly.
(*Couples dance the* grand-rond, *crossing the room from one door to the other. The first couple are Dasha and the Best Man, the last consists of Yat and Mrs Zmeyukin. These last two drop behind and stay in the ballroom. Zhigalov and Dymba come in and go up to the table.*) (H.1.120)

In this way, Chekhov rapidly sets up different centres of action: first, the festive off-stage quadrille; then the brief introduction of two guests and the Best Man; then, with the entrance of the groom and his mother-in-law, a different tone is introduced, one which hardly conforms to the tone of the quadrille; this, in turn, reaches its own disharmonious climax, only to be interrupted by the harmony of the *grand-rond* – a harmony, however, which an audience increasingly realises covers only discord. By the time the music stops, Chekhov has established two on-stage centres of action: Yat and the midwife on one side of the stage, Zhigalov and Dymba on the other side. Thus the movement, activity, and rhythm dictated by the off-stage music create the occasion of the wedding celebration and, initially, the mood. This is juxtaposed with the dialogue and behaviour of the characters on-stage which, in fact, creates a contrary rhythm: the Master of Ceremonies, or the 'keeper of the spirits', cannot infuse gaiety into the dancing.

Simonov provides this description of the opening of Vakhtangov's 1920 production of the play:

Vakhtangov started *A Wedding* with a brisk tempo. A noisy quadrille opened the play. A group of people, almost strangers to each other, danced to the shouted commands of the master of ceremonies, accompanied by the doleful, rattling sound of an out-of tune piano. The dancers were noisy and jolly; bumping into each other, then taking off in a different direction. Yet in their noise and seeming merriment one felt an emptiness, the heartlessness of this marital feast. Vakhtangov showed in the beginning of the play a parade of the characters, and thus introduced them to the audience.

The master of ceremonies (Gorchakov), in hired tails, dances showily, his pompadour bouncing on his forehead. A sailor, Mozgovoi (Zakhava), runs at top speed, squatting rather than dancing the quadrille. A foreigner of Greek descent, a confectioner, Kharlampy Spiridonitch Dimba (Simonov), the possessor of an immense moustache, with his shock of black hair standing on end, is also dancing, but God knows what. He has much difficulty keeping in rhythm with the music. The telegraphist, Yat (Lobashkov), tears about recklessly, struggling with his feet in his endeavor to make the figure of a 'pretzel'. A young high school boy, who just happens to be at the party by accident, hops about gaily. The midwife, Zmeyukina (Lyaudanskaya), in a bright red dress, floats along gracefully.

That quadrille parade, which Vakhtangov introduced, brought the audience into the atmosphere of a wedding – noisy, but not really gay, as it always is at gatherings of people who have just met. Especially when they are expecting an important guest – in this case, the General.[16]

In this way, Vakhtangov emphasised Chekhov's directions in order to use the music even more as a means of 'pointing', underlining, or emphasising the stage action – the arrival of the first course of the meal, for example, was accompanied by a brisk march as the waiters carried the tables on-stage. But, in fact, Vakhtangov altered the music directions which Chekhov gives at the end of the play:

The characters of the play now stand motionless with their backs to the audience; the dream is no more. In this world one cannot attract a genuine general even with money. Softer and softer sounds the sad quadrille. The feast is over; the working week begins. Thus Vakhtangov brought to an end the remarkable one-act play, *A Wedding*.[17]

In his stage directions, however, Chekhov ends the play with a very different mood:

NYUNIN:...(*Shouts*) To the health of bride and groom! You in the band! Play a march! Band! (*The band plays a march.*) To the bride and groom!
MRS ZMEYUKIN: I'm choking. Let me have air! Let me have air! I choke when I'm near you.
YAT: (*ecstatically*) Superb creature!
(*A lot of noise.*)
BEST MAN: (*trying to shout them down*) Ladies and gentlemen! On this, er, so to speak, day – (H.I.131)

The play ends noisily, even chaotically in the manner of a farce, but with a march – not the soft sound of a quadrille. It is essential, however, to understand Vakhtangov's production in the context of its time. Vahktangov's major production question in 1920–1 is described by Simonov as: 'in what way was it necessary to portray Chekhov's characters, defending them or accusing them?'[18] Thus Vakhtangov's interpretation was related to his view of the 'General's' function: 'The arrival of the General is in some degree the fulfilment of a dream about a more beautiful life.'[19] But Chekhov, writing as he was in 1889–90, was characteristically exposing falsity, pretentiousness and philistinism; sympathy is extended only to Revunov at the end of the play, while the other characters throw themselves back into the airless atmosphere and chaos of the interrupted festivities. The march keeps the audience at a distance, while taking in the whole scene: the music, therefore, works *against* the stage action. In Vakhtangov's production, by changing the musical direction, the grotesque farce of the wedding fades away and sympathy is extended to all the characters – they are no longer 'accused' in the same way. Chekhov, however, neither explicitly defends nor accuses: the march, crucially, raises the question in the minds of the audience in juxtaposition with the stage action and the preceding events. It is there, in effect, as a 'distancing' device.

In the last act of *The Three Sisters*, Chekhov's use of a march raises the same question, for the director, of mood and thus interpretation: 'A band is heard playing a march off-stage. Everyone listens.' It is as the music of the march grows louder that Irina – and the audience – hear of Tuzenbakh's death in the duel; Chebutykin sits on the bench and starts to read a newspaper.

(*The three sisters stand close together.*)

MASHA: Oh, listen to the band. They're all leaving us, and one has gone right away and will never, never come back, and we shall be left alone to begin our lives again. We must go on living, we must.

IRINA: (*puts her head on Olga's breast*) What is all this for? Why all this suffering? The answer will be known one day, and then there will be no more mysteries left, but till then life must go on, we must work and work and think of nothing else. I'll go off alone tomorrow to teach at a school and spend my whole life serving those who may need me. It's autumn now and it will be soon winter, with everything buried in snow, and I shall work, work, work.

OLGA: (*embraces both her sisters*) Listen to the band. What a splendid, rousing tune, it puts new heart into you, doesn't it? Oh, my God! In time we shall pass on for ever and be forgotten. Our faces will be forgotten and our voices and how many of us there were. But our sufferings will bring happiness to those who come after us, peace and joy will reign on earth, and there will be kind words and kind thoughts for us and our times. We still have our lives ahead of us, my dears, so let's make the most of them. The band's playing such cheerful, happy music, it feels as if we might find out before long what our lives and sufferings are for. If we could only know! If we could only know!

(*The music becomes fainter and fainter.*) (H.3.138–9)

Chekhov controls the pathos of this final scene, of the grouping of the sisters and their realisation of realities, by providing not just 'music', not merely a march of an unspecified nature, but, as Olga describes it, 'a splendid rousing tune' which 'puts new heart into you' – 'the band's playing such cheerful, happy music, it feels as if we might find out before long what our lives and sufferings are for.' The music, although it becomes fainter and fainter, nonetheless provides a strong contrast to the visual, and thus comments on what is seen and what is spoken. The juxtaposition of the off-stage sound with the on-stage action makes a strong interpretative comment – it simultaneously heightens the on-stage action *and* sets it in a wider perspective. In her speech, Olga sees herself and her sisters objectively, she 'pulls back' as she describes how history might one day see them, almost providing the audience with an 'aerial shot'; in the same way, the music of the march takes the audience beyond the immediate visual image. For an audience, sympathy is certainly not withheld from the three sisters, but the 'distancing' technique of the cheerful, happy music provides a call to thought, to objectivity. Even as the music grows fainter, the suggestion is of a world off-stage which increases in size as the band moves away. Thus the sisters are set in a context greater than themselves – just as the setting in Act 2 of *The Cherry Orchard* gives the characters their appropriate context and stature.

The contrapuntal rhythm is achieved largely through the use of various centres of action within the single 'frame', and extends also to sound effects other than music. At the very beginning of *The Three Sisters*, two conversations and laughter make apparently random comments on seemingly independent conversations: down-stage, in the drawing-room, sit Olga and Irina, as Masha reads her book; up-stage, 'beyond the columns near the table in the ballroom', are Tuzenbakh, Chebutykin and Solyony:

OLGA:...When I woke up this morning and saw the great blaze of light and knew that spring had come – I felt so happy and excited, I felt I just had to go back home to Moscow.

CHEBUTYKIN: (*to Solony and Tuzenbakh*) Not a chance in hell.

TUZENBAKH: Absolute nonsense of course.

(*Masha, absorbed in her reading, softly whistles a tune.*)

OLGA: Do stop whistling, Masha. Really! (*Pause.*) Being at school every day and then giving lessons till late in the evening, I'm always having headaches and the things that run through my mind – why, I might be an old woman already. And it's true that these four years I've been at the high

school, I've felt my youth and energy draining away drop by drop each
day. Only one thing grows stronger and stronger, a certain longing –
IRINA: To go to Moscow, to sell the house, have done with everything here
and go to Moscow.
OLGA: Yes, to Moscow! As soon as we can.
(*Chebutykin and Tuzenbakh laugh.*)   (H.3.73–4)

Such apparently artless coincidences make implied comment possible,
and allow an audience to shift perspective and attention from one focus
of action to another.

In *The Wedding*, this technique is used more overtly: the band playing
off-stage in the ballroom seems to lead a life of its own, but in fact
Chekhov structures its 'interventions' in such a way as to create a
comic-grotesque opposition to the on-stage action. Thus:

APLOMBOV:...(*to Yat*) Mr Yat, though you're a friend of mine, I won't have
you behaving so outrageously in other people's houses. Be so good as to
make yourself scarce!
YAT: I *beg* your pardon!
APLOMBOV: I wish you were as much of a gentleman as what I am. In a word,
kindly buzz off!
(*The band plays a flourish.*)   (H.1.124)

On other occasions, these 'flourishes' from the band serve as *over-
emphasis* of stage action, thus making the action appear ridiculous:

BEST MAN: (*shouts*) To the health of the bride's mother and father! Mr and
Mrs Zhigalov!
(*The band plays a flourish. Cheers.*)   (H.1.124)

And at other moments in this short play, the *omission* of a flourish from
the band, when it is expected or assumed, points a sense of anti-climax.
Revunov unwittingly gives a parody of the conventional cue for a kiss
at a wedding:

REVUNOV:...The herring tastes sour, and so does the blasted bread.
ALL: Blasted bread? Bless the bride! To the bride and groom!
(*Aplombov and Dasha kiss.*)   (H.1.127–8)

And there is no flourish from the band!

Thus, in *The Wedding*, the creation of an off-stage dramatic world
helps to control and motivate the rhythm of the action and – at significant moments – makes possible the juxtaposition of the off-stage sound
with the on-stage action. In *Ivanov* (1887–9), Chekhov had already

created a double-focus of action through his setting – a setting which allowed of fluid movement from up-stage to down-stage, and not only from stage left to stage right, as in *The Wedding*. The stage directions for Act 4 of *Ivanov* read:

A drawing-room in Lebedev's house. In the foreground an arch separating the drawing-room from the ballroom. Doors, right and left... Throughout the act guests in evening dress move about the ballroom. (H.2.215)

In Acts 1 and 2 of *The Three Sisters*, a similar depth, perspective and double-focus are achieved through the setting, though used with greater control and subtlety, and to greater effect:

The Prozorovs' house. A drawing-room with columns beyond which a ballroom can be seen. Midday. Outside the sun is shining cheerfully. A table in the ballroom is being laid for lunch. (H.3.73)

In this way, at the end of the first act, the lunch-party taking place up-stage forms the contrapuntal 'backcloth' for Andrey and Natasha who have moved down-stage.

But it is in Act 3 of *The Cherry Orchard* that Chekhov creates the most complex and subtle rhythm through the use of a multiple setting:

The drawing-room. Beyond it, through an archway, the ballroom. The chandelier is lit. The Jewish band mentioned in Act Two is heard playing in the entrance-hall. It is evening. In the ballroom they are dancing a grand rond. *Simeonov-Pishchik's voice is heard:* 'Promenade à une paire!' *They come into the drawing-room, the first two dancers being Pishchik and Charlotte. Trofimov and Mrs Ranevsky form the second pair, Anya and the Post Office Clerk the third, Varya and the Station Master the fourth and so on. Varya is quietly weeping and dries her eyes as she dances. The last couple consists of Dunyasha and a partner. They cross the drawing-room. Pishchik shouts,* 'Grand rond, balancez!' *and* 'Les cavaliers à genoux et remerciez vos dames!'

Firs, wearing a tail-coat, brings in soda-water on a tray. Pishchik and Trofimov come into the drawing-room. (H.3.175)

In addition, 'From an adjoining room comes the sound of people playing billiards.' At different moments in this act, the different rhythms of action separate, overlap, heighten each other, and are juxtaposed one with the other. And, as in *The Wedding*, the action of the dance allows characters to enter, exit, be seen up-stage, or leave the dancing to come down-stage in pairs. And the music of the band makes its own commentary at particular moments in the act: thus, at the end of Act 3, Lopakhin, the new owner, calls for music from the band as Ranevskaya weeps bitterly, but 'the band plays quietly'.

The Wedding is the only one of the one-act plays which is structured in a way which was to be highly developed in the later, full-length plays, and which uses setting and sound effects to create the rhythm of action. But it is a rhythm of action which also arises organically from what Simonov (who played Dymba in Vakhtangov's production) described as 'the overstrung rhythm that marked the inner life of the majority of the guests.'[20] Each of the characters has his or her own rhythm; as always in Chekhov's plays, conflicts arise simply by bringing people together. Out of a normally happy occasion and situation, the characters' interaction creates a stultifying and airless atmosphere. This may partly be seen in Chekhov's utilisation of certain conventions common to comedy, and found in his farce-vaudevilles and dramatic studies: the use of 'meaningful names' for the characters, the use of several 'comic' misunderstandings, but, in addition, the use of what appears to be a more conventional *dénouement* than in any of the other one-act works.

The 'meaningful names' are, in themselves, expressive of the tone and the dramatic intention of the play: the name 'Zhigalov' may be translated as 'Burning';[21] 'Aplombov' obviously relates to the word 'Aplomb'; the midwife is called 'Mrs Zmeyukin' or 'Mrs Snake'; 'Dymba' is a comically concocted 'foreign name'; the sailor in the Volunteer Fleet is called Mozgovoy, 'Brain'; while the unfortunate 'General' Revunov-Karaulov's name is associated with 'Guard' and 'Howl-for-Help'. It is these characters who take part in what may, on the level of a conventional vaudeville, be seen as 'a comic scene of daily life', but the characterisation is sharper, more exaggerated, and more grotesque than in any of Chekhov's farce-vaudevilles. The 'hyperbole' which is characteristic of comedy is used by Chekhov to create a gallery of largely unpleasant, but three-dimensional, portraits.

Simonov's description of Vakhtangov's production offers a fascinating insight into the tone of the production, and is worth quoting at some length given the illumination which is shed on the characters:

How then did Vakhtangov, together with his young actors, interpret the personages of Chekhov's *A Wedding*? Evdokim Zakharovitch Gigalov [Zhigalov], civil servant retired, as played by V. B. Schukin was a man who on first sight is kind and generous, but in fact is cruel and rapacious. The steady trickle of amiable, tender words, the tendency to feign a simpleton, a man who is not practical – all that was a mask behind which was hidden a functionary, an unquestionable grafter, a boring Philistine, one who was indifferent to everything except easy gain and position... The image created by Schukin, in compliance with Vakhtangov's demands, was a stark theme in relief, the theme of the spiritual bankruptcy and utter aloneness of the Philistine...

His better half, Nastasia Timofeevna Gigalova [Zhigalova], portrayed by Schukina, looked a worthy companion of her husband – narrow-minded, quarrelsome, lachrymose. She managed even at her daughter's wedding to quarrel with Yat, the telegraphist. I remember the uneasy, anxious look of Mrs Gigalova, always fearful lest she be taken advantage of. In the relationship of that married couple one could see immediately that it was the wife who had the upper hand. Schukina addressed her husband in angry severe tones: 'Don't poke your fork into the lobster. That is for the General. I still think he might appear.' The words rang out so sharply that one could easily suspect that if no one had been around she might have hit him. The image of Gigalov's daughter, Dashenka – the bride-to-be – was magnificently delineated plastically by Nekrasova. Little, plump, red-cheeked, awkward, lazy, she was not even quite aware of the significance of the day – her wedding day. Her indifference extended even to her young husband.[22] The food on the table interested her much more than the guests.

The role of the bridegroom, Apiminond Maximovich Aplombov, was played vividly and expressively by a young talented actor named Kudryavtzev. His monotonous, hollow voice, always on the same note, always with one intonation, bored into the audience as a drop of water wears away a stone. At times, in his most temperamental moments, his voice sounded like a dentist's drill...In appearance Aplombov was not prepossessing. He had a big nose, angry eyes, and a tuft of hair that fell carelessly on his forehead. A thin, long figure arrayed in a dresscoat – quite obviously purchased in a secondhand store – he wandered onto the stage with a dissatisfied look and manner that could not help but depress his guests. It would be impossible ever to get close to the heart of this man. He will end his life a grumbler, a bigot, a malcontent; he will fulfil his earthly occupation, that of an appraiser in a pawnshop, and on his deathbed he will still be recalling some unkept promises made by Gigalov.

The role of Andrey Andreevich Neunin – an agent in an insurance office, but a crook and a rascal – was played by Toltchanov. That profession requires the ability to talk a person into something, to force him to buy insurance, no matter how much he is against it. Neunin was pert, bald, with a husky voice, and saucily free in speech and actions. When he started to talk, he gave no one a chance to utter a word. From his point of view people existed for only one reason: so that he might extract money from them by hook or crook. Neunin undoubtedly gambles in cards and billiards, and most likely is physically beaten very often by his partners for cheating in games. Neunin, like Gigalov, caters to and flatters people who are well off and has no use for the rest of the world.

Anna Martinovna Zmeyukina, the thirty-year-old midwife, arrayed in a bright crimson dress, was played by Lyaudanskaya. The actress strongly emphasized in this role the traits of the Philistine. The narrow-mindedness was most sharply etched when the ridiculous bent for 'loftiness' possessed Zmeyukina. The midwife felt like the queen of the ball – a charming, irresistible woman surrounded by a coterie of admirers. In truth, there was only one admirer – the telegraphist Yat. But for Zmeyukina even that was satisfactory. She desired to give the

impression of an unusual, outstanding woman and Yat made an entirely suitable audience for her...Lobashkov, in the role of the telegraphist, Yat, created
a comic figure of an unlucky Don Juan, a romantic wooer from a very small
station in life. Not very tall, with short legs and a very long back, and with a
pince-nez dancing on his nose, he was ridiculous and rather pitiful.

The sailor from the Voluntary Fleet, as played by Zakhava, gave the impression of a cheerful person: an optimist, open-hearted and unassuming. The
important 'positive hero' of Vakhtangov's production of *A Wedding* was the
'General' – Captain Revunov-Karoulov – who was played by Basov with
warmth, simplicity, and much charm...

A foreigner of Greek origin, a confectioner by occupation, Kharlampy
Spiridonitch Dimba, looked in that surrounding like an exotic plant in a Russian
pine forest. Sociable, trusting, childishly hearty, he saw in every person at the
wedding a bosom friend. Warmed by wine, he felt as though he were in a blissful dream: the holiday, the music, the dancing, the festive table made an
enchanting impression on him. As soon as he found himself near the banquet
table, he reached a state of enthusiasm. I played the role of Dimba.[23]

And about the guests at the wedding, Simonov writes:

Look who surrounds the Gigalov family? Have they any true friends? No. All
the guests at the wedding – the midwife, the telegraphist, the sailor from the
Voluntary Fleet – are strangers who just happened to be at the wedding. The
Philistine's complacency leads to loneliness, and that is the frightening aspect of
Chekhov's *A Wedding*.[24]

This view is clearly supported by Nyunin's way of introducing the
'General' to the assembled guests – the majority are 'pretty small
beer'.

The loneliness, however, of *poshly* people is less immediately apparent
than the rows and conflicts which develop amongst them, rows caused,
in fact, by a succession of 'comic' misunderstandings: misunderstandings arising from 'irrelevancies', 'conversations-of-the-deaf', and the
situation.

The argument about the dowry which runs throughout the play, and
which is partly the cause of Aplombov's jaundiced attitude to the proceedings, is not in fact 'a misunderstanding'. It is one of the comparatively few arguments in any of the one-act plays in which the
characters understand each other only too well: clearly, the Zhigalovs
and Aplombov all know what was agreed on as the dowry. The
argument is, therefore, about *honouring* the understanding, and, as
such, becomes both more sordid and more revealing of the petty
philistine attitudes of a 'marriage of convenience'. The contestants are
equally matched: Aplombov will, no doubt, continue to be unpleasant

about his 'rights', while Mrs Zhigalov shows her ability to cope with the situation – she retreats into counting the places at the supper table while probably acutely aware of the empty chair waiting for the 'General'; and, subsequently, she either snaps at Aplombov or simply plays 'deaf' to his threats and demands. The conflict is not resolved with the ending of the play; clearly, it cannot be resolved given the personalities and values of the characters involved in the dispute.

The first real misunderstanding in the play arises, in fact, out of a 'comic irrelevance', and one which is an item on Chekhov's list of *Things Most Frequently Encountered in Novels, Stories and Other Such Things*: 'electricity – in the majority of cases dragged in for no particular reason'. Yat's totally irrelevant, apparently harmless, but unfortunate exposition of and pronouncement on the advantages and wonders of electric light is taken by Chekhov from his own list of clichés. It is irrelevant in the context in which it is brought into the supper table conversation; it is apparently harmless as a topic of conversation, but it is unfortunate in the way it is received by Yat's hosts. Even an apparently innocuous remark about electricity is taken as a slight by the Zhigalovs and by Aplombov: anything new is a threat to them; anything which they do not understand is seen merely as 'one-upmanship'. Yat may be, and is, pretentious, but he is also 'making conversation', and the fury with which his remark is received is only matched by the ignorance which it exposes. In a few lines, Chekhov turns the comic into an exposé of the truly ignorant, the bigoted and narrow-minded, indicative of social insecurity but, even more so, of *poshlost*:

YAT: I must say, ladies and gentlemen – always give credit where credit is due – this room and whole establishment are magnificent! They're terrific, charming! But you know, we do need one thing to set things off to perfection – electric light, if you'll pardon the expression. Electric light's come in all over the world – only Russia lags behind.

ZHIGALOV: (*with an air of profundity*) Electric light. I see. If you ask me, there's a lot of funny business about electric light. They shove in a little bit of coal and think no one will notice. No, dear boy, if we're to have light, don't give us your coal, but something with a bit of body to it, something solid that a man can get his teeth in. Give us real light, see? Natural light, not something imaginary.

YAT: If you'd seen what an electric battery's made of, you'd tell a different tale.

ZHIGALOV: I don't want to see. It's all a lot of funny business, to cheat the common man – squeeze him dry, they do, we know their sort! As for you, young feller-me-lad, don't you stick up for swindlers. Have a drink instead and fill up the glasses, that's my message to you!

APLOMBOV: I quite agree, Dad old man. Why trot out all the long words? Not that I mind discussing modern inventions, like, in a scientific manner of speaking. But there's a time and place for everything. (*To Dasha.*) What do you think, dear?

DASHA: The gentleman's only trying to show how brainy he is, talking about things no one understands.

MRS ZHIGALOV: We've lived our lives without book-learning, praise the Lord, and it didn't stop us finding good husbands for three daughters. If you think us so ignorant, why come here? Go and visit your smart friends.

(H.I.123)

It is ironic that Yat's initial remark about the light in the room is, in the first place, nonsense: as the opening stage directions make clear, the room is 'brilliantly lit'. It is also ironic that this argument provokes Aplombov into addressing his wife for the one and only time in the play – it is at this point that Dasha utters one of her two lines, and in so doing she conveys the essence of this wedding and the Zhigalov mentality: the worst motives are ascribed to other people (even if, in this case, accurately), and people are never given the benefit of the doubt; anything different and thus not understandable is dismissed as merely a new way of cheating, of squeezing, and of swindling. The Zhigalov mentality is projected onto everything and anything: people, in the Zhigalov milieu, are only either to be used or seen as a threat; modern inventions are part of a conspiracy to make them feel small: 'No, dear boy, if we're to have light, don't give us your coal, but...something solid that a man can get his teeth in. Give us real light, see? Natural light, not something imaginary.' It is also ironic that Zhigalov should demand 'the natural' and reject the invented or 'imaginary': the artificial has become natural to the Zhigalovs. It is partly this which is frightening in the play: the artificial, the pretentious, the second-rate, and the materially 'solid' are the only 'naturalness' which they understand, assume and expect. But in revealing this, in using the comic to expose the deeply serious and significant, Chekhov is not sneering at 'the little man' in the manner of many conventional vaudeville writers: Yat is no more enlightened or sympathetic than the Zhigalovs or Aplombov; he *is* pretentious and showing off, but, characteristically, the Zhigalovs are not simply ignorant, they are proud of their ignorance since they reject as unimportant or suspect anything which they do not understand. And it is this which colours their view of all relationships, whether their daughter's marriage, or Dymba the foreigner, or the General. The comic is used to communicate the dramatic.

Dymba is a confectioner but, more important, he is also a foreigner –

an 'exotic' Greek – and thus, in terms of the conventional vaudeville,
a source of comedy; in this way, Chekhov used a version or 'off-shoot'
of the comic 'conversation-of-the-deaf'. Dymba does not understand
the language of his hosts and fellow-guests but, equally, Zhigalov does
not understand the inanity of his own questions; in the nature of
Zhigalov's questions, his ignorance and his arrogance are again exposed.
The dialogue is extremely funny partly because (like Yat's speech) it is
composed of nonsense; but the fact that it *is* nonsense is also revealing.
Zhigalov and the other guests are incapable of simply accepting Dymba
as a fellow human being since they are not conscious of 'humanity' as
such, and thus, for them, Dymba is present in order to be 'exotic', and
to entertain them. His ignorance of their language has both curiosity
and entertainment value, but it also enables them to feel superior.
Zhigalov's 'conversation' with Dymba is, characteristically, both inane
and competitive:

ZHIGALOV: ...Tell me, are there tigers in Greece?
DYMBA: Yes, is tigers.
ZHIGALOV: And lions?
DYMBA: Is lions too. In Russia is nothing, in Greece is everything! In Greece is
    my father, my uncle, my brothers. Here is nothing, isn't it? (H.1.121)

Dymba is lonely, and – like the 'General' who will follow him as a
source of entertainment and the 'exotic' – he is not understood. This is
made evident also from a scene in an earlier version of the play which
Chekhov cut: in the 1889 version, Dymba is made to look even more
foolish when Mrs Zmeyukin gives him 'a prolonged kiss' in full view
of the wedding guests, and then faints with physical shock. Embarrassed
and perplexed, Dymba has retreated from her, but then tries desperately
to keep his balance; and when Mrs Zmeyukin recovers from her faint,
Dymba is only able to say: 'Why, pliss, isn't it?'[25] The more explicitly
farcical scene was cut by Chekhov in the script of 1890, and thus what
remains is more implicit in the use which the guests make of Dymba.
Thus:

ZHIGALOV: I see. And are there whales in Greece?
DYMBA: In Greece is every damn thing.
ZHIGALOV: Have you got lobsters in Greece?
DYMBA: We have. In Greece is damn all, I tell you!
ZHIGALOV: I see. Have you established civil servants too?
MRS ZMEYUKIN: I can imagine what a terrific atmosphere there is in Greece!
ZHIGALOV: And a terrific lot of funny business goes on too, I'll bet. The Greeks
    are just like the Armenians or gipsies, aren't they? Can't sell you a sponge
    or a goldfish without trying to do you down. (H.1.122)

Mrs Zmeyukin thinks only of 'atmosphere', Zhigalov thinks only of crooks and dirty deals, but Dymba, who understands almost nothing, falls silent. His function in the play is manifold: he is there as a source of the comic, but, in the treatment which he receives, Chekhov uses him also to reveal the serious; by being a foreigner, he broadens the horizon and perspective for the audience, and, in addition, he functions in the play partly as a dramatic preparation for Revunov-Karaulov. Both characters, for different reasons, are placed in a situation which they do not understand, both are treated as a source of entertainment and both are present because the Zhigalovs consider that they lend 'tone' to the proceedings. Thus, when the arrival of the 'General' is announced, Dymba's embarrassment at being forced into giving a public speech is ended:

ZHIGALOV: Are there mushrooms in Greece?

DYMBA: Is plenty. Is everything.

ZHIGALOV: Well, I bet there aren't any white and yellow ones like ours.

DYMBA: Is white. Is yellow. Is everything.

MOZGOVOY: Mr Dymba, it's your turn to make a speech. Let him speak, ladies and gentleman.

ALL: (*to Dymba*) Speech! Speech! Your turn!

DYMBA: Pliss? Do not understand –. What is which?

MRS ZMEYUKIN: Oh, no you don't – don't you dare try and wriggle out of it! It's your turn. Up you get!

DYMBA: (*stands up in embarrassment*) I speak, isn't it? Is Russia. Is Greece. Russian peoples is in Russia. Greek peoples is in Greece, isn't it? In sea is sailing-boots that Russians call sheep. Is railways on land. I am understanding very well, isn't it? We are Greeks, you are Russians and I am not needing anything, isn't it? I am also saying – . Is Russia. Is Greece –

(*Nyunin comes in.*)

NYUNIN: Just a moment, all of you – don't start eating just yet. One moment, Mrs Zhigalov, please come here. (*Takes Mrs Zhigalov on one side, panting.*) Listen. The General's on his way, I've got hold of one at last. Had a terrible time. It's a real General, very dignified, very old. He must be about eighty – ninety, even. (H.I.125)

The old man now takes Dymba's place as the centre of attention and, interrupted and forgotten, Dymba's value has come to an end. But it is with Nyunin's news that the climax of the wedding is reached for all the guests; at last the empty chair at the table will be filled, one part of the dowry will be 'paid in full', and the wedding will be made complete. As Simonov writes: 'These little people are growing in their own eyes.'[26] A real General is coming, and Mrs Zhigalov can hardly believe that she will get her money's worth:

NYUNIN: Any moment now. You'll be grateful to me all your life. He's a General and a half, a regular conquering hero! Not some wretched foot-slogging old square-basher, this – he's a General of the Fleet. His rank's Commander, and in naval lingo that's equal to a Major-General, or an Under-Secretary in the civil service, there's nothing in it. It's higher, in fact.

MRS ZHIGALOV: You're not pulling my leg are you, Andrew?

NYUNIN: What – think I'd swindle you, eh? Set your mind at rest.

MRS ZHIGALOV: (*sighing*) I don't want us to waste our money, Andrew.

(H.1.126)

And Nyunin, reassuring her, and raising his voice for the benefit of his audience, begins to improvise on his relationship with the General. The tension mounts as the guests hear of the imminent arrival of the General; Nyunin orders the band to play a march, and then follows a lengthy (in stage time) expectant 'pause' in the action as the band plays the march for 'a minute' and the frozen *tableau* of guests awaits the grand entrance. The waiter comes on to announce 'Mr Revunov-Karaulov', and as the guests stand 'Zhigalov, Mrs Zhigalov and Nyunin run to meet him'. By the guests' reactions, the formality of the announcement, the music of the march, and Mrs Zhigalov's introductory 'bow', Revunov's entrance is turned into the arrival of royalty. But for an audience, there is a comic disparity between expectation and the entrance of a rather surprised, puzzled old man of seventy-two. And once the introductions have been made, Chekhov introduces dramatic irony:

REVUNOV:...Excuse me, ladies and gentlemen, I must have a word with young Andrew. (*Takes Nyunin aside.*) I feel a bit awkward, my boy. Why all this 'General' stuff? It's not as if I was one – I'm a naval Commander, and that's even lower than a Colonel.

NYUNIN: (*speaks into his ear as if he was deaf*) I know, but please let us call you General, Commander. This is an old-fashioned family, see. They look up to their betters, they like to show due respect.

REVUNOV: Oh, in that case of course. (*Going to the table.*) Delighted!

MRS ZHIGALOV: Do sit down, General. Be so kind! And have something to eat and drink, sir. But you must excuse us, you being used to fancy things, like – we're plain folks, we are.

REVUNOV: (*not hearing*) What's that? I see. Very well. (*Pause.*) In the old days people all lived the simple life and were content. I live simply too, for all my officer's rank. Young Andrew comes to see me today and asks me to this wedding. 'How can I go,' I ask, 'when I don't know 'em? It's rather awkward.' 'Well,' says he, 'they're old-fashioned folk with no frills, always glad to have someone drop in.' Well, of course, if that's the way of

it – why not? Delighted! It's boring being on your own at home, and if
having me at a wedding can please anyone, they're only too welcome,
say I.

ZHIGALOV: So it was out of the kindness of your heart, General? I hand it to
you. I'm a plain man too. I don't hold with any sort of funny business, and
I respect people like myself. Help yourself, sir.   (H.I.127)

The dramatic irony is twofold, and creates the kind of tangle conventionally found in a farce-vaudeville: the audience and the guests
know that the General has been hired, but only the audience and Nyunin know that Revunov is not a *real* General. The levels of irony, however, are various: Nyunin, the smooth-talking insurance clerk, is
operating a 'double bluff'; Revunov has come because he was bored
and lonely, and out of kindness; Zhigalov is playing the man of simple
manners, honour and decency, and putting himself on the same plane
as Revunov; and all of them – with the exception of Revunov himself –
are playing out an elaborate charade, a ridiculous and snobbish custom.
Moreover, Revunov's discourse is, effectively, a monologue – Mozgovoy does not contribute a word, but his presence motivates Revunov's
tirade. It is, however, Revunov's naval 'irrelevancies' which provoke
Yat into further irrelevancies – instead of electricity, Yat brings in the
subject of morse. There is, almost, a competition in the irrelevant:

REVUNOV:…Every little word has its special meaning. For instance: 'Topmen
aloft! To the foresail and mainsail yards!' What does that mean? You can
bet your sailor knows! Tee hee hee! It's as tricky as geometry!

NYUNIN: To the health of General Theodore Revunov-Karaulov!

(*The band plays a flourish. Cheers.*)

YAT: Now, sir, you've just been telling us about the difficulties of naval service.
But telegraphing's no easier, you know. Nowadays, sir, no one can get a
job on the telegraph unless he can read and write French and German. But
the hardest thing we do is sending morse. It's a very tough job! Listen to
me, sir. (*Bangs his fork on the table in imitation of someone sending morse.*)

REVUNOV: What does that mean?   (H.I.128)

Yat's conversational offering, his flirtation with Mrs Zmeyukin in
morse, and his attempt to steal the limelight from Revunov are met
with total lack of interest from the old man; turning back to Mozgovoy,
Revunov carries on, lost in his own world and his own language. The
silence of the guests and the hosts is telling, but Revunov is deaf even to
Nyunin's plea: 'The guests can't make this out, and they're bored.'

Out of comic misunderstandings, and the resulting tangle, and out of
dramatic irony, Chekhov creates a situation arising organically from

the characters, in which expectations cannot possibly be rewarded – the expectations are based on the false and the pretentious, on trickery. But it is exactly because of Chekhov's use of dramatic irony that an audience's perception (and enjoyment) of the situation is increased, clarified, and controlled. The emphasis for an audience is, therefore, not on mystery and surprise, but on the working-out of a known situation: on the process. The audience is, in this way, prepared to watch the wedding party discover the truth about Revunov, and for Revunov to discover the true facts about the Zhigalovs' hospitality. The emphasis is not so much on *what* will happen next, as on *how* it will happen.[27] Simultaneously, however, Chekhov builds the action towards what appears to be a conventional *dénouement*.

The process of revelation begins to take place almost immediately, and it comes about by Chekhov's use of two conventional comic techniques: 'comic irrelevancies' and the 'conversation-of-the-deaf'. Spotting Mozgovoy in his sailor's uniform, Revunov recognises somebody who, he thinks, will speak his language, and he launches into a naval discourse which dominates the supper-table to the exclusion of everything and everyone else. This naval discourse, like Yat's introduction of the subject of electricity, is also found in Chekhov's 1880 list of clichés: 'an endless number of interjections, and attempts to use an appropriate technical term'. It relates also to one of the major requirements specified by Chekhov for a farce-vaudeville: 'each character must possess individual features and idiosyncrasies and must speak in a language of his own.' The Zhigalovs' earlier reaction to what they did not understand, namely Yat's brief remarks on electricity, have fully prepared an audience for their growing – if silent – fury and horror; the bride and groom are forgotten, the Best Man tries, and fails, to get a word in, and the guests are becoming restive. Implicit throughout Revunov's speeches is the reaction of his on-stage audience: the long-awaited event is going seriously wrong, and the 'General' is not behaving properly. And in the mounting tension, a fresh source of misunderstanding is at least clear to the Zhigalovs and their guests: Revunov is *literally* deaf!

BEST MAN: (*hastens to take advantage of the ensuing pause*) This evening, as we are, so to speak, gathered together to honour our dear –

REVUNOV: (*interrupting*) Yes, there's all that to remember, you know! For instance – let fly the foresheet, let fly the main!

BEST MAN: (*offended*) Why does he keep interrupting? We shan't get through a single speech at this rate.

MRS ZHIGALOV: We're poor benighted folk, sir, we can't make sense of all that. Why not tell us something about –

REVUNOV: (*not hearing*) I've already eaten, thanks. Goose, you say? No, thank you. Yes, it all comes back to me.   (H.1.129)

Revunov's deafness is, so to speak, the last straw; the guests and the Zhigalovs are no longer prepared to listen with respect and humility. The 'General', standing up and shouting, is excluding everybody, flattering nobody, and creating a disturbance. In Mrs Zhigalov's attempt to control him, and Revunov's deafness and incomprehension, the apparent *dénouement* is reached:

REVUNOV:...Then everything flies and cracks, a regular pandemonium, and it's all been done to perfection. We've brought her about!

MRS ZHIGALOV:(*flaring up*) And you a General! A hooligan, more like! You should be ashamed, at your time of life!

REVUNOV: (*mishearing*) A slice of tripe? Thanks, I don't mind if I do.

MRS ZHIGALOV:(*loudly*) I say you should be ashamed at your age! Call yourself a General, behaving like that!

NYUNIN: (*embarrassed*) Oh, look, everyone – why all the fuss? Really –

REVUNOV: Firstly, I'm not a General – I'm a naval Commander, which is equal to Lieutenant-Colonel in the army.

MRS ZHIGALOV: If you aren't a General, why take the money? We didn't pay good money for you to break up the happy home!

REVUNOV: (*bewildered*) Pay what money?   (H.1.130)

It is Mrs Zhigalov's fury at what she thinks of as a bad investment which finally outweighs the need to maintain the hypocritical pretence of the 'General's' presence at her daughter's wedding, and as she reveals the vulgar pretentiousness of the custom of hiring a general, Revunov at last realises how he has been used, and that 'a rotten, dirty trick' has been played on him. And, ironically, the Zhigalovs and Aplombov indict him for the very 'crimes' of which they themselves are guilty – pretending to be someone other than himself, and taking money under false pretences. Thus, it is in Revunov's response, in his realisation of the insults and humiliation meted out to him, that the real *dénouement* takes place – the dramatic indictment. The 'comic' *dénouement* has already taken place, but in Revunov's dazed response the seriousness of the play is encapsulated and exposed; until this moment in the play, the dramatic and serious implications have been implicit and subtextual, but with Revunov's 'Howl-for-help' and his exit, the milieu, the characters, and the atmosphere are explicitly indicted:

REVUNOV: I took no money. Get away from me! (*Stands up from the table.*) What a filthy, rotten trick! To insult an old sailor, an officer who's seen honorable service. If this was a respectable house I could challenge someone to a duel, but what can I do here? (*In despair.*) Where's the door? Which is the way out? Waiter, take me out! Waiter!²⁸ (*Moves off.*) What a filthy, rotten trick! (*Goes out.*) (H.1.131)

It is this which is the real climax of the play, but it is a climax of which only the audience are aware. Insulted and humiliated, but with his dignity re-established, Revunov leaves the table and exits – alone. The contrast between his entrance and his exit contains an indictment of an 'atmosphere' in which Generals are hired for weddings – and human beings are gratuitously insulted.

In the original *A Wedding with a General*, the story ends with the old man's exit:

The old man glanced from the suddenly blushing Andryusha²⁹ to his hostess, and saw it all. The 'prejudices' of a patriarchal family spoken of by Andryusha rose before him in all their loathsomeness...His tipsiness vanished in a moment ...Rising from the table, he shuffled into the hall, put on his coat and went away...He never again went to a wedding.

But in the play, Chekhov creates a different tone with the ending, and makes a different (and stronger) point: he shows clearly that for the Zhigalovs and their guests there was no climax, only an anti-climax which demands a reckoning. Revunov's feelings are ignored because they are neither understood nor recognised; all that is understood is that the Zhigalovs did not get their money's worth. Thus, when Revunov leaves, not a word is uttered about him: Mrs Zhigalov demands to know from Nyunin where the twenty-five roubles have gone, but for Nyunin what has happened is 'a lot of fuss about nothing'. Nyunin's dismissal of the situation is a dismissal not only of the money, but also of Revunov. Thus for the Zhigalovs what has happened is measured and calculated only in terms of money: it was a swindle and, no doubt, opens up a fresh source of future conflict; for the rest of the guests, *nothing* has happened. And the band starts up again, Yat pursues Mrs Zmeyukin, the Best Man reasserts his role of Master of Ceremonies, and thus the vulgarity and meanness of this philistine wedding starts up again with 'a lot of noise'.

The philistines, the *poshly* people, are indicated by their own behaviour, by their own values, and by their treatment of each other. Thus the true ending of the play is in the return to the previous action as if nothing has happened. The true ending, in fact, is that there is no ending, and certainly not a 'happy' one. The *dénouement* has taken place but the play, like *The Three Sisters*, is not resolved. In this atmosphere – as Mrs Zmeyukin constantly reminds the audience – there is no fresh air: it is 'brilliantly lit', but the air is stifling, congested and stale.

In a letter of 25 December 1901, Chekhov referred to the play as 'a farce'. The play *is* extremely funny: 'comic is represented here in all its many gradations – now caustic sarcasm, now quiet humour, now pointed satire or clever irony',[30] but the comedy is used as a critical weapon, as a means of ensuring objectivity, and as a means of controlling the audience's perception of character and milieu. The play may be seen as a 'comedy of manners', as a 'comic scene of daily life', but it utilises the comic conventions of the farce-vaudeville in a completely new way: the 'content' demands a new 'form', and thus Chekhov breaks down the barriers between comedy and drama – the farce-vaudeville becomes 'a play'.

6

A monologue in one act

Smoking is Bad for You (1886-1903)

In Act 2, scene i of Gogol's *The Government Inspector* (1835), the petty officials come on one by one to pay their respects to the 'government inspector' Khlestakov. Amongst them are Bobchinsky and Dobchinsky who, typically, go as a pair to see Khlestakov. Towards the end of their 'audience' with him, the following conversation takes place:

KHLESTAKOV:... (*he turns to Bobchinsky*) And is there anything I can do for you?
BOBCHINSKY: Yes, indeed, Excellency. A humble request.
KHLESTAKOV: Well? What is it?
BOBCHINSKY: When you go back to Petersburg, Excellency, I humbly beg you should say to these grand people, these admirals and senators and that, say to them, 'Your Grace...your Serenity...' or whatever it is...'in this little town there lives a man called Peter Ivanovich Bobchinsky!' Just you tell them that: 'There lives a man called Peter Ivanovich Bobchinsky!'
KHLESTAKOV: All right.
BOBCHINSKY: And if you should happen to meet the Tsar, Excellency, you say to him, 'Do you know, Your Imperial Majesty, in this little town there lives a man called Peter Ivanovich Bobchinsky!'[1]

In Act 4 of Chekhov's last play, *The Cherry Orchard* (1903-4), the neighbouring landowner Simeonov-Pishchik realises that Ranevskaya and Gaev are leaving – that their estate has not been saved, as his has been, by Englishmen finding clay on their land:

MRS RANEVSKY: We're just leaving for town and I'm going abroad tomorrow.
PISHCHIK: What! (*Deeply concerned.*) Why go to town? Oh, I see, the furniture and luggage. Well, never mind. (*Through tears.*) It doesn't matter. Colossally clever fellows, these English. Never mind. All the best to you. God bless you. It doesn't matter. Everything in this world comes to an end. (*Kisses Mrs Ranevsky's hand.*) If you should ever hear that my end has come, just remember – remember the old horse, and say, 'There once lived such-and-such a person, a certain Simeonov-Pishchik, may his bones rest in peace.' Remarkable weather we're having. (H.3.194)

Although differently emphasised, and in a different context, both Bobchinsky and Simeonov-Pishchik are asking for the same thing: in the realisation that they are nonentities, that they have left no mark, no trace of their existence, each – in his own way – is asking for a moment of immortality, a moment of recognition. It is this same tone which informs the ending of Nyukhin's monologue in *Smoking is Bad for You*:

I say, my wife's out there in the wings. She's turned up and she's waiting for me there. (*Looks at his watch.*) Time's up. If she asks, please, please tell her the lecture was, er – that the imbecile, meaning me, behaved with dignity.   (H.1.158)

In the eyes of his wife and in the eyes of the world, Nyukhin is 'an imbecile'; in his own eyes he is a ridiculous figure, but in this self-awareness there is a desperate longing for some dignity. It is in the discrepancy between what he used to be, or could have been, and what he now is that the tragi-comic point of the play lies. His ambition in life is now only for 'peace and quiet' or, comically, to be a scarecrow or a wooden post, but in the past Nyukhin had different ambitions; now he is only able to vent his frustrations on his tail-coat, and talk of his nagging, domineering wife in terms of comic exaggeration:

One glass is enough to make me drunk, I might add. It feels good but indescribably sad at the same time. Somehow the days of my youth come back to me, I somehow long – more than you can possibly imagine – to escape. (*Carried away.*) To run away, leave everything behind and run away without a backward glance. Where to? Who cares? If only I could escape from this rotten, vulgar, tawdry existence that's turned me into a pathetic old clown and imbecile! Escape from this stupid, petty, vicious, nasty, spiteful, mean old cow of a wife who's made my life a misery for thirty-three years! Escape from the music, the kitchen, my wife's money, and all these vulgar trivialities! Oh, to stop somewhere in the depths of the country and just stand there like a tree or a post or a scarecrow on some vegetable plot under the broad sky, and watch the quiet, bright moon above you all night long and forget, forget! How I'd love to lose my memory! How I'd love to tear off this rotten old tail-coat that I got married in thirty years ago (*tears off his tail-coat*), the one I always wear when I lecture for charity. So much for you! (*Stamps on the coat.*) Take that! I'm a poor, pathetic old man like this waistcoat with its shabby moth-eaten back. (*Shows the back.*) I don't need anything. I'm above all these low, dirty things.   (H.1.157–8)

Even the form which Nyukhin's rebellion takes – tearing off and trampling on his tail-coat – is farcical and ridiculous. It is ridiculous because it is petty and inadequate, but its symbolic significance is not petty: the tail-coat represents thirty years of a life; the waistcoat represents the shabby moth-eaten man beneath the tail-coat. And Nyukhin vaguely recognises the gulf which separates what he once was, and what he might have been, and the man he now is: 'Once I was young and clever and went to college. I had dreams and I felt like a human being.' In *Smoking is Bad for You*, an audience sees a man, Nyukhin, whose true face has already become hopelessly blurred, washed out by thirty-three years of married existence, but in *The Three Sisters* an audience watches the process of disintegration and blurring as it happens to Andrey over the time-span of the play. Thus in Act 1, Irina tells the audience that 'Andrey's probably going to be a professor'; in Act 2, after a year of marriage to Natasha, Andrey uses Ferapont's deafness to express thoughts which he knows Ferapont will not hear:

ANDREW:...Isn't it funny, my dear old fellow, how things change? And isn't life a swindle? Today I was bored and at a loose end, so I picked up this book, my old university lecture notes, and couldn't help laughing. God, I'm secretary of the county council and the chairman's Protopopov. I'm secretary, and the most I can ever hope for is to get on the council myself. Me - stuck here as a councillor, when every night I dream I'm a professor at Moscow University, a distinguished scholar, the pride of all Russia.   (H.3.94)

At the end of Act 3, after the birth of two children and several years of marriage to Natasha, Andrey aggressively justifies Natasha, his gambling, and his council work to his sister, and in the same act Irina makes explicit the disintegration which has taken place in Andrey:

IRINA: I must say, poor old Andrew has gone to seed. Living with that wretched woman has put years on his life and knocked all the stuffing out of him. At one time he was aiming to be a professor, and there he was yesterday boasting he'd got on the county council at long last. He's on the council and Protopopov's the chairman. The whole town's talking about it, everyone's laughing at him and he's the only one who doesn't know or see what's going on. And when everyone rushed off to the fire just now, there was he sitting in his room not taking the slightest notice and just playing his violin. (*Upset.*) Oh, it's frightful, absolutely frightful.   (H.3.118-19)

But in the last act of the play, Masha - watching Andrey walking up and down as he pushes the pram - puts into words the process of erosion and disintegration which time wreaks on the weak, the cowardly, or the unaware:

MASHA: There goes brother Andrew. All our hopes have come to nothing. Imagine thousands of people hoisting up a huge bell. Then after all the effort and money spent on it, it suddenly falls and is smashed to pieces. Suddenly, for no reason at all. That's how it's been with Andrew.

(H.3.128)

This, like the Button Moulder's words in *Peer Gynt*, 'You were going to be a shining button on the world's waistcoat, but your loop gave way,' expresses in graphic terms what happens when youth and promise are not fulfilled. But, like Nyukhin, Andrey is aware of what is happening to him; in the same act he confesses to Chebutykin what his real feelings are towards Natasha:

ANDREW:...there's something degrading about her too, as if she were some kind of blind, groping, scruffy little animal. She's not a human being anyway...I love Natasha, yes I do, but there are times when I find her thoroughly vulgar.

(H.3.130)

And a short time later, in the last act, Andrey expresses himself in words very similar to Nyukhin's:

ANDREW: Where is my past life, oh what has become of it – when I was young, happy and intelligent, when I had such glorious thoughts and visions, and my present and future seemed so bright and promising? Why is it we've hardly started living before we all become dull, drab, boring, lazy, complacent, useless and miserable?

(H.3.133)

In the same play, Kulygin comforts himself with the fact that he is a school teacher, and that he actually has 'the order of St. Stanislaus second class', but even he dimly realises that 'there's more to happiness than that'. Chebutykin, on the other hand, is too far eroded, too far removed, to care about anything (except Irina): 'Anyway, what does it all matter?' In this way a number of characters in Chekhov's plays have seduced themselves into making a virtue of what they gradually think of as an inevitability. In *The Three Sisters*, the movement of Andrey's erosion as a human being is spiritual and moral (although he is also 'getting stout'), but in *The Seagull*, again over the time-span of the play, Sorin is seen to degenerate physically, while in *The Cherry Orchard* Ranevskaya's failure to recognise Trofimov, and her subsequent reaction, indicates to an audience at his first entrance the extent to which he has physically altered:

MRS RANEVSKY:...Well, Peter? Why have you grown so ugly? And why do you look so old?

TROFIMOV: A woman in the train called me 'that seedy-looking gent'.

MRS RANEVSKY: You were only a boy in those days, just a nice little under-
graduate. But now you're losing your hair and wear these spectacles. You
can't still be a student, surely? (*Moves towards the door.*)

TROFIMOV: I'll obviously be a student for the rest of time.

MRS RANEVSKY: (*kisses her brother and then Varya*) Well, go to bed then. You
look older too, Leonid. (H.3.158)

Trofimov is not yet thirty, but it would seem that he is ageing pre-
maturely, he has not yet grown a beard, but is losing his hair; he has
not yet lost his ideals or enthusiasm (or priggishness), but his life-style
leaves its mark. From Chekhov's letters it is clear that Trofimov has
been several times expelled from the university and exiled for political
activities, but at the end of the play both Trofimov and Anya welcome
the future. Trofimov's potential is qualified by what an audience has
discovered about his character, but both Trofimov and Anya leave the
stage in Act 4 with the still unrealised potential of enthusiasm and youth.
The possibilities are qualified, but not resolved. This question, of the
potential of youth contrasted with the waste of thoughtless or deluded
existence or old age, is a central question running throughout much of
Chekhov's work, both literary and dramatic: in *A Tragic Role*, the henpecked Tolkachov realises that there must be more to life, that something has eluded him; in *Swan Song*, the old actor Svetlovidov measures
himself by what he was and what he might have been, and the same is
true of Vanya. The cause, however, is not always the same – this is not a
process of weathering, but of degeneration, of wasteful existence, not
fulfilled living; it happens, however, for one of two basic reasons:
either *poshlost* or self-delusion. But in all cases in Chekhov's plays, the
characters are brought to a point of recognition; and with the characters, so an audience is brought to a similar point of recognition and
realisation not to wallow in sad resignation, but – held at a distance – to
observe that things need not be so: in Gorky's quotation of Chekhov's
words, 'You live badly, my friends. It is shameful to live like that.'[2]
As in Brecht's plays, so the 'tragedy' in Chekhov's plays is, generally,
shown as avoidable. Thus Vanya 'endures' with his eyes open;
or Svetlovidov realises that it is too late for him, that he is too old, or
Konstantin – shamefully – kills himself while he is still a young, promising and talented man. Andrey and Nyukhin, however, have petty and
momentary rebellions and continue in the same way.

The similarity between Andrey and Nyukhin goes further than the
common disparity between what they might have been, and what they
are; in addition, each is 'the husband of his wife' or – as Nyukhin puts

it in the 1889 version of the play – each is 'my wife's husband'.[3] Andrey is both a cuckold and dominated by Natasha; Nyukhin is the stock character of the harassed, henpecked husband.

This, however, is but one feature of the play which utilises certain conventions of the farce-vaudeville: the play involves some farcical stage action which, however, emanates from the apparently 'stock' figure of the henpecked husband, and the form of the play is that of a 'monologue scene'. *Smoking is Bad for You* is the only apparently 'true' monologue scene which Chekhov wrote: *Swan Song*, written in 1887–8, is, initially and apparently, a monologue and, after Nikita's entrance, becomes a kind of 'false monologue'; *A Tragic Role*, written in 1889, is a 'false monologue' in that the presence of Murashkin motivates Tolkachov's frenzied tirade, but in *Smoking is Bad for You*, Nyukhin is alone on stage. But far from utilising an artificial and out-moded convention, Chekhov motivates the form of the play by its setting and context: 'The stage represents the platform in the hall of a provincial club', and Ivan Nyukhin, 'a henpecked husband whose wife keeps a music school and a girls' boarding-school', is giving a lecture for charity. But in what, at first glance, may appear to be one of the most artificial of Chekhov's one-act plays there are, in fact, the greatest number of innovations. Nyukhin is giving a lecture for charity; he 'struts in majestically... bows and adjusts his waistcoat' and begins with 'Ladies and er, in a manner of speaking, gentlemen.' He is addressing his audience in the hall of a provincial club but, in fact, he is addressing an audience in the theatre. The play is a reversal of the situation in *Swan Song*: Svetlovidov constantly refers to the audience as absent, but in *Smoking is Bad for You* it is not only present, but specifically addressed, appealed to and pleaded with by Nyukhin. It is therefore not only recognised, but is given a specific role: in *Swan Song*, Svetlovidov denies its presence; in a different way in this play, Chekhov extends the 'stage situation' into the auditorium and thus an audience is no longer a spectator, but a participant. It is, therefore, the active presence and participation of an audience for Nyukhin's lecture which makes the play, in some respects, a 'false monologue': if an audience was absent, Nyukhin's lecture would not take place at all, but its presence not only motivates the lecture, but also motivates the form which that 'lecture' takes.

This dual role of an audience (of both Nyukhin's lecture and the play) has, however, a double effect: on the one hand, an audience is in the same situation as Nyukhin, namely part of the lecture and in a provincial club; but, equally, the audience is also in a theatre. In this way, an audience is forced to take stock, to respond, and to assess a character who is addressing them directly. This dual effect is better-known to audiences of the twentieth century when watching any one of a number of Brecht's plays in which, for example, the staging of a trial in a courtroom makes an audience both spectator and involved in the stage situation as judge or jury. Thus, the physical placing on stage of Arturo Ui when he is addressing the mass-meeting of the Chicago grocers at the end of *The Resistible Rise of Arturo Ui* means that Ui is also addressing a theatre audience as an extension of his on-stage audience; in a similar way, the absence of a jury and the inadequacy of the judges in *The Good Person of Szechwan* or *The Caucasian Chalk Circle* means that the role of jury and judge is of dramatic and social necessity given to the audience. In *Smoking is Bad for You*, however, there is no trial; there is not even a token stage audience which would serve as a mirror or a conductor for the theatre audience, as there is in Act I of *The Seagull;* instead, there is a direct appeal from Nyukhin to fellow-participants at the lecture and to members of a theatre audience:

About tobacco as such, I just couldn't care less. But I suggest, ladies and gentlemen, that you attend to my present lecture with all due seriousness, or something worse may happen. If anyone's scared or put off by the idea of a dry, scientific lecture, he can stop listening and go. (H.1.155)

This 'back-handed' attitude to an audience is better known in music hall, and it has the immediate and apparently contradictory effect of making an audience pay closer attention. At the same time, however, Nyukhin's attitude to his audience forces them into an attitude towards him: he asks any doctors in the audience to pay particular attention, and then vaguely mutters a few incoherent sentences on a subject about which he clearly knows nothing, namely, the harmful effect of tobacco; he tells the audience that no doubt it would 'rather hear a song, a symphony or an aria or something', and then proceeds to sing a line from a song; and he uses the context of the lecture (clearly on instructions from his wife) to advertise both his wife's school and his daughters:

The wife's available at home to interview parents at any time, and if you want a prospectus, they're on sale in the porter's lodge at thirty copecks each. (*Takes several prospectuses from his pocket.*) Or I can let you have some of these if you like. Thirty copecks a whack. Any takers? (*Pause.*) None? All right then, I'll make it twenty. (*Pause.*) How annoying. (H.1.156-7)

This music hall approach is followed, a little later, by Nyukhin's attempt to advertise his daughters; he 'approaches the footlights' and says:

My wife's daughters are on view on high days and holidays at their Aunt Natalya's – that's the one who has rheumatism and goes round in a yellow dress with black spots on, looking as if she had black-beetles all over her. Snacks are served too, and when my wife's away you can get a bit of you know what. (*Makes a suitable gesture to indicate drinking.*) (H.1.157)

And at the end of the play, it is to the recipients of his lecture and thus to the audience in the theatre that Nyukhin says: 'If she asks, please, please tell her the lecture was, er – that the imbecile, meaning me, behaved with dignity.' It is, therefore, for the members of the audience to decide what they would say to Mrs Nyukhina; it is for the audience to assess whether 'the imbecile' did, in fact, behave with dignity; any doctors must decide whether they did, in fact, benefit from the lecture; any single men must decide whether they would wish to view these seven daughters, and any parents in the audience must question whether they would wish to send their daughters to the school. An audience must, in fact, assess Nyukhin's life and his attitude, partly because of his requests, partly because of his confidentiality, and partly because of the audience's own role.

In *A Tragic Role*, it is partly Murashkin's presence which helps to provide an audience with a sense of proportion; in *Swan Song*, it is largely the theatre setting which distances an audience; but in *Smoking is Bad for You*, it is the audience's own dual role which provides a sense of proportion which, with the comedy in the play, serves as a 'distancing' technique. Thus Chekhov uses the conventional and artificial form of the 'monologue scene', but he gives it a setting, motivation and context which, in effect, partly ensures objectivity and detachment from an audience. The audience is both participant and spectator, involved and detached.

The detachment, however, is also achieved by the comedy of the play – comedy which emanates organically from Nyukhin's personality and behaviour. The play is therefore a comedy of character – but, in addition, Chekhov uses the comedy technique of 'comic irrelevancies' as, in a sense, the content of the play. Thus, when Nyukhin begins his lecture he, eventually, states explicitly that 'the wife told me to give today's lecture on why tobacco's bad for you', but the lecture becomes almost a 'stream of consciousness' revelation of Nyukhin's situation, grievances, despair, dreams and reality – it is *not* on 'why tobacco's bad for you.' This is made clear, also, by the number of times Nyukhin himself interrupts his own thought-processes and 'irrelevant' wanderings with lines such as: 'time being short, let's not wander from the subject in hand', or 'However (*looks at his watch*), we've somewhat erred and strayed from our subject'. The whole play is composed of 'irrelevancies' but, as in *The Anniversary*, the apparently irrelevant becomes the real action of the play. Equally, part of the comedy, as in *The Proposal* or *The Anniversary*, arises from the conflict between the supposed action, namely the lecture, and the resulting action, namely the 'irrelevancies'. But whereas in *The Proposal* the conflict between what is intended and what actually happens is largely farcical, in *Smoking is Bad for You* it is not: the lecture becomes evidence of Nyukhin's burden, and an image of his situation, while the 'irrelevancies' are, in fact, the unburdening of a desperate and unhappy man. Glancing repeatedly into the wings, looking constantly at his watch, Nyukhin is truly terrified of his wife and terrified of not doing what he is supposed to be doing. The imminent arrival of Mrs Nyukhina adds an external tension and time-limit to the situation in a way not dissimilar to the imminent arrival of the deputation in *The Anniversary;* at the same time, however, it is her absence which allows Nyukhin to 'get a load off his mind'. As he says:

Anyway, I don't think she's turned up yet – she isn't here, so I can say what I like. I really get the willies when she looks at me. (H.1.157)

Out of the conventional laughing-stock of the henpecked husband Chekhov creates a character who is completely three-dimensional, and the balance between the pathetic and the comic is seen very clearly in the characterisation. Thus Nyukhin – to whom Chekhov gives the 'meaningful name' of 'Sniffer' – reveals not only his own (comic) situation, but his own serious attitude to that situation; not only a ridiculous way of life, but a frightening milieu, and not only the comic grotesque, but also the pathetic. His unhappiness is only matched by his dislike of his wife; his despair is only matched by his weakness. Nyukhin's constant frame of reference is either his wife or, as he aptly phrases it, his wife's daughters, or the girls at the school: he is surrounded by females, but he is completely dominated by them. As he puts it in the 1890 version of the play, 'There's only one man in the whole school – myself. But parents can rest assured as far as I'm concerned'.[4] This line was subsequently cut by Chekhov; it is, in any case, implicit in Nyukhin's character, and in his situation. In a complete reversal of the accepted role, it is Nyukhin, the only man, who performs the work conventionally done by the woman:

I'm the school matron. I buy food, keep an eye on the servants, do the accounts, make up exercise-books, exterminate bed-bugs, take the wife's dog for walks and catch mice. Last night I had the job of issuing flour and butter to Cook because we were going to have pancakes today. (H.1.156)

In addition, Nyukhin performs other tasks which increase an audience's perception both of his situation and of the nature of the school:

By the way, I forgot to say that besides being matron in the wife's school of music, I also have the job of teaching mathematics, physics, chemistry, geography, history, singing scales, literature and all that. My wife charges extra for dancing, singing and drawing, though I'm also the singing and dancing master. (H.1.156)

No other teacher in the school is mentioned, but it is in this ridiculous excess, the hyperbole, that the comedy also lies. At the same time, however, the origins of Nyukhin's situation are explained by his financial position:

Between you and me, my wife likes to complain of being hard up, but she's got a tidy bit salted away – a cool forty or fifty thousand – while I haven't a penny to my name, not a bean. But what's the use of talking? (H.1.156)

Thus the school, the seven daughters, the dog, the mice, the bed-bugs, everything, belongs to 'the wife'.

Nyukhin also communicates his situation and his character by his clear knowledge and awareness of other people's attitude to him:

I'm a complete failure, I've grown old and stupid. Here I am lecturing and looking pretty pleased with myself, when I really feel like screaming or taking off for the ends of the earth. There's no one to complain to, it's enough to bring tears to your eyes. You'll say I have my daughters. What of my daughters? They only laugh when I talk to them. (H.1.157)

Nyukhin's daughters laugh at him, and so too does an audience; he wants someone to complain to, and he complains to the audience; but as the play progresses the laughter is increasingly *with* Nyukhin, and not *at* him. Time and again he anticipates the audience's response to him, and it is by this disarming self-awareness that Nyukhin engages the sympathy and compassion of the audience. This sympathy is still, however, combined with detachment about his faults, weaknesses and inadequacy. Nyukhin is superstitious, and his endless harping on the number '13' is both comic and ridiculous. He makes the number '13' responsible for everything which is wrong with his life, including the twitch in his right eye:

I'm a nervous wreck by and large, and this eye-twitching business started back in September 1889, on the thirteenth of the month – the very day when my

wife gave birth, in a manner of speaking, to our fourth daughter Barbara. My
daughters were all born on the 13th.   (H.1.155–6)

And:

Our school of music is at Number Thirteen, Five Dogs Lane.[5] That's probably
why I've always had such bad luck – living at Number Thirteen. My daughters
were born on the thirteenth of the month too, and the house has thirteen
windows. But what's the use of talking?   (H.1.156)

It is part of the comic hyperbole of the whole play that each of the seven
daughters should have been born on the 13th. At the same time,
Nyukhin conjures up a vivid picture of himself obsessively counting
the windows of the house. Equally, the constant reiteration of the
number '33' – the years of his marriage – reveals his attitudes and
obsessions. And in everything he says, Nyukhin builds up a picture of a
milieu in which 'we've even got bugs in our piano'. Thus, just as
Tolkachov creates a whole world and milieu in *A Tragic Role*, so
Nyukhin creates the school, the family, Aunt Natalya, and the character
of a wife who becomes as real to an audience as do Protopopov and
Vershinin's wife. It is inevitable that an audience, listening to Nyukhin's
comically exaggerated picture of his wife, would question the truth of
this 'characterisation *in absentia*': 'this stupid, petty, vicious, nasty,
spiteful, mean old cow of a wife who's made my life a misery for
thirty-three years'. But however exaggerated Nyukhin's portrait of his
wife may be, he builds up a picture of a *poshly* life and *poshly* people, a
world of trivialities, vulgarity and meanness. In these terms, he does
demonstrate an awareness, albeit paralysed, of something better in life,
but it is like Andrey's awareness in *The Three Sisters*, that he is being
sucked in by Natasha to a way of life quite different from his dreams
and earlier aspirations. Natasha, like Mrs Nyukhina, is stupid, petty,
spiteful, and mean:

NATASHA:...I must look a sight. (*Stands in front of the mirror.*) People say I've
    put on weight. But it's not true, not a bit of it. Masha's asleep – tired out,
    poor girl. (*To Anfisa, coldly.*) How dare you be seated in my presence?
    Stand up! Be off with you! (*Anfisa goes out. Pause.*) Why you keep that
    old woman I don't understand.
OLGA: (*taken aback*) I'm sorry, I don't quite understand either.
NATASHA: There's no place for her here. She came from a village and she
    should go back to her village. This is sheer extravagance. I like to see a
    house run properly, there's no room for misfits in this house.   (H.3.111)

By the same token, Mrs Nyukhina's attitude to her husband is indicated
by her rhetorical question: '"Why feed you, imbecile?" she asks.'

Nyukhin, however, is spineless and weak: he accepts insults and humiliation and thus colours other people's view of him. His fear of his wife leads him into both hypocrisy and pseudo-intellectual pretensions:

I'm not a professor, of course, and university degrees have passed me by. Still, for the last thirty years I've been working – non-stop, you might even say, ruining my health and all that – on problems of a strictly academic nature. I've done a lot of thinking, and even written some learned scientific articles, believe it or not – well, not exactly learned, but in the scientific line, as you might say. By the way, I wrote a great screed the other day on 'The Ill Effects Caused by Certain Insects.' (H.1.155)

Characteristically, Nyukhin writes on the harmfulness of insects, and lectures on the harmfulness of tobacco (although, as he says, he is a smoker himself), but he is not able to write, lecture, or talk about the benefits of anything – except Keating's Powder.

Nyukhin's movements and gestures make their own telling comment on his character: when he first enters, he 'struts in majestically', and at the end of his monologue his exit is the same, 'Bows and struts out majestically'; he says, in Latin worthy of Kulygin, 'That's the end. *Dixi et animam levavi* !', but all he has done is to get a load off his mind. Nothing has changed; he does not escape from his 'rotten, vulgar, tawdry existence' which has turned him into a 'pathetic old clown and imbecile'. He comes on as a pathetic old clown, and he goes off in the same way. But for an audience, the balance between sympathy and detachment is upheld: his 'right eye usually twitches', but Nyukhin has a 'majestic strut'. The 'little man' who gives a lecture for charity is, himself, deserving of charity: his frustration and his despair are clearly expressed by the farcical action of stamping on an old coat, but this farcical and ridiculous action also reveals the inadequacy of his rebellion. It is the impotent rage of a child which is expressed by this act, not the significant rebellion of a grown man. In this way, the physical is used comically to expose a serious moral and spiritual state.

The writing of *Smoking is Bad for You* occupied Chekhov at intervals over sixteen years of his creative life, starting in 1886, after *On the High Road* and before *Swan Song* and *Ivanov*, and ending, with the sixth and final version of the play, in 1903, after *The Three Sisters*, and while he was planning *The Cherry Orchard*. The first version was completed on 14 February 1886, on which day Chekhov wrote in a letter: 'I've just finished my monologue *Smoking is Bad for You*, which was intended in my heart of hearts for the comic actor Gradov-Sokolov',[6] but instead Chekhov sent it to the *Peterburgskaya Gazeta*, in which it was published

on 17 February. It was published, revised, in January 1887; revised
again by 30 May 1889, and then revised again in 1890, in 1902, and in
1903, by which time Chekhov regarded the play as an 'entirely new
work'.[7] This constant reworking of what has been effectively dismissed
as simply 'an amusing trifle'[8], illustrates clearly the significance which
Chekhov attached to this short 'monologue in one act'. In addition,
however, his view that the play was a different one in 1903 from the
first and earlier drafts is justified by the major alteration of the mood
and tone: from the farce of 1886, it became the tragi-comedy of 1903.[9]
These alterations, over a sixteen-year period, relate to the characterisation of Nyukhin, the treatment of his situation, and – as a result – the
attitude and response of an audience: the point of the play is made more
and more by implication. This is evident, for example, in the change
which Chekhov made to Nyukhin's Christian name: in the versions of
1889 and 1890, Nyukhin is given the more pretentious and unlikely
name of Marcellus; in the 1903 script of the play, however, he is given
the commonplace and ordinary Russian name, Ivan. In the same way,
the 'sixth daughter, Veronica' of 1889, becomes 'the fourth daughter'
of 1890 and, in turn, the 'fourth daughter Barbara' in the last versions.
Equally, the number of Nyukhin's daughters was cut down from nine
to seven. In this way, Chekhov reduced the completely farcical hyperbole, and gave his characters ordinary, everyday names. By the
same token, Chekhov reduces the comic effect of Nyukhin's physical
sufferings, yet the economy utilised still conveys the same point: in the
1889 version, Nyukhin has a violent attack of asthma; by 1890, this has
been altered into the – funnier – attack of hiccups which interrupts the
lecture; but by the last revision of the play this has been reduced to the
more subtle nervous twitch in Nyukhin's right eye, a twitch which
does not stop the lecture, but of which both Nyukhin and his audience
are equally conscious. Nyukhin's suffering at the hands of the girls in
the school is implied in the last revision of the play, but in the earlier
versions he takes a snuff-box out of his pocket only to discover that
'these wretched, miserable girls' have been 'mucking around with it
again'; 'Yesterday they put face-powder in my snuff-box, today it's
something burning and poisonous'. This, in fact, increases the sympathy
for Nyukhin, as he continues, 'What a dirty trick, to make fun of an
old man like that! (*Sneezes.*) After all, I'm old – I'm sixty-eight.
(*Pause.*)'[10] By cutting this very explicit unkindness out of the play, and
by cutting any specific reference to Nyukhin's age, Chekhov reduced
the possibility of sentimentality in an audience's response. He also cut
down on the number and nature of Nyukhin's gestures and move-

ments – whereas in the earlier versions, he went through a succession of very different gestures, in the final version Nyukhin makes fewer gestures, but they are repetitive: he consistently looks at his watch, glances into the wings, and adjusts his tailcoat.

As a result of these (and other) alterations, the emphasis of the play shifts increasingly from the 'comic scene' of a man giving a lecture on a subject about which he clearly knows nothing, to a tragi-comic emphasis on the man himself; the language is simplified; a number of farcical elements are reduced and decreased, and more is implied about the tragi-comedy of a 'little man'. An audience is increasingly kept at a distance, rather than at any time wallowing in a sentimental response to Nyukhin – as a result, the emphasis is on an unhappy 'nonentity' who himself wallows passively in his own despair.

Out of the artificial form of the 'monologue scene' Chekhov created an exposé of a man, a milieu, and an attitude to life. In *A Tragic Role*, Tolkachov desperately makes the point that 'This isn't funny, it's downright tragic'; the reverse, however, may also be true: 'This isn't tragic, it's downright funny.' The resolution of the question is left to an audience; but it may be that *Smoking is Bad for You* concerns the tragedy of a 'little man', and the farce of a man who is not big enough. The point is made by Lopakhin in Act 2 of *The Cherry Orchard:* 'the Lord gave us these huge forests, these boundless plains, these vast horizons, and we who live among them ought to be real giants.'

7

A conclusion

I write a play and get it produced, and only after it has become a smash-hit do I realise that a play exactly like it was written by V. Alexandrov, and by Fedotov before him, and by Shpazhinsky before him.

These words are spoken by the main character in Chekhov's *feuilleton* written in 1891 and significantly titled *A Moscow Hamlet*. The story begins:

I am a Moscow Hamlet. Yes. I go to houses, theatres, restaurants, and editorial offices in Moscow, and everywhere I say the same thing:
'God, how boring it is, how ghastly boring!'
And the sympathetic reply comes:
'Yes, indeed, it is terribly boring!'

In *Tatyana Repina*, written two years earlier, Chekhov debunked the myth of people 'doing a Tatyana Repina'; similarly presented for critical appraisal are people who see themselves as Hamlet. This is not Shakespeare's Hamlet, but the popular nineteenth century Russian idea of Hamlet which Turgenev analysed in his lecture of 1858, *Hamlet and Don Quixote*: Hamlet was viewed as passive, resigned, incapable of action, and representing people like Chekhov's Ivanov who 'don't solve problems' but 'cave in under the weight'.[1] The *feuilleton A Moscow Hamlet* demonstrates the aimlessness of such a character, and in the story Chekhov typically deflates the 'Moscow Hamlet' through the ludicrous and unnecessary causes of his boredom: first, absolute ignorance; second, the belief that he is 'very clever and extraordinarily important'. But this boredom has its dangerous aspects – it is symptomatic of a deeper social malaise; it results in passivity and resignation; it becomes an excuse for lethargy, frustration and despair, and it is also infectious:

I'm catching, like the influenza. I complain of boredom, look important, and slander my friends and acquaintances from envy, and lo, a young student has

already taken in what I say. He passes his hand over his hair solemnly, throws away his book, and says:
    'Words, words, words...God, how boring!'

It is not accidental that quotations, or deliberate misquotations, from *Hamlet* recur in Chekhov's plays, whether in *The Anniversary* or, to different effect, in *Ivanov* or, again differently, in *The Seagull* or *The Cherry Orchard*. But it is in *A Moscow Hamlet* that the alternatives or options available to someone 'being Hamlet' are made quite explicit:

And yet I could have learned anything. If I could have got the Asiatic out of myself, I could have studied and loved European culture, trade, crafts, agriculture, literature, music, painting, architecture, hygiene. I could have had superb roads in Moscow, begun trade with China and Persia, brought down the death-rate, fought ignorance, corruption and all the abominations which hold us back from living. I could have been modest, courteous, jolly, cordial; I could have rejoiced sincerely at other people's success, for even the least success is a step towards happiness and truth.

    Yes, I could have! I could have! But I'm a rotten rag, useless rubbish. I am a Moscow Hamlet. Take me off to the Vagankov cemetery!

    I toss about under my blanket, turning from side to side. I cannot sleep. All the while I think about why I am so tortured with boredom, and these words echo in my ears until the dawn: 'You take a piece of telephone cord and hang yourself on the nearest telegraph pole. That's all that's left for you.'

The refrain 'I could have' is one which is echoed in different ways by a number of characters in Chekhov's plays. Only Ivanov and Konstantin (for differing reasons) take the 'solution' of suicide, while Vanya, lacking the resolve for suicide, takes the alternative of work, albeit as a drug. But it is the characters themselves who generally provide the only major obstacle to self-fulfilment or enjoyment, to living as opposed to merely existing, and it is in this way that 'tragedy' is usually presented either as avoidable and unnecessary or not as 'tragic' at all. This point is perhaps brought out in a comment made by Kenneth Tynan in a review of Orlov's performance as Vanya when the Moscow Art Theatre came to London in 1958: 'This Vanya always looks capable of tragedy: his tragedy is that he is capable only of comedy'.[2] More often than not, a character in a Chekhov play turns out to be not Hamlet, but Tartuffe.

    Chekhov's reaction to the performances of his plays, and to his audience's response, is expressive of his dramatic intention:

You tell me that people cry at my plays. I've heard others say the same. But that was not why I wrote them. It is Alexeyev [Stanislavsky] who made my characters into cry-babies. All I wanted was to say honestly to people: 'Have a look at yourselves and see how bad and dreary your lives are!' – The important thing is that people should realise that, for when they do, they will most certainly create another and better life for themselves. I shall not live to see it, but I know that it will be quite different, quite unlike our present life. And so long as this different life does not exist, I shall go on saying to people again and again: 'Please, understand that your life is bad and dreary!' – What is there in this to cry about?[3]

Chekhov's conviction that life must be faced 'as it is' in order to 'create another and better life', or 'life as it should be', is both a denial of the inevitability of tragedy, and an affirmation of man's potential. But this affirmation is never glib or easy, and rarely explicit: it emerges through an exposé of 'life as it is'; through the characters' unhappiness, frustration or inadequacy, or through some characters' realisation and recognition of realities. This recognition of reality is frequently brought about in the plays through the shattering of illusions because, as Vanya puts it, 'When people aren't really alive, they live on illusions. It's better than nothing anyway' (H.3.37). And it is in this sense that what Chukovsky called 'the struggle between human will and the lack of will-power' provides a major source of the content of the plays – and of the tragicomic. Moreover, an audience, too, is brought to a point of realisation: the discrepancy between cause and effect, the inadequacy or irrelevance of a character's response to reality, and the use of juxtaposition and counterpoint are amongst the methods Chekhov utilises in an attempt to ensure that an audience recognises some of the characters as crybabies, and does not simply cry with them:

Take my *Cherry Orchard*. Is it my *Cherry Orchard*? With the exception of two or three parts nothing in it is mine. I am describing life, ordinary life, and not blank despondency. They either make me into a cry-baby or into a bore.[4]

It was perhaps inevitable that Chekhov's contemporaries, whether Stanislavsky or the audience of the Moscow Art Theatre, should identify with the characters in the plays, but in so doing they were 'Chekhov characters in a Chekhov scene'. Chekhov demands of his audience something much more rigorous than easy identification – a demand which is more readily understood in a theatre which has experienced both Brecht and Beckett. Writing about Shakespeare, Peter Brook states:

Brecht and Beckett are both contained in Shakespeare unreconciled. We identify emotionally, subjectively – and yet at one and the same time we evaluate politically, objectively in relation to society.[5]

Without pursuing an analogy between Shakespeare and Chekhov, it is nonetheless the case that the emotional identification and the objective evaluation are both demanded by Chekhov's plays; they are, as Trevor Griffiths puts it, 'both subjectively painful and objectively comic'.[6] Objective evaluation is ensured in a variety of ways: partly through comedy, and partly through techniques which need not be comic in form or effect, but which may be described as 'distancing effects' in the Brechtian sense of the term. Chekhov's method is designed to provoke thought, to maintain objectivity and a sense of proportion in his audience, to ensure understanding of cause and effect and not simply identification with result, and to suggest man's ability and potential (albeit unrealised) to change himself and his world.

Chekhov's characters are always seen in a context, in relation to each other, to a milieu, and to a society. It is this context which frequently defines the stature of the characters: a character's ability or inability to cope, awareness of reality or blindness to it, are to a certain extent measured. Thus Nyukhin's ambition to be a scarecrow both reduces his stature and intensifies his situation; the setting of Act 2 of *The Cherry Orchard* creates a horizon, a perspective against which the characters are viewed; the three sisters stand grouped together as the cheerful music of the military band grows fainter, and the world grows, correspondingly, larger. Such examples, however, serve only to indicate a further rich source of study: the 'distancing' techniques in Chekhov's later full-length plays relate to characterisation, to setting, to sound effects, to the visual gesture and action, to the structure of the plays and the use of juxtaposition and counterpoint, to the patterning of the dialogue, or to the situation in a play which is, for example, 'not a drama but an incident', or 'not a tragedy but a comedy and in places even a farce'. The 'distancing' techniques work through the relationship of one component or organic element with another, through antithesis, parody, farce, the use or reversal of conventions, the incongruous or the grotesque, the deflation or reduction of characters at a moment of 'drama' or self-dramatisation, through the under-cutting or defusing of atmosphere, and the acceleration or, more significantly, the deceleration of rhythm and pace.

The result in the full-length plays is a more complex extension of the techniques of balance to be found in the one-act plays: a balance between objectivity and commitment, comic detachment and sympathetic involvement, the creation of theatrical illusion, and the exposure of social reality. Through the exposure of the illusory, reality is revealed.

Chekhov's technique has been described by Peter Brook in *The Empty Space* in these terms:

Any page of *The Three Sisters* gives the impression of life unfolding as though a tape-recorder had been left running. If examined carefully it will be seen to be built of coincidences as great as in Feydeau – the vase of flowers that overturns, the fire-engine that passes at just the right moment; the word, the interruption, the distant music, the sound in the wings, the entrance, the farewell – touch by touch, they create through the language of illusions an overall illusion of a slice of life.[7]

And Brook concludes:

This series of impressions is equally a series of alienations: each rupture is a subtle provocation and a call to thought.

Not only is this borne out by the major plays but these techniques, and the philosophy which motivates them, may be seen emerging as a tendency in the one-act plays which span the period of Chekhov's creative life from 1885 to 1903.

Appendix 1

Dishonourable Tragedians
and
Leprous Dramatists

A terrible-awful-disgraceful
desperate trrragedy.
Many acts, more scenes.

Dramatis Personae:

M. V. LENTOVSKY a male and an impresario.

TARNOVSKY a heart-rending male; on intimate terms with devils, whales and
crocodiles; his pulse is 225, his temperature is 42.8°.

THE PUBLIC a lady, pleasant in all respects; she eats anything served up.

CHARLES XII The Swedish King; has the manners of a fireman.

BARONESS a brunette, not without talent; does not refuse trivial parts.

GENERAL ERENSVERD a frightfully big man with the voice of a mastodon.

DELAGARDI an ordinary male; acts his part with the free-and-easy manner of a
prompter.

STELLA sister of the impresario.

BURL' a man, brought out on Svobodin's shoulders.

HANSEN

OTHERS

Epilogue[1]

*The crater of a volcano. Tarnovsky sits at a desk covered in blood; instead of a head on
his shoulders, he has a skull; brimstone burns in his mouth; green little devils, smiling
disdainfully, jump from his nostrils. He dips his pen, not into the inkstand, but into lava
which witches keep stirring. It is frightening. The air trembles with cold shivers. At the
back of the stage, shaking knees hang on red hot hooks. Thunder and lightning. The
calendar of Alexsei Suvorin* (the provincial secretary) *lies on this very spot, and foretells, with the impartiality of a bailiff, the collision of the earth with the sun, the destruction of the universe and the increased prices of pharmaceutical goods. Chaos, horror, fear
. . . The rest may be embellished by the reader's imagination.*

TARNOVSKY: (*gnawing his pen*) The Devil take it, what is one to write? It seems
impossible to think of anything! *A Voyage to the Moon* has already been

[1] I would have wanted to put down 'Prologue', but the editors say that the less
likely everything is, the better. As they wish.   (Type-setters' footnote.)

193

done... *The Tramp* has also been done...(*He drinks burning oil.*) One has to invent something else, something which would make the merchants' wives from Zamoskvoreichye dream of devils for three days on end. (*Rubs his frontal bone.*)...Hmm...Get a move on, you great brain! (*He thinks.*)

Thunder and lightning. A volley is heard from a thousand guns executed according to the design of Mr Shekhtel. Dragons, vampires and snakes crawl out of chinks. A big chest falls into the crater, out of which steps Lentovsky dressed in a large poster.

LENTOVSKY: Hullo, Tarnovsky!

TARNOVSKY
WITCHES } (*in unison*) Sir!
OTHERS

LENTOVSKY: Well, what about it? Is the play ready, devil take it? (*He brandishes a truncheon.*)

TARNOVSKY: I'm afraid not, Mikhail Valentinych. I keep on thinking, I keep on sitting, and nothing comes to mind. You've set me too hard a task! You want the public's blood to curdle, you want an earthquake to occur in the hearts of the merchants' wives from Zamoskvoreichye, you want my monologues to extinguish all the lamps...But you must agree, this is beyond the strength of even such a great playwright as Tarnovsky. (*He gets embarrassed, having praised himself.*)

LENTOVSKY: Rubbish, the devil take it! What we need is more gunpowder, Bengal lights, and more ringing monologues, that's all! So there should be frequent costume changes, the dddevil take it! Make it broader... Treachery...the prison...the prisoner's sweetheart is made to marry the villain...Let us give the part of the villain to Pisarev...And then, the flight from prison...Shots...I shall not spare the gunpowder...Further on, a child whose noble origin is only subsequently discovered...Finally, shots again; again a girl, and virtue triumphs...In a word, concoct it according to cliché, the same way Rocambole and the Counts of Monte-Cristo are concocted...

Thunder, lightning, hoar-frost, dew. The volcano erupts. Lentovsky is thrown out.

Act 1

The audience, the ushers, Hansen and Others.

USHERS: (*helping the public out of their coats.*) For a pint, please, your worship! (*Not getting a tip, they seize the public by their tailcoats.*) Oh, blackest ingratitude! (*They feel ashamed for humanity.*)

ONE PUBLIC VOICE: Well, what about Lentovsky, is he well again?

USHER: He's already started fighting, that means he's better.

HANSEN: (*dressing in his dressing-room*) And how I'll stun them! I'll show them! All the papers will be talking!

The action continues, but the reader is impatient; he is longing for Act 2 and therefore the curtain comes down.

Act 2

The palace of Charles XII. (We see Val'ts with his back to the audience swallowing swords and burning coal.) Thunder and lightning.

Charles XII and his courtiers.

CHARLES: (*Walks about the stage and rolls the whites of his eyes.*) Delagardi! You've betrayed your country. Surrender your sword to the captain and kindly march to prison!

Delagardi says a few heartfelt words and leaves.

CHARLES: Tarnovsky! In your heart-rending play you have forced me to live an extra ten years! Kindly betake yourself to prison! (*To the Baroness.*) You love Delagardi and you have a child by him. In the interest of the plot, I must not know this fact and I must marry you to a man you do not love! Marry General Erensverd.

BARONESS: (*Marrying the General*) Ah!

GENERAL ERENSVERD: I'll wear them out! (*He appoints himself the warder of the prison in which Delagardi and Tarnovsky are languishing.*)

CHARLES: Well, now I'm free right up to Act 5. I shall go to the dressing-room.

Acts 3 and 4

STELLA: (*As usual, she acts quite well.*) Count, I love you!

THE YOUNG COUNT: And I love you too, Stella, but I exorcise you in the name of love. Tell me, what the devil made Tarnovsky drag me into these goings-on? What does he need me for? What have I got to do with his plot?

BURL': It's all Sprit's fault! I became a soldier because of him. He beat me, he chased me, he bit me...If my name isn't Burl', if it isn't he who has written this play! He's capable of anything just to annoy me!

STELLA: (*Discovering her origin.*) I'm going to my father, and I will free him. (*On the way to the prison she meets Hansen. Hansen cuts capers.*)

BURL': Through Sprit's kindness, I landed up as a soldier and I am taking part in this play. Probably just to annoy me, this Sprit has made Hansen dance. Just you wait!

They bring up bridges. The stage is collapsing. Hansen makes a jump, which makes all the old maids present feel sick.

Acts 5 and 6

STELLA: (*Stella makes her Papa's acquaintance in prison, and with him she thinks up a plan of escape.*) I shall save you, Father. But how can one arrange for Tarnovsky to escape with us? As soon as he leaves the prison, he's sure to write a new play.

GENERAL ERENSVERD: (*He torments the Baroness and the prisoners.*) Since I'm a villain, I must in no way resemble a human being. (*He eats raw meat.*)

Delagardi and Stella escape from the prison.

ALL: Hold them! Catch them!

DELAGARDI: Whatever happens, we shall in any case escape and remain in one piece!

A shot.

I don't give a damn! (*He falls down dead.*) I couldn't care less about this! The author kills but he also resurrects.

Charles emerges from his dressing-room and orders virtue to triumph over vice. General rejoicing. The moon smiles, and the stars also smile.

THE AUDIENCE: (*Pointing out Tarnovsky to Burl'*) Catch him!

Burl' strangles Tarnovsky. Tarnovsky falls down dead, but jumps up at once. Thunder, lightning, hoar-frost, the murder of Koverlei, the great migration of peoples, shipwreck, and the assemblage of all parts.

LENTOVSKY: But all the same, I'm not satisfied. (*Disappears through the stage.*)

BROTHER OF MY BROTHER (1884)

Appendix 2

A Forced Declaration

In 1876, on 7 July at 8.30 p.m. I wrote a play. Should my opponents wish to know its contents – here it is. I submit it to the verdict of society and the press.

The Sudden Death of a Horse
or the Magnanimity of the Russian People!

A Dramatic Sketch in 1 Act

Dramatis personae:

LYUBIN, a young man.

COUNTESS FINIKOVA, his mistress.

COUNT FINIKOV, her husband.

NIL YEGOROV, cab driver No. 13326.

The action takes place on Nevsky Prospect in broad daylight.

Scene i

The Countess and Lyubin are travelling in Nil Yegorov's cab.

LYUBIN: (*embracing the Countess*) Oh, how I love you! But I won't be at peace until we reach the station and get into the carriage. My heart senses that your scoundrel of a husband is rushing after us at this very moment. I am shaking in my shoes. (*To Nil.*) Drive faster, you devil!

COUNTESS: Faster, driver! Lash it with your whip! You don't know how to drive, you son of a bitch!

NIL (*lashing the horse*): On! On, blast you! The gentleman and lady are bound to give us a bit extra.

COUNTESS: (*shouting*) That's it! That's it! Get this rotten beast moving or we'll be late for the train!

LYUBIN: (*embracing her, admiring her unearthly beauty*) Oh, my dear one! Soon, soon the hour will come when you belong entirely to me, when you will no longer belong to your husband! (*Looks round, then with horror*) Your husband's following us! I can see him! Cabby, drive faster! Faster, you scoundrel, a hundred devils on your tail! (*Lyubin lashes Nil's back.*)

COUNTESS: Hit him on the back of his head! Wait, I'll do it myself with my umbrella. (*She beats Nil.*)

NIL (*whipping his horse with all his might*) Come on, come on! Get a move on, accursed animal!

The exhausted horse falls and dies.

LYUBIN: The horse has died! Oh, horror! Now he'll catch up on us!
NIL: Woe is me, now how will I make a living?

He falls on the corpse of his beloved horse and sobs.

Scene ii

The very same and the Count.

COUNT: You'd run away from me?! Stop! (*Seizes his wife by the hand.*) Traitress! Didn't I love you? Didn't I provide for you?
LYUBIN (*faintheartedly*) I'll take to my heels! (*He runs away accompanied by the noise of the assembled crowd.*)
COUNT (*to Nil*) Cabby! The death of your horse has saved my hearth from desecration. If your horse had not suddenly died, I would never have caught up with the fugitives. Here, take a hundred roubles!
NIL (*magnanimously*) Noble Count! I don't need your money! A totally satisfying reward for me is the knowledge that the death of my beloved horse has served to protect the foundations of a family!

The delighted crowd lifts him shoulder high.

Curtain

On 30 February 1886, this very play was performed at the shore of Lake Baikal by drama amateurs. That was when I enlisted as a member of the Society of Playwrights, and received a suitable fee from the Treasurer, A. A. Maikov. I have not written any other plays since, and have not received any fee whatsoever.

And so, as a member of the above-named Society with the rights stipulated by this calling, and in the name of our party, I urgently demand that: first, the chairman, treasurer, secretary and committee publicly apologise; second, that all the above-named official persons should be rejected and replaced by members of our party; third, that twenty-five thousand of the Society's annual budget should be annually assigned to the purchase of tickets for the Hamburg lottery, and that each win should be shared equally by all members; fourth, that military music should be played at public and extraordinary meetings of the Society, and that decent *zakuski* should be served; fifth, since the Society's whole revenue is received only by those 30 members whose plays are running in the provinces, and as the rest of the members don't receive a penny because their plays are not running anywhere, it is necessary to petition the highest authorities in the interests of justice and equality, so that these 30 members be forbidden to put on their plays. And by this action upset the balance which is so very necessary for the normal course of events.

In conclusion, I consider it necessary to issue a warning that if a negative reply follows at least one of the above-mentioned points, I shall be forced to resign and renounce the membership of the Society.

Member of the Society of Playwrights and Opera Composers.

AKAKY TARANTULOV

FROM THE EDITORS: In publishing this declaration from the honourable member of the Society of Playwrights and Opera Composers, we flatter ourselves with the hope that it will arouse the fullest sympathy from at least half of the worthy members of this Society, the merits of whom are just as great as those of Mr Akaky Tarantulov. Russian drama is precisely that important aspect of poetry, in which the Akaky Tarantulovs can acquire everlasting fame from the cold Finnish rocks all the way to the passionate wings, from the overwhelming Kremlin to the chatter of General Meetings of the Society of Playwrights and Opera Composers. (1889).

Appendix 3

A note on the vaudeville writers Khmelnitsky, Pisarev, Koni, Karatygin, Nekrasov and Lensky

Nicholas Ivanovich Khmelnitsky (1789–1846): regarded as one of the best comic dramatists prior to Griboyedov because of the simplicity and flexibility of his verse, masterly dialogue, and fidelity as a translator. The majority of his plays were either translations or adaptations of (primarily French) plays: when translating, for example, Molière's *Tartuffe* or *L'Ecole des femmes*, Khmelnitsky did not follow the contemporary (and by then artificial) custom of automatically 'Russifying' the plays, and out of his adaptations he created genuinely Russian vaudevilles. Khmelnitsky was prolific, and his work offers the reader a range of examples of different kinds of vaudeville, from 'opera-vaudeville' in *The New Paris* to 'parody-vaudeville' in *Greek Ravings, or Iphigenia in Tauris*. Probably his most famous vaudeville is *The Prattler (Govorun)* which was adapted from a comedy by Boissy, and is an example of a vaudeville 'portraying an amusing and unusual character'. The tone and basic situation of some of his other vaudevilles is indicated by their titles: *The Pranks of the Enamoured; The Irresolute; A Fashionable Incident; The Russian Faust; Actors in their Own Circles; Marriages are Made in Heaven; Chief Cook Felten; Mutual Trials; Grandmother's Parrots*, or *Castles in the Air* which was popular and regularly performed up to the end of the nineteenth century.

Alexander Ivanovich Pisarev (1803–28): the author of twenty-three plays, the majority of which were either translations or adaptations of foreign plays. Generally considered the best Russian vaudeville writer. His most famous plays are the comedy *Lukavin*, and the vaudeville *Busybody* in which the character of Repeikin 'the busybody' is a renowned character in Russian comedy – a part played with resounding success by the great actor Shchepkin. Pisarev's particular talent was characterisation, but the beginnings of social criticism can also be seen in his vaudevilles, such as *The Caliph's Amusement* (an 'opera-vaudeville' which required considerable scene and costume changes), and *The Tutor and the Pupil* (a 'parody-vaudeville' which mocked at the then highly regarded philosopher Schelling).

F. A. Koni (1809–79): a playwright and *littérateur*. Koni's wife was the famous actress of the Alexandrinsky Theatre, Sandunova-Koni, and his son, A. F. Koni, was a famous jurist and friend and contemporary of Chekhov, Dostoyevsky, Tolstoy, and others. Koni is regarded as a 'progressive' vaudeville writer, as his plays *Petersburg Lodgings* (a five-act vaudeville) and *The Prince with a Toupee and a Cataract* managed to escape censorship and are overtly critical of the political *status quo*. An example of Koni's overt criticism of the police and censorship reads:

> Nothing critics know but cursing!
> Lock them up with the insane!
> Let them there keep on rehearsing –
> This is wisdom true and plain.
> To maintain both peace and order
> All the students should be placed
> In the care of a strict warder –
> This is wisdom pure and chaste!
> No oppression or vexation!
> Revenues are to be raised
> Through additional taxation
> Of the sot by liquor crazed.
> Vengeance now will freely flutter,
> But my spies will put a curb
> On whoever dares to utter
> Words that public peace disturb.
> And all folks, with great elation,
> Will exclaim: Here's freedom's age!
> Let them dream of liberation:
> We shall keep in store our rage.[1]

The majority of Koni's vaudevilles are, however, 'character anecdotes' albeit set in a specific social milieu: *The Husband of All Wives, The Husband in a Chimney, Titular Councillors at Home, The Deceased Husband, Devils Dwell in a Calm Pool*, and others.

P. A. Karatygin (1805–79): brother of the famous tragic actor V. A. Karatygin, he wrote 46 vaudevilles of which 20 were originals, while the rest were translated and adapted from the French. When compared with Pisarev, Koni or Lensky, Karatygin is generally considered second-rate.

Nikolai Alexeyevich Nekrasov (1821–77): the great poet and publicist. Edited *Peterburgskii Sbornik* with Herzen and Turgenev, and edited the *Sovremennik* (*The Contemporary*) with Belinsky, a literary review which became the most prominent in Russia. The authorities stopped publication in 1866. Nekrasov was the first to publish Dostoyevsky's *Poor Folk*, and was in the forefront of progressive thought. Under the pseudonym of Perepelsky, Nekrasov wrote such vaudevilles as: *That's the Meaning of Being in Love with an Actress*, *An Awl Cannot be Hidden in a Sack*, and *Grandfather's Parrots*. Undoubtedly many serious writers were shame-faced about writing vaudevilles and used pseudonyms – a practice which makes tracing the true authorship of some vaudevilles difficult. It is known, for example, that the vaudeville writer N. I. Bakhtin asked Pushkin to compose couplets for a benefit vaudeville, instead of the mediocre French couplets of the original. It is not known, however, whether Pushkin complied with the request.

D. T. Lensky (1805–60): the pseudonym of the actor Vorobyov, and the author of nearly 72 plays.[2] Lensky wrote for the actors Shchepkin, Repina and Saburova, and his plays enjoyed tremendous popularity. Amongst his admirers was Pushkin,[3] and for twenty years Lensky's plays drew audiences to the Bolshoi Theatre. His work spans the period from the 1820s to the 1850s, and all of his plays, both translations and originals, were written on the French pattern. By this time, the 'French pattern' partly meant, for example, the plays of Eugene Scribe who was the author of (amongst other works) no less than 216 *comédies-vaudevilles*, vaudevilles which combined the light satirical tone of the vaudeville with techniques from the *comédie d'intrigue*. With his collaborators, Scribe developed these light sketches into the lengthier comedy of manners which became the established prototype of the *pièce bien faite*. Lensky's play *And Pretty and Ugly and Stupid and Clever* (1833) was based on a play by Scribe.[4] Another play by Lensky, *Leo Gurich Sinichkin* (a five-act vaudeville), is considered a direct precursor of Ostrovsky's plays portraying theatrical customs (*The Forest*, *Guilty Without Guilt*, and *The Girl Without a Dowry*), and closely resembles Ostrovsky's *Talents amd Their Admirers*. Today, Lensky's play is worth reading for its vivid portrayal of theatrical customs in the provinces. A number of vaudevilles (whether French, Russian adaptations, or native Russian originals) were set in a theatrical background, and it is thus possible to see Chekhov's *Swan Song (Calchas)* as an inheritor of this tradition.

The titles of the plays mentioned have all been rendered in English in order to give the non-Russian reader an indication of tone, and of the common practice in naming vaudevilles: the titles describe either the leading character or the basic situation of the play.

The following collections provide a primary source of various kinds of vaudeville (opera-vaudeville, comedy-vaudeville, or joke-vaudeville), some of which are one-act vaudevilles, others are in five acts or 'pictures':

D. T. Lensky, *Vodevili*, Moscow, 1937.
V. V. Uspensky, ed., *Russkiy vodevil*, Leningrad-Moscow, 1959 (contains vaude-

villes by Khmelnitsky, Griboyedov, Pisarev, Karatygin, Lensky, Koni, Grigoriev, and Nekrasov).

N. Shantarenkov, ed. *Russkiy vodevil*, Moscow, 1970 (contains vaudevilles by Pisarev, Lensky, Koni, Karatygin, Nekrasov, Grigoriev, Sollogub, and Fedorov).

Notes

1. Objectivity and commitment: the evolution of a philosophy

1 Quoted in S. Laffitte, *Chekhov 1860–1904*, London, 1974, p. 16.
2 Alexander Kuprin (1870–1938), a writer and young contemporary of Chekhov.
3 Quoted in D. Magarshack, *Chekhov the Dramatist*, New York, 1960, p. 16.
4 Quoted in S. Karlinsky, ed., *Letters of Anton Chekhov*, London, 1973, p. 337.
5 D. MacCarthy, *The New Statesman*, 27 January 1945.
6 L. Shestov, *Anton Tchekhov and other essays*, Dublin–London, 1916, p. 5.
7 Karlinsky, *Letters of Chekhov*, p. 337.
8 E. Braun, *Meyerhold on Theatre*, London, 1969, pp. 27–8.
9 *Ibid*. p. 30.
10 T. Wolff, tr., *Pushkin on Literature*, London, 1971, pp. 264–5.
11 Quoted in E. Braun, *The Director and the Stage*, Milton Keynes, 1977, p. 31.
12 Braun, *Meyerhold on Theatre*, p. 271.
13 P. Brook, *The Empty Space*, London, 1968, p. 79.
14 Braun, *Meyerhold*, p. 30.
15 C. Stanislavski, *My Life in Art*, London, 1962, p. 415.
16 See T. K. Shakh-Azizova, *Chekhov i zapadno-evropeiskaya drama ego vremeni*, Moscow, 1966.
17 *Fragments*, a humorous magazine based in St Petersburg, to which Chekhov contributed a column and many of his stories of 1883–5.
18 Critics such as Vukol Lavrov, Alexander Skabichevsky, Nikolai Mikhailovsky, and others.
19 N. A. Toumanova, *Anton Chekhov, The Voice of Twilight Russia*, New York, 1937.
20 Quoted in Karlinsky, *Letters of Chekhov*, p. 88.
21 *Ibid*. p. 112.
22 *On the High Road* (1885) was never passed by the Censor's office.
23 Letter to Suvorin, 11 September 1888.
24 Karlinsky, *Letters of Chekhov*, p. 104.
25 *Ibid*. p. 109.
26 Quoted in Wolff, *Pushkin*, p. 264.
27 Letter to L. A. Avilova, 29 April 1892.
28 Letter to M. Kiselyova, 14 January 1887.
29 *Ibid*.

30 Reminiscent of Ibsen's line in his poem *A Letter in Rhyme:* 'I only ask. My task is not to answer.' Quoted in M. Meyer, *Henrik Ibsen*, vol. 2, *A Farewell to Poetry*, London, 191, p. 210.

31 Karlinsky, *op. cit.* pp. 116–17.

32 Letter to Suvorin, 27 March 1894.

33 Letter to Suvorin, 28 July 1893.

34 Karlinsky, *op. cit.* p. 367.

35 Letter to Nikolai Leykin, 20 May 1884.

2. Conventions and innovations in Russian comedy

1 Quoted in Magarshack, *Chekhov the Dramatist*, p. 30.

2 Stories such as *The Jeune premier, A Cure for Drunkenness, Boots, An Actor's End, Calchas, Stage Manager under the Sofa, A Tragic Actor, In the Graveyard, A Dreary Story, A Moscow Hamlet.*

3 V. Nemirovitch-Dantchenko, *My Life in the Russian Theatre*, London, 1968, p. 27.

4 Victor Krylov, a prolific and popular 'hack' playwright.

5 See V. Nemirovitch-Dantchenko, *My Life in the Russian Theatre*, pp. 28–31.

6 B. V. Varneke, *History of the Russian Theatre*, New York, 1971, p. 427.

7 *Ibid.* p. 428.

8 *The Seagull*, Act 1, H.2.236.

9 L. Weiner, in *The Contemporary Drama of Russia*, New York, 1971, provides a detailed bibliographical appendix in which he lists the plays of the 1870s, 1880s and 1890s (pp. 192–242) and some of the now unknown playwrights (p. 74). The new *Istoriya russkogo dramaticheskogo teatra*, Vols. 1–7, Moscow, 1977–, also contains invaluable lists of the theatrical repertoire.

10 S. Laffitte, in *Chekhov*, pp. 52–4, quotes the memories of Marie Steiger, born Drossi, dictated to A. Roskin (Moscow, 1959) in which she describes Chekhov's first visit at the age of thirteen to the theatre in Taganrog to see *La Belle Hélène*. This is substantiated by A. B. Derman, *Moskva v zhizni i tvorchestve A. P. Chekhova*, Moscow, 1948. For the Taganrog repertoire in Chekhov's youth, see Semanova, *Teatral'nyye vpechatleniya Chekhov-gimnazista*, quoted in D. Rayfield, *Chekhov, The Evolution of his Art*, London, 1975, p. 245.

11 E. Bentley, 'Apologia', *The Brute and Other Farces*, 1958, p. i.

12 Quoted in Magarshack, *Chekhov*, p. 54.

13 V. P. Burenin, author of dramas from 1885 (*Messalina*) to 1898 (*The Heart of Princess Azra*).

14 Letter to Suvorin, 2 January 1894.

15 M. P. Chekhov, *Anton Chekhov i ego syuzhety*, Moscow, 1923, p. 41.

16 G. P. Berdnikov, *Chekhov-dramaturg*, Moscow, 1972, p. 31.

17 *Ne darom kuritsa pela; Nashla kosa na kamen*, and *Brityi sekretar s pistoletom*. In *A New Life of Chekhov* (London, 1976, p. 26), Hingley refers to *Nashla kosa na kamen* as an early vaudeville of which the bare title survives: *Deadlock*. In *Chekhov the Dramatist* Magarshack mentions two titles: *Laugh It Off*

If You Can, and *Diamond Cut Diamond*, but does not provide the Russian titles. Alexander Chekhov refers to Chekhov's early vaudevilles by titles in a letter of 14 October 1878 (*Letters*, Moscow, 1939).

18 J. L. Shcheglov, *Chekhov v vospominaniyakh sovremennikov*, Moscow, 1952, p. 117.

19 S. D. Balukhaty, *Dramaturgia Chekhova*, Moscow, 1935, p. 4.

20 A. P. Chekhov, *Things Most Frequently Encountered in Novels, Stories and Other Such Things*, Vol. 1 (1880–2) pp. 17–18: *Polnoe sobranie sochineniy i pisem A. P. Chekhova*, Moscow, 1944–51.

21 E. S. Smirnova-Chikina, '"Tatyana Repina" Antona Chekhova', an article in *V tvorcheskoy laboratorii Chekhova*, Moscow, 1974, p. 116.

22 See A. S. Dolinina, 'Parodiya li, "Tatyana Repina" Chekhova?', in *A. P. Chekhov, Zateryannye proizvedeniya*, Leningrad, 1925, and *Russkaya teatral'-naya parodiya XIX nachala XX veka*, Moscow, 1976.

23 Quoted in D. Rayfield, *Chekhov, the Evolution of his Art*, London, 1975, p. 20.

24 Chekhov, *Works*, Vol. 1, pp. 483–8: 'Opyat o Sare Bernar'.

Chekhov expresses his opinion in rather more restrained tones than did Turgenev, who wrote to Savina on 15 December 1881: 'I am annoyed with my compatriots who behave so foolishly over the intolerable Sarah Bernhardt. She has nothing to boast of but a charming voice – everything else in her is falsehood, coldness, affectation – and a repulsive Parisian swank.' *Letters to An Actress*, London, 1973, p. 83. In another letter, this time to Yakov Polonsky, Turgenev again stressed the artificiality which both he and Chekhov disliked so much: 'I can't tell you how furious I am with the frenzied acclamations of Sarah Bernhardt, that arrogant fraud, that insufferable *poseuse*, who reminds me of a toad every time I think of her, and whom nature, by some incomprehensible caprice, has endowed with such a delightful voice, having deprived her of anything else'. Quoted in David Magarshack's *Turgenev*, London, 1954, p. 303.

25 Letter to Suvorin, 25 November 1889.

26 Hauptmann's play was finally performed by the Society of Art and Literature on 3 April 1896. Nemirovitch-Dantchenko suggests the often confusing nature of censorship at the time which sometimes varied according to the individual censor, created evident differences between what was allowed in Moscow as opposed to St Petersburg, for example, and varied in stringency according to the efficiency of the bureaucracy at any one time, and also depended on whether there was a sudden surge of reaction from the Government, as there was, for example, after the assassination of Alexander II in 1881. There was Government censorship of all performed works for the stage, whether in the Imperial or private theatres; of all publications, whether of newspapers, journals or books; and there was also Church censorship which concerned itself with matters of morality and ecclesiastical themes (as in the case of Chekhov's censored short story, *The Bishop*). In addition, directors and editors applied pre-censorship, and then there was the self-censorship exercised by the writers on themselves; as Chekhov put

it, 'It's like writing with a bone stuck in your throat.' It was no doubt for this reason that in the 1880s and 1890s it became increasingly common that writers (such as Tolstoy) had uncensored Russian editions of their works printed abroad.

27 See Nemirovitch-Dantchenko, *My Life*, pp. 176–8.

28 Quoted in H.1.170.

29 Quoted in W. H. Bruford, *Chekhov and His Russia*, London, 1971, p. 106.

30 Such as Berdnikov, *Chekhov. Ideynye i tvorcheskiye iskaniya*, Moscow, 1961.

31 Quoted in Varneke, *History of the Russian Theatre*, p. 190.

32 That this same method of writing often took place in Russia is made clear by Repetilov in Griboyedov's comedy of 1823, *Woe from Wit* (4, iv):

> But still, if I sit tight and strain my poor old mind
> It doesn't take an hour of labour,
> Before, casual-like, out pops a pun.
> The others jump on my idea;
> Six of them to cook up a little vaudeville,
> Another six to write the music for it
> The rest to clap when it's performed.

(J. Cooper, *Chatsky* in *Four Russian Plays*, Harmondsworth, 1972, p. 198.)

33 R. Simonov, *Stanislavsky's Protégé: Eugene Vakhtangov*, New York, 1969, Part 1: 'Vakhtangov Directs *A Wedding*', p. 202.

34 Ibsen regarded Heiberg's essay as required reading for every would-be critic in Scandinavia. Several of Heiberg's vaudevilles, modelled on French vaudevilles but with Danish settings and topical Danish themes, were staged by Ibsen in Bergen and Christiania.

35 Quoted in M. Meyer, *Henrik Ibsen*, London, 1967, vol. 1, Appendix C, p. 242.

36 *Ibid.* p. 243.

37 *Ibid.* p. 242.

38 Quoted in Varneke, *History of the Russian Theatre*, p. 139.

39 *Ibid.* p. 199.

40 Three weeks after her coronation in September 1762, Catherine the Great had imported a French company from Paris, partly because of her own French-influenced education, and partly because the French stage still reigned supreme in Europe, as it had since Molière. It was only from this time onwards that some kind of national consciousness began to emerge in a Russian theatre which had been officially established at Court for only a decade.

41 Varneke, *History of the Russian Theatre*, p. 129.

42 *Ibid.* p. 191.

43 N. Shantarenkov, *Russkiy vodevil*, Moscow, 1970, p. 7.

44 *Ibid.* pp. 7–8.

45 V. G. Belinsky, *Polnoe sobranie sochineniy v 13-ti tomakh*, Moscow, 1954, Vol. 3, p. 492.

46 For a more detailed note on these vaudeville writers and their plays, see Appendix 3.

47 N. V. Gogol, *Diary of a Madman and Other Stories*, ed. R. Wilks, Harmondsworth, 1972, p. 23.

48 N. V. Gogol, *Works*, Moscow, 1952, vol. 8, p. 396.

49 This change of setting is reflected in Gogol's own plays; not only in the best-known, full-length plays, but also in the lesser-known one-act plays or scenes: *The Lawsuit*, *The Servant's Hall*, and *An Official's Morning*.

50 Berdnikov, *Chekhov-dramaturg*, p. 34.

51 *Masquerade* really only received the production it merited in Meyerhold's production of 1917, and subsequent productions.

52 A. S. Pushkin, *Table-talk*, Sovremennik, vol. 8, 1837, in Wolff, *Pushkin on Literature*, pp. 464–5.

53 D. J. Welsh, *Russian Comedy 1765–1823*, The Hague, 1966, p. 98.

54 V. V. Uspensky, *Russkiy vodevil*, Leningrad–Moscow, 1959, p. 364.

55 A. Slonimsky, 'The Technique of the Comic in Gogol', in *Gogol from the Twentieth Century*, Princeton, 1974, p. 352.

56 *Ibid.* p. 353.

57 Discussed by V. Orlov, 'The Problems of Griboyedov's Art', Moscow, 1946, *Lit. nasledstvo*, 47–8, pp. 40–3.

58 It is interesting that Strindberg observed conventional scene divisions in *The Father*, but not in *Miss Julie*.

59 Welsh, *Russian Comedy*, p. 104.

60 Letter to A. A. Bestuzhev, January 1825.

61 Such as Uspensky, in his *Russkiy vodevil*, and N. Shantarenkov and E. K. Lepkovskaya in *Russkiy vodevil*.

62 Welsh, *Russian Comedy*, p. 108.

63 Varneke, *History of the Russian Theatre*, p. 190.

64 Uspensky, *Russkiy vodevil*, p. 5.

65 The notable exception is to be found in Ostrovsky's comedies, which are justly regarded as realistic partly because action emanates from character and is motivated by the characters' interaction.

66 The play, if written, has never been traced.

67 Letter to Yakov Polonsky, 22 February 1888.

68 A. S. Pushkin, 'Draft Notes on Tragedy', 1825, in Wolff, *Pushkin on Literature*, p. 130.

69 Simonov writes about 'the tradition of Shchepkin and Martinov, two great Russian actors, who, when playing vaudeville, used to move their audience not only to hearty laughter but also to compassionate tears'. *Stanislavsky's Protégé: Eugene Vakhtangov*, p. 202.

70 Slonimsky, 'Technique of the Comic in Gogol', p. 329.

71 Quoted by Slonimsky, *op. cit.* p. 338.

72 The pen-name of Captain Ivan Leontyev (1856–1911), an army officer, playwright and novelist, friend and correspondent of Chekhov's. Author of *Chekhov v vospominaniyakh sovremennikov*, Moscow, 1952.

73 Berdnikov, *Chekhov-dramaturg*, pp. 33–4, quoting the *Theatrical Chronicle*, *Moscow Gazette*, 1888, No. 274, p. 4.

74 Chekhov, *Works*, vol. 14, p. 176.

75 E. P. Karpov, later a producer at the Alexandrinsky Theatre, and largely responsible (as the director) for the failure of *The Seagull*. Author of *Crocodile Tears*, *On the Meadow*, *The Committee-Supported Widow*, *The Workers' Quarter*, *The Free Bird*, etc. Chekhov gives a detailed opinion of *Crocodile Tears* in a letter to Suvorin on 11 November 1888.

76 Quoted in Magarshack, *Chekhov the Dramatist*, p. 32.

77 Berdnikov, *Chekhov-dramaturg*, p. 34.

78 *Ibid.* p. 46.

79 See Appendices 1 and 2, and S. D. Balukhaty, *Chekhov-dramaturg*, Leningrad, 1936, p. 29.

80 Quoted in Magarshack, *Chekhov the Dramatist*, p. 44.

81 *Ibid.* p. 45.

82 Members of F. A. Korsh's company. Korsh's well-known Moscow theatre specialised in farces. It was at Korsh's Theatre that *Ivanov* and *Swan Song* were first performed.

3. The farce-vaudevilles

1 V. Mayakovsky, 'Dva Chekhova', in *Polnoe sobranie sochineniy v trinadtsati tomakh*, Moscow, 1955, Vol. 1, p. 301.

2 After seeing a performance of *Uncle Vanya* at the Moscow Art Theatre on 24 January 1900, Tolstoy is reported to have said to Chekhov: 'You know I cannot stand Shakespeare, but your plays are even worse than his.' Quoted in S. Karlinsky, *Letters of A. Chekhov*, p. 375.

3 Quoted in V. Lakshin, *Tolstoy i Chekhov*, Moscow, 1975, pp. 104–5.

4 Quoted in Simonov, *Stanislavsky's Protégé*, p. 22.

5 Magarshack, *Chekhov the Dramatist*, p. 59.

6 *The Seagull*, Act 1, H.2.233.

7 Yu. Yuzovsky, 'Chekhov u Meyerkholda', *Razgovor zatyanulsya za polnoch*, Moscow, 1966, p. 252.

8 The choice of names here serves as an example of Chekhov's employment of 'meaningful names'. While there is an obvious danger in sometimes 'reading in' a significance which may not have been intended, in this case the association of the names is part of the comic effect: Gruzdev's name is associated with the Russian word for 'mushroom'; Yaroshevich with 'spring wheat', and Kuritsyn with 'chicken'.

9 *The Three Sisters*, Act 2, H.3.106.

10 See Chekhov's 1880 list of clichés and conventions, Chapter 2, p. 17.

11 See Chapter 2, p. 35, and H.1.175.

12 Quoted in H.1.174.

13 Letter to Suvorin, 6 January 1889.

14 See C. Stanislavski, *My Life in Art*, London, 1962, p. 358.

15 Simonov, *Stanislavsky's Protégé*, p. 55.

16 *Ibid.* pp. 24–5.

17 Similarly, Serebryakov's first entrance in Act 1 of *Uncle Vanya* tells the audience a great deal about him – as Vanya says: 'It's hot and stuffy today, but the great sage is complete with overcoat, galoshes, umbrella and gloves' (H.3.21). The extremity and disparity of dress is comic and telling.

18 Such as Pushkin's *Dubrovsky*, or *Tales of Belkin*; Gogol's *The Two Ivans*, or in several of Ostrovsky's plays.

19 Lakshin, *Tolstoy i Chekhov*, p. 105.

20 Yuzovsky, *Razgovor zatyanulsya za polnoch*, pp. 256–7.

21 *Ibid.* p. 259.

22 See K. L. Rudnitsky, *Rezhissyor Meyerhold*, Moscow, 1969, pp. 473–81, and Braun, *Meyerhold on Theatre*, p. 248.

23 Lomov is looking for his own shoulder!

24 In *The Wedding*, Zmeyukina keeps asking for air: 'Give me air, do you hear?'; and in *Uncle Vanya*, Astrov says: 'You know, I don't think I should survive a single month in your house, this air would choke me' (H.3.38). The demand for air invariably relates to atmosphere and situation, and is rarely simply a comment on the weather.

25 In Meyerhold's production, Chubukov's plea was answered – a giant knife and pistol appeared, and no doubt motivated a 'relapse' from the reviving Lomov.

26 See Berdnikov, *Chekhov-dramaturg*, pp. 38–9.

27 Konstantin Varlamov, a well-known Petersburg actor.

28 Letter to Suvorin, 4 May 1889. Karlinsky, *Letters of Chekhov*, p. 140.

29 Letter to Leontyev, 6 May 1889. Quoted in H.1.180.

30 H.1.105–14.

31 Quoted in B. Eichenbaum, 'Chekhov at Large', an essay in R. L. Jackson, ed., *Chekhov: A Collection of Critical Essays*, Englewood Cliffs, N.J., 1967, p. 28.

32 W. Gerhardi, *Anton Chekhov: A Critical Study*, London, 1974, pp. 100–1.

33 Yuzovsky, *Razgovor zatyanulsa za polnoch*, p. 248.

34 See Rudnitsky, *Rezhissyor Meyerhold*, pp. 473–81.

35 Yuzovsky, *op. cit.*, pp. 248–9.

36 *Ibid.* p. 250.

37 From the aria in the final act of Tchaikovsky's opera, *Eugene Onegin*. Significantly, the aria is sung by Tatyana's *husband*.

38 A similar comic technique was used by Gogol in *How Ivan Ivanovich quarrelled with Ivan Nikiforovich*: '"*Please* have some more, Ivan Ivanovich." "I can't stop, thank you very much." With these words Ivan Ivanovich bowed and sat down again.' Gogol, *Diary of a Madman and other Stories*, Harmondsworth, p. 132.

39 Yuzovsky, *op. cit.*, p. 249. The part of Merchutkina was played by Serebryannikova.

40 See Gogol, *Diary of a Madman and other Stories*, pp. 96–7.

41 Chekhov, *Works*, Moscow, 1944–51, vol. 13, p. 391. For a similar view

expressed by Ibsen, see his letter of June 1883 to August Lindberg, quoted in Meyer, *Henrik Ibsen*, vol. 3, p. 26.

42 Like Lomov in *The Proposal*.

43 Magarshack, *Chekhov the Dramatist*, p. 65.

44 Such as *Tatyana Repina*, the two little-known sketches, *Dishonourable Tragedians and Leprous Dramatists* and *A Forced Declaration* (see Appendices 1 and 2), and some of Chekhov's early parodies on the work of Gaboriau, Jules Verne, Victor Hugo, Alphonse Daudet, and others.

45 H.1.201.

46 In a letter to Leykin on 20 May 1884, Chekhov wrote: 'I would now enjoy writing a satirical medical text in two or three volumes.'

47 Possibly a reference to Turgenev's *Asya*.

48 It was exactly because of this 'access' that hairdressers, barbers, and chambermaids were well-placed to create intrigue – as in *The Barber of Seville*, *The Marriage of Figaro*, or many vaudevilles.

49 Letter to Axel Lundegård, October 1887, quoted in M. Meyer, *Strindberg: The Father, Miss Julie and The Ghost Sonata*, London, 1976, pp. 17–18.

4. The dramatic studies

1 Quoted in H.1.171.

2 Chekhov did not include the play in the 1902 Collected Edition of his work.

3 See Appendix 1.

4 Taken over from Ossip, a character in Chekhov's untitled play generally known as *Platonov*.

5 *The Cherry Orchard*, Act 2, H.3.173.

6 Mention is also made of a brick-works in *The Three Sisters*: Tuzenbakh resigns from the army to work in a brick-works.

7 'An impoverished nobleman', one of the *Things Most Frequently Encountered in Novels, Stories and Other Such Things*.

8 See Chapter 3, p. 80.

9 Quoted in Magarshack, *Chekhov the Dramatist*, p. 84.

10 Like Telegin's wife.

11 Quoted in H.1.2.

12 See Appendix 1.

13 The Kuban District, an area north of the Caucasus.

14 Or the three sisters dreaming of Moscow.

15 K. Chukovsky, *Chekhov the Man*, London, 1945, p. 60.

16 Quoted in S. D. Balukhaty, *M. Gorky i A. Chekhov; perepiska, stati i vyskazyvaniya*, Moscow–Leningrad, 1937, p. 84.

17 *Troilus and Cressida* – Act 3, scene iii.

18 Karlinsky, *Letters of Chekhov*, pp. 62–4.

19 Letter to A. N. Pleshcheyev, 17 October 1888.

20 Letter to A. P. Lensky, 26 October 1888.

21 Revised for the 1897 collection of *Plays*, in which *Uncle Vanya* appeared in print for the first time.

22 H.1.2.
23 There are, of course, precedents in Molière: the preparations in *L'Impromptu de Versailles*; Harpagon's search for gold amongst the audience in *L'Avare*, or Argan's indignant reference to 'that fellow Molière' in *Le Malade imaginaire*.
24 Published in *Teatr*, 1883, Nos. 10 and 11.
25 E. S. Smirnova-Chikina, '"Tatyana Repina" Antona Chekhova', an article in *V tvorcheskoy laboratorii Chekhova*, Moscow, 1974, p. 109.
26 *Ibid.*
27 Chekhov's sister, Maria Pavlovna Chekhova, maintained that the play is a parody, and as recently as 1976, Chekhov's *Tatyana Repina* was included in a collection of nineteenth and twentieth century Russian theatrical parodies. See Appendices 1 and 2.
28 See Appendix 1.
29 The critic Smirnova-Chikina makes out a strong case for Chekhov's *Tatyana Repina* as a parody on the work of 'Gip', the pseudonym of the Countess Gabriele de-Martel-de-Janvil (1850–1932), whose light novels were popular in Russia at the time; her novels are to be found in Chekhov's bookcase in the Chekhov Museum in Yalta, and it is likely that he saw the stage adaptation of her *Autour du mariage*, performed in Petersburg in December 1888 when Chekhov was there to see the premiere of Suvorin's play. According to Smirnova-Chikina, Chekhov's *Tatyana Repina* bears a strong resemblance to *Autour du mariage*.
30 A. S. Dolinina, 'Parodiya li, "Tatyana Repina" Chekhova?', an article in *A. P. Chekhov, Zateryannye proizvedeniya*, Leningrad, 1925, p. 60.
31 *Ibid.*
32 Quoted in Dolinina, 'Parodiya li, "Tatyana Repina"?', p. 70.
33 Hingley, *A New Life of Chekhov*, p. 108.
34 Suvorin owned the reactionary *Novoe Vremya*.
35 *Syn Otechestva*, No. 332.
36 *Novosti*, No. 343.
37 *Peterburgskie Vedomosti*, 13 December 1888, No. 344.
38 Quoted in Dolinina, 'Parodiya li, "Tatyana Repina"?', p. 70.
39 *Ibid.*, p. 75.
40 Smirnova-Chikina, 'Tatyana Repina', p. 109.
41 *Ibid.*
42 Dolinina, 'Parodiya li, "Tatyana Repina"?', p. 74.
43 *Ibid.*
44 Chekhov, *Works*, vol. 14, p. 257.
45 Quoted in Smirnova-Chikina, 'Tatyana Repina', p. 111.
46 Dolinina provides the most detailed documentation of Chekhov's contribution to the Maly Theatre's production in 'Parodiya li, "Tatyana Repina"?', pp. 59–84.
47 Chekhov, *Works*, vol. 14, p. 257.

48 Letter to Suvorin, 15 November 1888.
49 Quoted in Dolinina, 'Parodiya li, "Tatyana Repina"?', p. 72.
50 See Chapter 4, page 123.
51 *Miss Julie* was written in July–August 1888, the Preface and publication came later.
52 See Appendix 1.
53 See Appendix 2. Published in *Novoe Vremya*, April 1889, under the pseudonym of Akaky Tarantulov.
54 Smirnova-Chikina, 'Tatyana Repina', p. 117.
55 Yarmolinsky, *Letters of Anton Chekhov*, p. 94.
56 Letter to Suvorin, 5 March 1889.

5. A play in one act – The Wedding

1 Only *Ivanov*, of the full-length dramatic works, is subtitled 'a play'.
2 M. Gorky, *Reminiscences of Tolstoy, Chekhov and Andreev*, London, 1968, p. 108.
3 Written in 1830.
4 Vakhtangov's diary, 26 March 1921, quoted in Simonov, *Stanislavsky's Protégé*, pp. 7–8.
5 Gorky, *Reminiscences*, p. 107.
6 Gogol, *Marriage*, Act 1, Scene i, trans. B. Costello, Manchester, 1969, p. 5.
7 *Ibid.* Act 1, Scene ii, pp. 17–18.
8 *Ibid.* Act 2, Scene i, pp. 33–4.
9 Variously translated as *A Nasty Joke* and *An Unpleasant Incident*.
10 There is no record of *Skverny anekdot* in dramatic form in F. M. Dostoyevsky, *Polnoe sobranie sochineniy v tridtsati tomakh*, Leningrad, 1973, Vol. 5, pp. 5–45 and 352–6, but Simonov may well have seen a subsequent dramatisation of the story. Dramatisations, whether of Chekhov's stories or Dostoyevsky's, have been frequently done. See Stanislavski, *My Life in Art*, pp. 211–14, on the production of Dostoyevsky's *The Village of Stepanchikovo;* dramatisations have also been made of *The Gambler, The Idiot, The Brothers Karamazov, Crime and Punishment, My Uncle's Dream*, and others.
11 Until the chairs collapse noisily, and the bride's mother takes her off for the night.
12 Simonov, *Stanislavsky's Protégé*, pp. 69–70.
13 F. M. Dostoyevsky, *A Disgraceful Affair*, trans. N. Gottlieb, London, 1959, pp. 70–1.
14 *Ibid.* pp. 79–80.
15 Simonov, *Stanislavsky's Protégé*, p. 71.
16 *Ibid.* pp. 55–6.
17 *Ibid.* p. 69.
18 *Ibid.* p. 23.
19 *Ibid.* p. 66.
20 *Ibid.* p. 34.

21 Strangely, Simonov calls the character 'Gigalov', 'Cunning Rogue'.
22 Dasha has only two lines in the whole play.
23 Simonov, *Stanislavsky's Protégé*, pp. 29–34.
24 *Ibid.* p. 30.
25 H.1.182.
26 Simonov, *Stanislavsky's Protégé*, p. 66.
27 As in Brecht's plays, where an audience observes the process in the full knowledge of the situation.
28 The Russian word *chelovek* carries the meaning of 'Man' in addition to the word 'waiter' in this context; it therefore possibly carries a more universal plea or 'howl for help'.
29 Andryusha Nyunin.
30 Simonov, *Stanislavsky's Protégé*, p. 21.

6. A monologue in one act – Smoking is Bad for You

1 *The Government Inspector*, an English version by Edward Marsh and Jeremy Brooks, London 1968, p. 77.
2 Gorky, *Reminiscences*, p. 111.
3 See H.1.192.
4 *Ibid.* .
5 Five Dogs Lane is also the setting for Chekhov's short story *A Marriage of Convenience*. See p. 148.
6 H.1.189.
7 *Ibid.*
8 Hingley, *A New Life of Chekhov*, p. 88.
9 A similar progression may be seen in Gogol's alterations to *The Government Inspector* from the first performance in April 1836 to the final version published in 1842. See Braun, *Meyerhold on Theatre*, pp. 210–11.
10 H.1.199.

7. A conclusion

1 Letter to Suvorin, 30 December 1888.
2 K. Tynan, *Tynan on Theatre*, Harmondsworth, 1964, p. 278.
3 'Chekhov v neizdannykh dnevnikakh sovremennikov', in *Literaturnoe nasledstvo*, LXVIII, Moscow, 1960, pp. 479–80.
4 Quoted in Magarshack, *Chekhov the Dramatist*, p. 14.
5 Brook, *The Empty Space*, p. 87.
6 T. Griffiths, *The Cherry Orchard: A New English Version*, London, 1978, p. vi.
7 Brook, *The Empty Space*, p. 79.

Appendix 1. Dishonourable Tragedians and Leprous Dramatists

See: *Polnoe sobranie sochineniy i pisem A. P. Chekhova*, 20 vols, Moscow, 1944–51, vol. 3 (1946), p. 483. *Russkaya teatral'naya parodiya XIX nachala XX veka*, Moscow, 1976, pp. 434–8; commentary by M. Polyakov, p. 798.

Commentary:
Published for the first time in the journal *The Alarm Clock*, 1884, No. 4.

Signed: My Brother's Brother. Published in accordance with *A. P. Chekhov: Complete Collected Works and Letters* in 20 vols., vol. 3 (Goslitizdat, 1946), p. 483. This is a parody on the production of the play *The Pure and the Leprous* (from the German original by K. Tarnovsky) performed in the theatre of M. V. Lentovsky.

M. V. Lentovsky: Impresario of the private Moscow Theatre, The Buffoon. Among melodramas and farce-vaudevilles, Lentovsky rather surprisingly produced Tolstoy's *The Power of Darkness.*

K. Tarnovsky: adaptor and writer of vaudevilles.

Stella, sister of the impresario: Lentovsky's sister played the main part in *The Pure and the Leprous.*

Svobodin: an actor who worked in Lentovsky's theatre in 1883–4.

Hansen: the ballet-master in Lentovsky's theatre.

The calendar of Alexsei Suvorin: A. S. Suvorin was the publisher of *New Times*, and his firm published calendars.

the increased prices of pharmaceutical goods: a topical item, to which newspapers and journals devoted considerable attention.

A Voyage to the Moon... The Tramp (in the original *Forest Tramp*): plays in the repertory of Lentovsky's theatre.

Let us give the part of the villain to Pisarev: the artist M. I. Pisarev who at that time was acting in Lentovsky's theatre.

Rocambole: the hero of the adventure novels by Ponson du Terrail.

Val'ts: designer of productions in Lentovsky's theatre.

the murder of Koverlei: a hint at the bloody effects of the French melodrama *The Murder of Koverlei.*

Appendix 2. A Forced Declaration

See: *Polnoe sobranie sochineniy i pisem A. P. Chekhova*, 20 vols. (Moscow, 1944–51) vol. 7 (1947), p. 482. *Russkaya teatral'naya parodiya XIX nachala XX veka*, Moscow, 1976, pp. 439–41; commentary by M. Polyakov, p. 799.

Commentary:
Published for the first time in *New Times*, 22 April 1889, No. 4721.

Unsigned. Published in accordance with *A. P. Chekhov: Complete Collected Works and Letters* in 20 vols., vol. 7 (Goslitizdat, 1947) p. 482. This play was regarded as a parody by N. Efros who produced it successfully at his theatre The Bat (See N. Efros, *Theatre: The Bat*, p. 40).

Society of Playwrights: 'The Society of Russian Playwrights and Opera Composers' was formed in 1874. V. Rodislavsky was elected secretary, and the treasurer was A. Maikov. The parody is connected with Chekhov's attendance of one of the Society's General Meetings, on 10 April 1889. At that meeting, Chekhov was elected to the committee of the Society, as were Yuzhin-Sumbatov, Nemirovich-Danchenko, Shpazhinsky, and others. In the resolution arising from that meeting it was noted that the General Meeting 'had revealed certain weaknesses in the workings of the Society and this has led to the thought of a review and change of the regulations' (See *A Survey of the Activities of the Society of Russian Playwrights and Opera Composers*, M.1899, p. 43).

publicly apologise to me, a reference to the second point of the notice resulting from the meeting on 10 April 1889: 'about the insulting expressions of one of the members of the Society in 1888.' (See, as above.)

only by those 30 members: Chekhov's figure corresponds almost exactly to the real situation. In 1889, there were 426 members of the Society.

Appendix 3. A note on the vaudeville writers Khmelnitsky, Pisarev, Koni, Karatygin, Nekrasov and Lensky

1 Translated by Boris Brasol in B. V. Varneke's *History of the Russian Theatre*, edited by B. Martin, New York, 1971, p. 195.

2 Published in a six-volume *Theatre of D. T. Lensky*, Petersburg, 1874, and available in D. T. Lensky, *Vodevili*, Moscow, 1937.

3 Shantarenkov describes a meeting between Pushkin and Lensky in the Summer Gardens in Moscow, *Russkiy vodevil*, Moscow, 1970, p. 9.

4 N. Shantarenkov, *Russkiy vodevil*, p. 13.

Selected Bibliography

Chekhov: Works and Correspondence

Chekhov, A. P. *Polnoe sobranie sochineniy i pisem A. P. Chekhova*, ed. S. D. Balukhaty and others, 20 vols. Moscow, 1944–51.

Polnoe sobranie sochineniy i pisem A. P. Chekhova, 30 vols. Moscow, 1974–82.

A. P. Chekhov, *Izbrannie proizvedeniya v trekh tomakh*, Moscow, 1964.

Nechistye tragiki i prokazhennye dramaturgi (Dishonourable Tragedians and Leprous Dramatists); Vynuzhdennoe zayavlenie (A Forced Declaration), and *Tatyana Repina*, in *Russkaya teatral'naya parodiya XIX nachala XX veka*, ed. M. Polyakov, Moscow, 1976.

Letters of Anton Chekhov, selected and edited, A. Yarmolinsky, New York, 1973.

Letters of Anton Chekhov, tr. M. H. Heim in collaboration with S. Karlinsky. Selection, Commentary by Karlinsky, London, 1973.

Chekhov: Letters on the short story, the drama and other literary topics, selected and edited by L. Friedland, London, 1965.

The Oxford Chekhov, ed., tr. R. Hingley, London, 1964–.

The Brute and Other Farces, ed. E. Bentley, tr. T. Hoffman, New York, 1958.

Works wholly or largely about Chekhov

Balukhaty, S. D. *Dramaturgia Chekhova*, Moscow, 1935.

Chekhov-dramaturg, Leningrad, 1936.

M. Gorky i A. Chekhov, perepiska, stati i vyskazyvaniya, Moscow–Leningrad, 1937.

Berdnikov, G. P. *Chekhov. Ideynye i tvorcheskiye iskaniya*, Moscow, 1961.

Chekhov-dramaturg, Moscow, 1972.

Chekhov, Moscow, 1974.

Bruford, W. H. *Chekhov*, London, 1957.

Chekhov and his Russia, reissued, London, 1971.

Chekhov, M. P. *Anton Chekhov i ego syuzhety*, Moscow, 1923.

Chekhova, M. P. *Dom-muzey A. P. Chekhova v Yalte*, Moscow, 1958.

Chukovsky, K. *Chekhov the Man*, tr. P. Rose, London, 1945.

Derman, A. *Anton Pavlovich Chekhov: Kritiko-biograficheskiy ocherk*, Moscow, 1939.

Moskva v zhizni i tvorchestve A. P. Chekhova, Moscow, 1948.

Dolinina, A. S. 'Parodiya li, "Tatyana Repina" Chekhova?' in *A. P. Chekhov*,

Zateryannye proizvedeniya, ed. M. D. Belyaeva and A. S. Dolinina, Leningrad, 1925.

Elton, O. *Chekhov*, The Taylorian Lecture, Oxford, 1929.

Gerhardi, W. *Anton Chekhov, A Critical Study*, revised collected edition, London, 1974.

Gitovich, N. I. ed., *A. P. Chekhov v vospominaniyakh sovremennikov*, Moscow, 1960.

Gorky, M. *Reminiscences of Tolstoy, Chekhov and Andreev*, tr. Mansfield, Koteliansky and Woolf, 3rd edit., London, 1968.

Hahn, B. *Chekhov, A Study of the Major Stories and Plays*, Cambridge, 1977.

Hingley, R. *Chekhov*, London, 1966.

A New Life of Chekhov, London, 1976.

Jackson, R. L. ed., *Chekhov, A Collection of Critical Essays*, New Jersey, 1967.

Laffitte, S. *Tchekhov par lui-même*, Paris, 1955.

Chekhov 1860–1904, tr. M. Budberg and G. Latta, London, 1974.

Lakshin, V. *Tolstoy i Chekhov*, Moscow, 1975.

Magarshack, D. *Chekhov the Dramatist*, New York, 1960.

Mayakovsky, V. 'Dva Chekhova', in *Polnoe sobranie sochineniy v trinadtsati tomakh*, vol. 1, Moscow, 1955.

Pitcher, H. *The Chekhov Play, A New Interpretation*, London, 1973.

Rayfield, D. *Chekhov, The Evolution of his Art*, London, 1975.

Shakh-Azizova, T. K. *Chekhov i zapadno-evropeiskaya drama ego vremeni*, Moscow, 1966.

Shcheglov, J. L. *Chekhov v vospominaniyakh sovremennikov*, Moscow, 1952.

Shestov, L. *Anton Tchekhov and other essays*, Dublin–London, 1916.

Simmons, E. J. *Chekhov: A Biography*, Chicago, 1962.

Smirnova-Chikina, E. S. '"Tatyana Repina" Antona Chekhova' in *V tvorcheskoy laboratorii Chekhova*, Moscow, 1974.

Speirs, L. *Tolstoy and Chekhov*, Cambridge, 1971.

Styan, J. L. *Chekhov in Performance*, Cambridge, 1971.

Toumanova, N. A. *Anton Chekhov, The Voice of Twilight Russia*, New York, 1937.

Valency, M. *The Breaking String, The Plays of Anton Chekhov*, New York, 1966.

Yermilov, V. *Dramaturgia Chekhova*, Moscow, 1948.

A. P. Chekhov, tr. I. Litvinov, Moscow, n.d.

Background works: Russian theatre and literature

Belinsky, V. G. *Polnoe sobranie sochineniy v 13-ti tomakh*, Moscow, 1954.

Braun, E. *Meyerhold on Theatre*, London, 1969.

The Theatre of Meyerhold, London, 1979.

Dobrolyubov, N. A. *Sobranie sochineniy v tryokh tomakh, Russian Satire in the Time of Catherine II*, vol. 2, Moscow, 1952.

Dostoyevsky, F. M. *A Disgraceful Affair*, tr. N. Gottlieb, London, 1959.

Evreinov, N. *Histoire du théâtre russe*, Paris, 1947.

Bibliography

Gifford, H. *The Hero of his Time*, London, 1950.

Gogol, N. V. *Polnoe sobranie sochineniy v 14-ti tomakh*, Moscow, 1940–42.

The Government Inspector, tr. Marsh and Brooks, London, 1968.

Marriage, tr. B. Costello, Manchester, 1969.

Diary of a Madman and Other Stories, tr. R. Wilks, Harmondsworth, 1972.

Kholodov, E. G. ed., and others, *Istoriya russkogo dramaticheskogo teatra*, vols. 1–7, Moscow, 1977– (vol. 1, 1977; vol. 2, 1977; vol. 3, 1978; vol. 4, 1979; vol. 5, 1980. Vols. 6 and 7 of this invaluable work are not yet available).

Magarshack, D. *Turgenev*, London, 1954.

Nemirovitch-Dantchenko, V. *My Life in the Russian Theatre*, tr. J. Cournos, London, 1968.

Pushkin, A. S. *Pushkin on Literature*, tr. T. Wolff, London, 1971.

Rudnitsky, K. L. *Rezhissyor Meyerhold*, Moscow, 1969.

Shantarenkov, N. ed., *Russkiy vodevil*, Moscow, 1970.

Simonov, R. *Stanislavsky's Protégé: Eugene Vakhtangov*, tr. M. Goldina, New York, 1969.

Slonimsky, A. 'The Technique of the Comic in Gogol,' in *Gogol from the Twentieth Century*, ed., tr. R. A. Maguire, Princeton, 1974.

Stanislavski, C. *My Life in Art*, tr. J. J. Robbins, London, 1962.

Turgenev, I. S. *A Month in the Country*, tr. G. R. Noyes in *Masterpieces of the Russian Drama*, vol. 1, New York, 1961.

Letters to An Actress, tr., ed. N. Gottlieb and R. Chapman, London, 1973.

Uspensky, V. V. ed., *Russkiy vodevil*, Leningrad–Moscow, 1959.

Varneke, B. V. *History of the Russian Theatre*, tr. B. Brasol and B. Martin, reprint of 1951, New York, 1971.

Weiner, L. *The Contemporary Drama of Russia*, reprint of 1924, New York, 1971.

Welsh, D. J. *Russian Comedy 1765–1823*, The Hague, 1966.

Yuzovsky, Yu. *Razgovor zatyanulsya za polnoch*, Moscow, 1966.

Further reading

Bakshy, A. *The Path of the Modern Russian Stage and other essays*, London, 1916.

Braun, E. *The Director and the Stage*, Milton Keynes, 1977.

Brereton, G. *French Comic Drama from the Sixteenth to the Eighteenth Century*, London, 1977.

Brook, P. *The Empty Space*, London, 1968.

Campbell, O. J. *The Comedies of Holberg*, reprint of 1914, New York–London, 1968.

Gourfinkel, N. *Le Théâtre russe contemporain*, Paris, 1931.

Gorki par lui-même, Paris, 1967.

Holtzman, F. *The Young Maxim Gorky 1868–1902*, New York, 1948.

Meyer, M. *Henrik Ibsen*, London, vol. 1, 1967 and vols. 2 and 3, 1971.

Mirsky, D. *Modern Russian Literature*, London, 1925.

Slonim, M. *Russian Theatre*, London, 1963.
Tynan, K. *Tynan on Theatre*, Harmondsworth, 1964.
Vsevolodsky-Gerngross, V. N. *Istoriya russkogo teatra*, Moscow-Leningrad, 1929.

Index

Index